OXFORD GUIDES TO COMPUTING
FOR THE HUMANITIES

*Series Editor*: Susan Hockey

# A HISTORIAN'S GUIDE TO COMPUTING

OXFORD GUIDES TO COMPUTING
FOR THE HUMANITIES

The computer is becoming an indispensable tool in many areas of the humanities, yet the range of possibilities which it opens up is often not fully appreciated. This series will provide a comprehensive survey of computer applications in humanities disciplines, from the perspective of the humanities scholar. It will explore the range of electronic sources which are available and examine their usefulness for research and teaching. It will take the reader well beyond the word processor and the bibliographical database to provide a critical overview of the field, concentrating on tools and techniques which are appropriate for scholarly use, drawing attention to those which are less appropriate, and providing an introduction to the relevant literature. The volumes in the series will be useful not only for research but also for the teaching of undergraduate and graduate courses.

# A Historian's Guide to Computing

DANIEL I. GREENSTEIN

OXFORD UNIVERSITY PRESS
1994

Oxford University Press, Walton Street, Oxford OX2 6DP
Oxford New York Toronto
Delhi Bombay Calcutta Madras Karachi
Kuala Lumpur Singapore Hong Kong Tokyo
Nairobi Dar es Salaam Cape Town
Melbourne Auckland Madrid
and associated companies in
Berlin Ibadan

Oxford is a trade mark of Oxford University Press

Published in the United States
by Oxford University Press Inc., New York

British Library Cataloguing in Publication Data
Data available

Library of Congress Cataloging in Publication Data
A historians' guide to computing / Daniel I. Greenstein.
(Oxford guides to computing for the humanities)
Includes bibliographical references and index.
1. History—Data processing. I. Title. II. Series.
D16.12.G74 1994 902'.85—dc20 93–46381

ISBN 0-19-824235-2
ISBN 0-19-823521-6 (pbk.)

Set by Hope Services (Abingdon) Ltd.
Printed in Great Britain on acid-free paper by
Biddles Ltd., Guildford & King's Lynn

*For*
*Hannah and Melissa*

# Contents

# List of Figures

# Introduction

HISTORIANS have used computers now for over thirty years in their research. The advent of inexpensive microcomputers in the 1980s and the enthusiasm for word processing that they encouraged ensured the broadening out of what was once a minority interest. Despite this there is no comprehensive guide to computer applications expressly written for historians.[1] Certainly, any good bookshop will boast shelves of computer textbooks and manuals. But these are either too technical in their approach or written with examples which are instantly comprehensible in the world of commerce but rather unhelpful for anyone faced with a medieval charter or parish register. The gap in the literature is more than just a publisher's opportunity. It reflects historians' unwillingness to dissociate computers from quantitative social science history with which they made their first debut in the 1960s. To many, the computer is still viewed as the natural ally of the once 'new' historians who challenged 'traditional' narrative with theoretical models and methods borrowed from the social sciences and thus prolonged a seventy-year-old controversy about the nature of Clio's craft.[2] One consequence is that in the 1990s the computer is still tarred with the same brush as the social science historians. Too rarely is it treated for what it essentially is: a tool which, like many other tools, has some general utility for the historian. One of the primary aims of this book, and consequently the focus of its first chapter, is to demystify the computer; to show that its use neither makes nor requires a quantitative or 'number-crunching' social science historian.

[1] Until recently the only available guide was E. Shorter's outdated *The Historian and the Computer: A Practical Guide* (Englewood Cliffs, NJ, 1971). There is at last some new activity in the field; see E. Mawdsley and T. Munck, *Computing for Historians: An Introductory Guide* (Manchester, 1993).

[2] For a recent and comprehensive contribution to the debate, R. W. Fogel and G. R. Elton, *Which Road to the Past: Two Views of History* (London, 1983). Other contributions are listed in the bibliography, section IVA.

There are, however, two more compelling reasons to produce a historian's guide to computers at this point in time. First, what was once 'new' history has aged considerably and is now arguably in decline; some of its more eminent practitioners have sounded a retreat to narrative or admitted that borrowed social science models and methods never really lived up to expectations.[3] With the move away from the 'new' history in full swing, literature on the use of computers in history is increasingly confined to *Computing and Blah*—the journals and conference proceedings prepared for and consumed by a small cadre of the converted. To all but the cognoscenti, its language is impenetrable. Historians are thus in danger of missing out on recent technical advances which have made computation accessible to non-specialist and non-technical historians in a way which promises to benefit their work. Indeed, it is recognized here that few historians are likely to apply their energies to research that requires sophisticated computer applications or quantitative methods. Most, however, stand to benefit directly by using the computer to prepare and manage bibliographies, research notes, and teaching materials. Still more may gain from the electronic communications which promise to bring a world of information—including distant library catalogues—onto the historian's desk. It is for this audience that Chapter 2 has been provided as guidance to the computer-assisted conduct of day-to-day tasks.

Secondly, without better documentation on how computers can be integrated effectively into historical research, novice (and not so novice) users remain in danger of recreating techniques. already tried and tested by others. Despite this tendency to 'recreate the wheel', we shy away, on the whole, from a methodological literature which might minimize if not end the practice entirely. Arguably no such literature can replace first-hand experience of archival immersion when coming to terms with how to 'understand' the past. But the same does not apply where computer techniques are concerned. Attempting to use computers in the solitude which still characterizes so much historical investigation can be a frustrating and unnecessarily time-consuming experience. At worst it can produce costly mistakes and spectacular errors. The book consequently takes on two other aims. First, to

[3] For a classic statement see L. Stone, 'The Revival of Narrative: Reflections on a New Old History', *Past and Present*, 85 (1971), 2–34.

provide non-specialists with a comprehensive and approachable guide that points out the promise but also the pitfalls of those computing applications which are most commonly used in historical research. Secondly, to inform novice users sufficiently so they may concentrate their experimental energies on techniques which promise to advance their particular research rather than on those which have been known and well documented (though buried perhaps in a specialist literature) for some time.

These rather more methodologically oriented aims are fulfilled in the book's central chapters, 3–6, and in its comprehensive bibliography and resource guide provided in an appendix. Chapter 3 explains how databases can be used to manage information which is highly structured, such as that which might be found in a census or parish register, or easily summarized, such as that found in a collective biography. Chapter 4 moves from management to measurement. It explains how statistical measures and graphical and tabular display are used to summarize information succinctly, and how computers can help in this process. The chapter deals largely but not exclusively with numbers as they are found in the historical record (e.g. in financial accounts), and as they emerge whenever the historian counts occurrences of almost anything. Chapter 5 discusses how computers can help manage and analyse our most familiar source—the text—and in doing so open up untried areas of historical enquiry. The chapter launches out with word processing and document preparation if only to show that these familiar computer applications are merely the beginning where texts are concerned. Thereafter, it looks at the management, storage, and retrieval of machine-readable texts and at methods of text analysis. The latter are rarely used in historical research despite the fact that they promise to shed new light on a whole range of historical problems. Chapter 6 offers an eight-point guide on how to design and implement computer projects of any size and complexity. It has two aims: to ensure that projects are directed from the outset towards successful completion, and that they harness the computer to the task of managing and analysing information in the most cost-effective way possible.

Throughout the book, explanations of different research methods and computing techniques are presented in simple and precise language, with reference to real historical problems and 'data sets', and with comprehensible diagrams. Given the coverage, discussion is necessarily general. The book cannot possibly serve as a 'how to' guide or a 'Which Computer'. It is hoped that in future, such specialist guides written expressly for historians will emerge. In the meantime signposts are provided throughout this volume and extensively in the bibliography and resource guide that will show the historian how and to what effect computers have been introduced into the research agenda. They will also direct the historian where to go in search of more detailed help with specific computer applications or analytical techniques.

There are numerous debts. The Leverhulme Trust and the Economic and Social Research Council funded a large-scale computer-aided investigation into the social origins, university experiences, and career destinations of Oxford University's twentieth-century members. The project acted as a valuable training ground in many of the methods and techniques which are discussed herein and a rich source of materials for their exemplification.[4] The Text Encoding Initiative has facilitated more formal exploration of historians' computational requirements from which I have benefited enormously.[5] The Association for History and Computing has also been particularly important. Its conferences, its journal, and its recent president, Manfred Thaller, have given me many new insights and corrected some of my erroneous assumptions.

Personal debts are more numerous still. Susan Hockey's timely and expert interventions helped give shape to the text in its conception and direction to the author. Brian Harrison was always supportive of my attempts to bring new methods to bear on Oxford's twentieth-century history, and taught me by his own impeccable examples about historical methods less easily docu-

---

[4] ESRC research Grant R000 23 2286. The project collected rudimentary information on every male matriculant, 1900–67, and every female matriculant 1920–67 (*c*.12,000 matriculants in all), and comprehensive biographical information on a 10 per cent stratified sample thereof. Comprehensive biographical information was also collected for an estimated 10 per cent sample of male and female matriculants, 1968–79, and for members of the women's societies, 1900–19. D. I. Greenstein, 'The Junior Members, 1900–90: A Profile', in B. H. Harrison (ed.), *The History of the University of Oxford*, viii: *The Twentieth Century* (Oxford, forthcoming).

[5] For the results see D. I. Greenstein (ed.), *Modelling Historical Data: Towards a Standard for Encoding and Exchanging Machine-Readable Texts* (St Katharinen, 1991); D. I. Greenstein and L. D. Burnard, 'Speaking with one Voice: Encoding Standards and the Prospects for an Integrated Approach to Computing in History', *Computers and the Humanities* (forthcoming).

mented than those described here. Lou Burnard remained good humoured in the face of unsolicited phone calls and electronic mail messages which went begging after advice. Friendly competition with Thomas Munck and Evan Mawdsley helped see a first draft of the manuscript to completion; the encouragement of my editor, Frances Morphy, sealed a similar fate of the final version. Richard Alexander, Christopher Black, and Donald Spaeth read selected chapters and offered helpful advice. Michael Moss also took part in the reading and shouted encouragement at every opportunity, even when clinging to the side of the Aonach Eagach. Thomas Munck and Hamish Maxwell-Stewart suffered the manuscript in its entirety and bolstered the author with their comments and enthusiasm. Dr Maxwell-Stewart was particularly persistent with Chapter 3, which he saw in several different guises and which eventually incorporated a database of his own design. Jonathan Andrews, Morna Black, and Philip Taylor also provided example data sets and expert advice on particular methods. Mike Black maintained a remarkably friendly and useful computing environment, in which most of the book was produced. Needless to say, despite all the support and assistance, the book has many shortcomings for which I alone am responsible.

# 1

## Myths and Legends

In the 1990s, computers have become essential items in the historian's tool-kit. Few are completely unfamiliar with word processing, and the prospects of instantaneous access to remote library catalogues and other on-line databases find the last of the computer illiterates approaching workstations, albeit with some trepidation. In short, the computer revolution is near complete. And yet one senses amongst colleagues within the humanities generally a degree of scepticism and distrust. The use of computers in humanities teaching and research is still stigmatized for forcing measurement and a scientific outlook onto what is essentially a literary craft. Though understandable in the 1970s as a reaction to the 'new' history which was boldly overstating its claims, this view is no longer well founded. Indeed, in the 1990s it only serves to constrain us from exploiting the new technology beyond simple word processing and forcing it to serve our own aims irrespective of whether they are conceived of as being literary, scientific, or purely administrative. This chapter then attempts to debunk the myths which have grown up amongst historians about the computer and how it is used in history, so it may be embraced for what it is. That is, an implement which, taken together with many other implements, is part of the historian's tool-box. It is this rather benign view of the computer as implement which must by necessity be embraced before guidance about its use can be given and received in measured and non-controversial tones.

'COMPUTERS FACILITATE A KIND OF MEASUREMENT
WHICH IS NOT SUITED TO HISTORICAL QUESTIONS AND
SOURCES'

The first myth surrounding the computer's use in history might be stated thus: that computers, developed by and for the military, industrial, and scientific establishments, are principally used for measurement, and measurement is not something which historians are interested in. At least the important questions of history 'are important precisely because they are not suited to quantitative measurement'.[1] We might agree that complex statistical measures that have been used, for example to estimate the cost of gradual emancipation to slave-holding planters in the *ante bellum* American south, are a minority interest.[2] None the less, measurement is fundamental to all historical interpretation irrespective of whether or not the sources on which interpretation is based contain any numbers. The point is easily made. Simply choose a historical text at random, open it to any page, and count up the quantitative statements found there.[3] Take T. S. Ashton's discussion of changes in the textile industry found in *An Economic History of England: The Eighteenth Century*, for example: 'In the *early* years of the century', Ashton writes,

there were in the mines of Northumberland and Durham *quite as many* putters or barrowmen *as* hewers: by the *beginning* of the following century *the number* of men at the face (*the best paid* of the workers) *far exceeded* those who transported coal underground. The same thing occurred in the textile industry. Here the *chief cost* was the *poorly paid* women spinners, who *greatly outnumbered* the fullers and weavers, and the employment of whom, in their *scattered* homes, involved *high* expenditure on transport and book-keeping. It was not *high* wages but *high* labour costs that led to the introduction of the devices of Hargreaves, Arkwright, and Crompton. It is true that, *long before* these came into being, James Kay had turned his attention to improvements in weaving. But one object, and result, of the flying shuttle was to make it possible for the craftsman to weave a broad piece of cloth without an assistant. The progress of the device was *far less* rapid *than* that of the jenny, the frame, and the mule; but it had a similar effect in eliminating the *less* well paid of the weavers.[4]

[1] A. Schlesinger, Jr., 'The Humanist Looks at Empirical Social Research', *American Sociological Review*, 27 (1962), 770; G. Himmelfarb, 'History with the Politics Left Out', in G. Himmelfarb (ed.), *The New History and the Old* (Cambridge, Mass., 1987), 14–15.

[2] R. W. Fogel and S. L. Engerman, *Time on the Cross: The Economics of American Negro Slavery* (Boston, 1974), 35–6, and the calculation as explained in *Time on the Cross: Evidence and Methods—A Supplement* (Boston, 1974), 33.

[3] As recommended in R. W. Fogel, 'The Limits of Quantitative History', *American Historical Review*, 80 (1975), 329–50.

[4] I am grateful to Hans Christian Johansen who demonstrated the effectiveness of this method in teaching undergraduates and for ensuring that my random

The italic print indicates Ashton's reliance upon quantitative measures. Perhaps this should come as no surprise. The sources of modern economic history consist of company ledgers, reports of economic conditions commissioned by private or public associations, and census-like documents. Along with national population censuses, electoral rolls, and government statistical compilations such sources proliferated in Western Europe from at least the mid-eighteenth century. Taken together they share two things in common: they are made up largely of numbers, and they are often highly structured, that is presented as lists or tables. To summarize this sort of evidence, historians are forced to measure and to produce the kinds of quantitative statements indicated above in italic.

If economic history is all too obvious a prop on which to support an argument that historians rely on measurement, then Rowse's celebratory history of an Oxford college and its role in shaping British foreign policy in the 1930s seems a rather more unlikely selection. None the less we find that Rowse also relies very heavily on quantitative statements in his description of the Chamberlainites:

What was *characteristic* of this inner group, *especially* of Chamberlain, Simon and Hoare, but of the egregious Runciman, Kingsley Wood and Ernest Brown *too*—the Chamberlainites as such? There were *several* things that united them. They were 'men of peace', i.e. no use for confronting force, or guile, or wickedness. That they did not know what they were dealing with is the most charitable explanation of their failure; but they might at least have taken the trouble to inform themselves. There were *plenty* of people to tell them, but they would not listen. They *all shared* a Non-conformist origin, and its characteristic self-righteousness—all the more intolerable in the palpably wrong. These things are more important than people realise; to the historian they are significant elements. One way or another *they had none* of the old 18th-century aristocracy's guts—*they were* middle-class men with pacifist backgrounds and no knowledge of Europe, its history or its languages, or of its diplomacy.[5]

Ashton is concerned with wages, expenditure, cost, and the relative size and composition of different groups of workers; informa-

selection included T. S. Ashton, *An Economic History of England: The Eighteenth Century* (London, 1977), 109.

[5] A. L. Rowse, *All Souls and Appeasement: A Contribution to Contemporary History* (London, 1961), 19.

tion which, when it is discovered in the historical record, will often be expressed in terms of numbers. Rowse, on the other hand, is interested in information about particular people—their religion, social class, and education—which is normally found in running prose. In autobiographies and the like, the prose may be narrative: 'I was born on 12 January 1891. According to my nurse . . .'.[6] Elsewhere it may appear in more highly structured lists, such as those which appear in city directories, associations' membership lists, collective biographies, and hospital admission registers. Despite the fact that the information is not itself numeric, Rowse relies as much as Ashton does on measurement in order to summarize it. He is effectively counting up the number of people who share particular characteristics in common. Thus he can tell us that the Chamberlainites '*all* shared a Non-conformist background', or 'were [implying all] middle-class men'. The exercise is one frequently undertaken by historians when systematically characterizing groups of people, objects, or events.

If the selection from Rowse seems somewhat contrived because its historical subject-matter is less than significant, we might turn to debates about who supported the National Socialists in Germany during the 1930s. Here, too, one discovers any number of unsubstantiated quantitative claims being used to answer some of the weightier questions of contemporary history. For Karl Dietrich Bracher, for example, the NSDP drew disproportionately on the support of 'the petty-bourgeois, middle-class, and small landholding groups which had been hardest hit by the outcome of war, the economic crisis, and the structural changes of modern society'. Underlying this essentially quantitative statement, however, there is no attempt to determine more precisely who voted for Hitler. Instead the claims are inferred from the tenor of the party's ideological position as evident in *Mein Kampf* and from its institutional connections with 'middle-class organizations'.[7]

The reader also might object that the systematic description engaged by Rowse and by the historians of Germany between the wars is itself idiosyncratic. It is, in fact, not at all dissimilar to Ashton's summary of numeric information which was itself a speciality interest. All involve a degree of measurement (counting in

[6] J. C. Masterman, *On the Chariot Wheel: An Autobiography* (London, 1975), 13.

[7] K. D. Bracher, *The German Dictatorship: The Origins, Structure and Consequences of National Socialism*, trans. J. Steinberg (London, 1973), 195.

the case of Rowse and Bracher), but none is at all representative of what most historians get up to. Instead, most historical evidence is literary, and few historical questions are so well defined as Rowse's and Bracher's as to enable systematic categorization and counting. But even where the researcher is exclusively interested in the subjective interpretation of literary sources as, for example, are historians of ideas, there is a degree of measurement involved. Take as a final example a selection from Patricia Bonomi's analysis of religion and its role in shaping the revolutionary spirit in the American colonies. After having quoted brief passages from Edmund Burke's parliamentary address on the subject of the American rebellion in 1775 and Joseph Galloway's *Historical and Political Reflections on the Rise and Progress of the American Rebellion* (1780), Bonomi concludes:

Burke and Galloway were describing a tradition of popular resistance that was *rooted* in sixteenth-century religious dissent and in the religious politics of Stuart England. This ideology of dissent—as *improved* by Enlightenment whigs and eighteenth-century radical publicists—was *amplified* in America, where dissenters formed a majority of the inhabitants. By the 1760s it had also taken on certain features *from* evangelical religion, such as a concern for individual accountability and the rights of minorities in matters of conscience. Nonetheless, the American ideology of dissent was *firmly grounded* in reason as well as emotion, which gave it special force among provincial leaders—including many Anglicans—who *prided themselves* on taking a rational approach to Revolution issues. No doubt *millenial expectations* and *evangelical preaching* helped *to move* a good many Americans into the patriotic camp. But by 1775–1776 the *emotionalism* of the Great Awakening had *subsided* or been *diluted* by a *widening* current of Enlightenment rationalism. Thus evangelical Calvinism and religious rationalism did not carve separate channels but *flowed* as one stream toward the crisis of 1776.[8]

The quantitative statements emphasized here are of an entirely different order from those so far encountered. They relate and compare bodies of ideas defined by the author. That is, they are concerned with the contents of the literary evidence and the concepts addressed therein. But in every instance, the author is engaged in some form of measurement. Purely descriptive statements—'the American ideology of dissent was *firmly grounded*

[8] P. U. Bonomi, *Under the Cope of Heaven: Religion, Society, and Politics in Colonial America* (New York, 1986), 187–8.

in reason as well as emotion'—indicate the author's impressionistic measure of rational and emotive words and phrases found in the literature of American dissent. Comparative statements which attempt to establish the ecology or genealogy of ideas are quantitative in the same way. In the statement, 'Burke and Galloway were describing a tradition of popular resistance that was *rooted* in sixteenth-century religious dissent and in the religious politics of Stuart England', measures are based on synonymous words and phrases appearing in two bodies of literary work. And underlying the comparative statement lies another quantitative measure. This one categorizes and counts the use of similar stylistic devices, words, or phrases in two bodies of literature to assess the influence that the earlier of the two might have had on the later. Still other statements—'the *emotionalism* of the Great Awakening had *subsided* or been *diluted* by a *widening* current of Enlightenment rationalism'—measure how certain concepts changed over time, here perhaps by categorizing and counting adjectival expressions used in discussions of religious ideas. With quantitative processes involved in the historian's interpretation of literary evidence, then, it is fair to say that measurement is at least indirectly at the heart of historical research.

The point, however, is not simply to show that measurement is fundamental to history but that computers are capable of conducting the task better than tried and tested manual methods. Numeric calculations such as those conducted by Ashton with data about the number, composition, and pay of textile workers in the north of England may be conducted more quickly, easily, and accurately with statistical packages or spreadsheets—computer applications discussed in Chapter 4. Computers are particularly good at 'number crunching'. The first digital computers emerged from the military-industrial establishment in order to handle the number crunching involved in ballistics. It should come as no surprise, therefore, to learn that computers were first harnessed to historical investigations which involved calculations with numeric data.[9] Classifying, counting, and tabulating information—processes upon which Rowse and Bracher rely—

[9] R. P. Swierenga, 'Clio and Computers: A Survey of Computerized Research in History', *Computers and the Humanities*, 5 (1970), 1–4; G. G. S. Murphy, 'Historical Investigation and Automatic Data Processing Equipment', *Computers and the Humanities*, 3 (1968–9), 3.

also may be done more quickly and accurately with computer databases, as discussed in Chapter 3. Data classification and analysis have been automated since at least the late nineteenth century, when Herman Hollerith's tabulating machine was used to compile 1890 US census returns. Similar 'tabulating' machines were used to a limited extent with historical sources from at least the 1930s.[10] The textual analyses that Bonomi employs are further areas where the computer's assistance has been sought with some success, as discussed in Chapter 5. Computer-aided textual analyses were central to military intelligence during the Second World War and were adapted to research in the humanities in the late 1940s and eventually to historical research in the mid-1960s. Here, too, the computer's speed and accuracy is its greatest asset, in this case in its ability to identify word and phrase patterns in great volumes of text.[11]

There are advantages other than speed and accuracy which may be gained by computerizing the measurement upon which so much historical research is based. Let us return to our three examples where central parts of the arguments hinge on the vaguest quantitative expressions. Ashton is imprecise in comparing wages and labour costs, yet the comparison is central to his explanation about why the jenny, frame, and mule were introduced into the textile industry. Similarly, Rowse explains the political motivations of the Chamberlainites with reference to their social-class background but tells us almost nothing about the characteristics that the Chamberlainites shared which led Rowse to conclude that they were middle class. Finally, Bonomi has identified emotion and reason in the literature of eighteenth-century American dissent because of her familiarity with eighteenth-century literature generally and her appreciation of the words and symbols which indicate these concepts. Her assertion that this eighteenth-century American literature is a direct descendant of a sixteenth-century religious one is similarly grounded. Nowhere, however, does Bonomi indicate precisely what linguistic, semantic, or stylistic features she has found in both bodies of literature to support her conclusions. In each case,

[10] Swierenga, 'Clio and the Computers', 2–4, and his 'Computers and Comparative History', *Journal of Interdisciplinary History*, 5 (1971), 267–86.
[11] S. Hockey, 'An Historical Perspective', in S. Rahtz (ed.), *Information Technology in the Humanities* (Chichester, 1987), 22.

the reader is unable to evaluate the authors' respective findings or to rework them from a slightly different perspective or in the light of newly discovered information or assumptions. The authors ask us simply to trust their judgement, their reading of the sources, and their impressionistic feel for the subject at hand. They then proceed to make pronouncements on some of the weightiest historical questions: Ashton on the causes of technological innovation and the impact of technologies on the structure and composition of the work-force; Rowse and Bracher on the relationship between social-class background and political motivation; and Bonomi on how inherited ideas influence both individuals' world-views and their political actions.

Had computers been used to conduct the more important measures in each of these studies, other historians would have access to the information upon which the measures were based. Conclusions could thus be verified or amended. Computers also would have lent greater precision to the studies. Using a computer Ashton would have documented the precise differences between wages and labour costs in the eighteenth-century English textile industry. Rowse would have revealed his assumptions about social-class structure. Bonomi would have documented the literary features she focused on in her research. And there would be other spin-off benefits as well from the machine-readable data left behind as by-products of these computerized studies. Ashton's would be available for comparison with similar data from other industries perhaps in other countries, on the eve of technological revolution. Rowse's would offer a computerized index of occupational classifications which might be used with collective biographical data for other studies. And Bonomi's data would contribute important literary works to the corpus of materials already available in machine-readable form, furnishing a valuable resource for linguists and philologists, as well as for historians of religion and of eighteenth-century Britain and America.

Obviously not all of the measures with which historians are involved require computer precision and efficiency. Explicit quantification might have provided substance to Ashton's description of the labour-force in eighteenth-century English textiles, but quite possibly at the expense of readability. Rowse's handling of information on the Chamberlainites' confessional status is beyond reproach. One either is or is not a Nonconformist. No more explicit formulation is required, nor would it add anything to the argument. And it would be sheer pedantry to demand from Bonomi the exact size of the dissenter majority or the number of Americans driven into the patriotic camp by millenial expectations and evangelical preaching.

Elsewhere, historical sources may be insufficiently reliable to support anything other than vague or impressionistic quantitative treatment. Analyses of unreliable data can yield unreliable results, as encapsulated nicely in the well-known acronym, GIGO, or 'Garbage In Garbage Out'.[12] With corruption and piracy rife in eighteenth-century shipping, for example, cargo registers and records of port duties can disguise more than they reveal about international trade. The same might be said of election returns for some nineteenth-century American cities. 'The government', cautioned one historian about the use of census records,

are very keen on amassing statistics. They collect them, add them, raise them to the Nth power, take the cubed root and prepare wonderful diagrams. But you must never forget that every one of these figures comes in the first instance from the village watchman, who just puts down what he damn pleases.[13]

Some quantifiable sources are not only unreliable, they are also potentially unrepresentative. Is there something peculiar about those few ports which keep detailed records reaching back into the seventeenth century? And what of those few large plantation owners in the *ante bellum* American south who kept detailed records of their transactions in human chattel? Were they sufficiently representative of the slave-owning public?

These considerations about the potential benefits offered by computer-aided research and the reliability and representativeness of the sources on which it is based effectively amount to a cost–benefit analysis. Are the sources sufficiently robust? Do the likely results justify the effort involved in obtaining them with the

---

[12] L. Stone, 'History and the Social Sciences', in L. Stone, *The Past and the Present* (Boston, 1981). But also see R. W. Fogel, who argues that sophisticated analytical techniques are especially necessary where data are most unreliable in 'The New Economic History: Its Findings and Methods', in D. K. Rowney and J. Q. Graham, Jr. (eds.), *Quantitative History: Selected Readings in the Quantitative Analysis of Historical Data* (Homewood, Ill., 1969), 320–35.

[13] Cited in R. E. Beringer, *Historical Analysis: Contemporary Approaches to Clio's Craft* (Malabar, Fla., 1986), 198.

computer's assistance? Do the end-products which may include both substantive historical results and machine-readable data sets, promise some lasting contribution to knowledge? In the end, informed answers to these questions, not debate about the place of measurement in history should determine where and how computers are integrated into historical research. Given the proven accessibility of some historical sources to computer-aided analysis and the growing amount of primary materials already coming to us in machine-readable form (e.g. late twentieth-century government records), it would be absurd to assume that computers have absolutely no place in history.[14]

'COMPUTERS FORCE AN UNSUITABLY SCIENTIFIC OUTLOOK ONTO THE HISTORIAN'

A second myth associates computing with a so-called scientific history which self-consciously sets out its research aims as testable hypotheses. This is poor historiography, surely. Computers did not cause the ground swell of enthusiasm for a scientific history which was determined to transcend narrative description and concentrate instead on the social forces and structures underlying historical events.[15] In the decades before the Second World War, the progressive historians in the USA, including Charles Beard, Carl Becker, and Frederick Jackson Turner, and historians in Europe who were associated with *Annales: économies, sociétés, histoires* gave an important non-computerized boost to what had hitherto been a minority interest.[16] After the

[14] Many of the data of late twentieth-century political, diplomatic, and military history will only be available in machine-readable form. See J. M. Clubb, 'Computer Technology and the Source Materials of Social History', *Social Science History* 10 (1986), 97–114; D. I. Greenstein, 'Historians as Producers or Consumers of Standard-Conformant, Full-Text Datasets? Some Sources of Modern History as a Test Case', in D. I. Greenstein (ed.), *Modelling Historical Data: Towards a Standard for Encoding and Exchanging Machine-Readable Texts* (St Katharinen, 1991), 179–94; R. W. Zweig, 'Virtual Records and Real History', *History and Computing*, 4 (1992), 174–82.

[15] F. Furet, 'From Narrative History to Problem Oriented History', in F. Furet (ed.), *In the Workshop of History* (London, 1984); and his 'Introduction', ibid. 8–10. Also see L. Benson, *Towards the Scientific Study of History* (Philadelphia, 1972).

[16] Stone, 'History and the Social Sciences' adds that Britain's *Economic History Review* was as influential. See L. Benson, *Turner and Beard: American Historical*

Second World War, historians' rush to fashion themselves after the social scientists whose star was in the ascendant contributed additional momentum. There were other factors as well. To some, narrative history seemed unable to address questions which were particularly pressing in the post-war world. Invidious comparisons made in an era of Cold War between communist and non-communist countries placed emphasis on the relationship between social and economic structures on the one hand, and on political formations, attitudes, and behaviour on the other. So did the 'new left' as it emerged in Western Europe and in the USA with its emphasis on class and economy as determinant historical forces.[17]

In the heady political milieu of the 1960s, scientific history promised useful moral and practical lessons. By documenting the inarticulate masses' past experience, for example, of economic change, urban growth, poor relief, education, and class and racial conflict, the scientific historian might provide hard evidence which could be brought to bear on contemporary policy decisions. Together these influences pushed historians closer to sources which had hitherto been little used. Censuses and census-like lists, parish registers, probate inventories, tax assessment rolls, and the accounts and statistics compiled by legislative, judicial, and corporate bodies all promised to illuminate changes in the material world over the *longue durée*. But the data in these sources were vast, and they required extensive manipulation before they could be summarized. The scientific historian's quest, in other words, exalted both social science theory and the measurable, and from the 1960s drifted quite naturally towards the computer.

The myth that computers are near or at the root of a scientific history is based as well on a failure to differentiate between the developmental trajectories of the 'new' social histories which

*Writing Reconsidered* (Glencoe, Ill., 1960); G. G. Iggers, *New Directions in European Historiography* (London, 1985), 60–6.

[17] M. Kammen, 'The Past before Us', in M. Kammen (ed.), *The Past before Us: Contemporary Historical Writing in the United States* (Ithaca, NY, 1980), 22. The 'revolutionary' activity in Latin and South America and in Paris in 1968 also demanded that the social basis of political stability be reconsidered by left and right alike. See C. G. Pickvance, 'Introduction: Historical Materialist Approaches to Urban Sociology', in C. G. Pickvance (ed.), *Urban Sociology: Critical Essays* (London, 1976), 1–2.

emerged from the late 1950s. Many social historians adopted quantitative methods and computational techniques to organize and summarize information found in sources which had hitherto been unused in historical research. Few, however, pressed the claim that their work was at all scientific, and their influence over the profession should not be overestimated. The economic historians were first to press a scientific claim in part because their territories had been invaded by economists in the 1950s.[18] Economist Simon Kuznets's attempts to model general laws of contemporary economic behaviour were particularly influential. A model in this sense is a hypothesis expressed in terms of a mathematical formula which postulates a relationship between different factors—the price of labour, supply of raw materials—thought to shape economic development, for example. Once defined, the formula can be applied to data which are gathered to test the relationships specified therein. Where the model is at odds with the data, it can be refined and retested until the best fit between them is obtained.[19]

Within economic history, the controversial science of 'cliometrics' was born at Williamstown, Massachussetts, in 1957 when two economists, Alfred Conrad and John Meyer, showed how economists' modelling techniques could be applied to historical data.[20] Though initially controversial, economists' modelling methods slowly met with general if grudging acceptance at least amongst economic historians in the USA. Economist Robert Fogel's 1964 analysis of the railway's contribution to nineteenth-century American economic development, for example, provoked a hostile response because his argument was based on modelling techniques.[21] Ten years later in 1974, the Bancroft-winning economic history of slavery which Fogel co-authored with Stanley Engerman, also provoked hostility, but as much on account of its

[18] Murphy, 'Historical Investigation'.

[19] R. W. Fogel, 'The New Economic History, Its Findings and Methods', in Rowney and Graham, *Quantitative History*, 320–35.

[20] L. E. Davis and S. L. Engerman, 'The State of the Science (or is it Art or, perhaps Witchcraft?)', *History Methods Newsletter*, 20 (1987). Also see the bibliography section IVв.

[21] R. W. Fogel, *Railroads and American Economic Growth: Essays in Economic History* (Baltimore, 1964); F. Redlich, '"New" and Traditional Approaches to Economic History and their Interdependence', *Journal of Economic History*, 25 (1965), 480–95.

emotive subject as its methods.[22] By then, cliometric methods were already entrenched. In 1971, for example, the *Journal of Economic History*, a bell-wether of developments within economic history, had embraced the new methods as a permanent fixture by devoting much of volume 31 to their evaluation.

The 'new' political history also rode on the coat-tails of the behavioural sciences at a time when political scientists were attempting to measure the social and economic determinants of political behaviour in the post-war world and beginning to benefit from consultancies and from their experience with political opinion polls.[23] Sir Lewis Namier's work on the biographical characteristics of Elizabethan parliamentarians is an early example of a historian emulating the political scientist's survey research techniques.[24] By 1957 political science had stolen the initiative from political history, at least in the USA. In that year a group of US political historians were found begging after political scientists for methodological advice at a meeting in Rutgers.[25] Thereafter, narrative descriptions about 'what President Lincoln did next', which had served so long as a model for political history, appeared inadequate compared to measures of how class, ethnicity, religion, party, and race determined electors' and legislators' respective behaviour.[26] The new political history offered more than just an analytical style. It proposed that political behaviour, like the different causes of economic growth, could be modelled and that

[22] Fogel and Engerman, *Time on the Cross*. Two book-length refutations are P. A. David *et al.*, *Reckoning with Slavery: A Critical Study in the Quantitative History of American Negro Slavery* (New York, 1976) and H. Gutman, *Slavery and the Numbers Game* (Urbana, Ill., 1975).

[23] A. G. Bogue, 'United States: The "New" Political History', in Rowney and Graham, *Quantitative History*, 109–26; A. G. Bogue, 'The Quest for Numeracy: Data and Methods in American Political History', *Journal of Interdisciplinary History*, 21 (1990), 89–116; A. H. Barton, 'Paul Lazarfeld and Applied Social Research', *Social Science History*, 3 (1979).

[24] Sir L. Namier, *The Elizabethan House of Commons* (London, 1949). Other early examples cited in A. G. Bogue's 'United States: The "New" Political History'.

[25] Conference proceedings published as R. P. McCormick, 'Report: Conference on Early American Political Behaviour, Social Science Research Council', *Items* (Dec. 1957). Also see A. G. Bogue, 'Great Expectations and Secular Depreciation: The First 10 Years of the Social Science History Association', *Social Science History*, 11 (1987).

[26] A. G. Bogue, 'Quantification in the 1980s: Numerical and Formal Analysis in US History', *Journal of Interdisciplinary History*, 12 (1981). For more on quantitative and computer-aided approaches to the "new" political history see the bibliography section IVc.

the models could be tested scientifically against hard historical data.[27]

But the development of the new economic and political histories was to some extent unique and the inroads that scientific methods made there unusual. Elsewhere quantifiable evidence was increasingly sought but rarely to test hypotheses rigorously laid down as mathematical formulae. Urban history, for example, increasingly turned to census data to describe material changes in the nineteenth-century city but did very little to test explicitly formulated theoretical propositions.[28] Historical demography was as 'unscientific' in its use of quantifiable data from parish registers.[29] This does not imply a complete absence of theory from most social history. On the contrary, social history was increasingly influenced by theory. Few historical investigations, however, were conducted in the laboratory-like environments that were established for analyses of nineteenth- and twentieth-century economic development and political behaviour. Consequently, where theory informed a social historical investigation it was introduced as a set of general propositions, not as testable hypotheses. Stephen Thernstrom's 1964 social mobility study, *Poverty and Progress*, is therefore far more representative of the new social histories than Fogel's *Railroads and American Economic Growth*. Both looked at history from the bottom up and attempted to document material changes. Thernstrom, however, articulated general historical problems rather than testable mathematical theorems, and offered quantitative evidence to illuminate but not to prove prospective solutions.[30]

[27] Lee Benson was particularly influential. See his 1957 publication reprinted as 'Research Problems in American Historiography', in Benson, *Towards the Scientific Study of History*, and his 'Quantification, Scientific History, and Scholarly Innovation', *AHA Newsletter* (June 1966).

[28] Early examples include O. Handlin, *Boston's Immigrants, 1790–1880* (Cambridge, Mass., 1941); M. Curti *et al.*, *The Making of an American Community: A Case Study of Democracy in a Frontier County* (Stanford, Calif., 1959). Later works never deviated significantly from the trend even as their quantitative methods became more sophisticated. See S. B. Warner, Jr., *Streetcar Suburbs: The Process of Growth in Boston (1870–1900)* (Cambridge, Mass., 1962); T. Hershberg *et al.* (eds.), *Philadelphia: Work, Space, Family, and Group Experience in the 19th Century* (New York, 1981).

[29] See D. Eversley and E. A. Wrigley (eds.), *An Introduction to English Historical Demography from the Sixteenth Century to the Nineteenth Century* (London, 1966), and the bibliography section IVf.

[30] S. Thernstrom, *Poverty and Progress: Social Mobility in a Nineteenth Century*

Elsewhere, the sources of social history could not sustain even the simplest statistical treatment that became the stock-in-trade of those modern historians who worked with population and manufacturing censuses, poll books, legislative and electoral voting records, and financial and commercial data.[31] Medieval and early modern historians in particular were forced to contend with sources that contained both ambiguities and vast lacunae simply unknown to the modernist.[32] Alan MacFarlane's early attempts to document the day-to-day life of Earle's Colne over a 400-year period by building up a detailed collective biography of its inhabitants is a particularly good example.[33] MacFarlane's sources were very unlike those of the nineteenth-century urban historians whose community studies he was trying to emulate. For MacFarlane, biographical evidence was not to be found in census manuscripts, city directories, probate inventories, and tax assessment records where individuals were easily located in lists organized alphabetically by name or street address. Instead, MacFarlane relied on the occasional references to individuals which might occur by serendipity in whatever literary evidence remained for Earle's Colne for the relevant period. Where analyses of nineteenth- and twentieth-century communities had problems with too much evidence, MacFarlane had problems with too little. Moreover, MacFarlane's sources did not, on the whole, comprise highly organized and easily usable lists but thickets of dense prose. Consequently, tasks which proved reasonably straightfor-

*City* (Cambridge, Mass., 1964) and his 'Poverty and Progress: A Retrospective After Twenty Years', *Social Science History*, 10 (1986).

[31] Swierenga, 'Clio and Computers', 1–21, and R. Zemsky, 'Numbers and History: The Dilemma of Measurement', *Computers and the Humanities*, 4 (1969–70), 31–40.

[32] The use of computers in medieval history is a particularly interesting story. Take-off there seems to have awaited technological advances from the mid- to late 1970s which permitted the management and representation of both ambiguous data and eccentric characters. See the bibliography section IVᴅ.

[33] A. MacFarlane *et al. Reconstructing Historical Communities* (Cambridge, 1977). For a more recent study of Languedoc society, 1750–1850 see J. Smets, 'Histoire régionale sur concept international: effort de recherches communes', in J.-P. Genet (ed.), *Standardisation et échange des bases de données historiques* (Paris, 1988), 65–70; 'South French Society and the French Revolution: The Creation of a Large Database with CLIO', in P. R. Denley and D. Hopkin (eds.), *History and Computing* (Manchester, 1987), 49–57; 'La Base de Données de l'IRHIS: Dévelopments et Perspectives' in Centre National de la Recherche Scientifique, *L'Ordinateur et le métier d'historien. IVe Congrès 'History and Computing': volume des actes* (Bordeaux, 1990), 141–4.

ward (if perhaps time consuming) for the census-equipped modern historian, for example, in estimating a regional population were at best nightmarish and at worst impossible wherever the evidence was less complete.

It is no surprise, then, that as historians became interested in measuring phenomena other than nineteenth- and twentieth-century economic development and political behaviour, Thernstrom's mode of analysis prevailed over that offered by cliometrics and the 'new' political history. The latter simply proved unworkable given the fallibility inherent in many of the social historian's sources, particularly those drawn from pre-industrial periods and/or nations. One consequence was that social science historians beat a retreat from the limelight of publicity they had enjoyed in the 1960s and 1970s, into a small number of professional associations and specialist journals. In the expansive phase of the 1960s the Mathematical Social Science Board (MSSB) and the Ad Hoc Committee of the American Historical Association to Collect the Quantitative Data of History, were particularly important in the USA, as was the social survey data archive in Ann Arbor, the Inter-University Consortium for Political Research (ICPR). The MSSB sponsored summer schools and an important publication series while the Ad Hoc Committee and the ICPR worked together to computerize US election and census data and to prepare the groundwork for similar initiatives in Europe.[34] Quantum was Europe's only equivalent association. It was founded in Cologne in 1975 to promote research along lines already laid down by the new political and economic historians in the USA.[35] When enthusiasm for scientific social history waned in the late 1970s, such organizations folded altogether, redirected their activity, or became highly introspective. By the 1980s, anyway, it was evident that social science historians had paddled out of the main swim of the profession into the quieter waters offered by the Economic History Association, the Social Science History

[34] See A. G. Bogue's, 'Great Expectations and Secular Depreciation'; 'United States: The "New" Political History'. For the European dimension see V. R. Lorwin and J. M. Price (eds.), *The Dimensions of the Past: Materials, Problems, and Opportunities for Quantitative Work in History* (New Haven, Conn., 1972).

[35] The collaboration came to fruition in a 1976 conference which resulted in J. M. Clubb and E. K. Scheuch (eds.), *Historical Sociological Research: The Use of Historical Process Produced Data* (Stuttgart, 1980). Also see E. A. Johnson, 'Counting "How it Really Was": Quantitative History in West Germany', *History Methods Newsletter*, 21 (1988), 63.

Association (founded in 1976), and Germany's Quantum (founded in 1975).[36]

If enthusiasm for a scientific social history waned or was channelled into specific journals and associations, that attracted by computer-aided analyses of hitherto underused sources, waxed lyrical. The evidence is everywhere apparent in the summer schools and journals that sprung up at least in part to spread information about new methods and the use of new sources in history.[37] Non-specialist manuals also proliferated from the late 1960s offering simple measures and computing techniques to the uninitiated.[38] The holdings of historical data archives, indeed the very number of such archives established to house the machine-readable data of history, furnish another measure of the increasing use historians were making of the scientific historians' sources and tools.[39] Recent European developments have in some ways been most spectacular. There historical demography precipitated the only institutional developments before the mid-1970s. The French had *Annales*, the British the Cambridge Group for Population Studies, the Scandinavians had projects at Umeå and at Stockholm, and the Germans a research establishment at the Max Planck Institut für Geschichte in Göttingen. Elsewhere there was only the occasional data archive, summer school, and well-

[36] The journals belonging to these associations—*Journal of Economic History*, *Social Science History*, and *Historical Social Research*—are still the principal outlets for the results and methods of scientific social history. For comments on the retreat of social scientific political and economic history see J. H. Silbey, 'Delegates from the People? American Congressional and Legislative Behaviour', *Journal of Interdisciplinary History*, 3 (1983), 603–27; P. Temin, 'Economic History in the 1980s: The Future of the New Economic History', *Journal of Interdisciplinary History*, 12 (1981), 179–97; D. McCloskey, 'Ancients and Moderns', *Social Science History*, 14 (1990), 289–303.

[37] Summer schools and conferences were established from the 1960s with support from the ICPR, IBM, the Council of Social Science Data Archives, the National Archive Record Service, the American Historical Association, the American Council of Learned Societies, and by history departments at different universities. Most were reported in *History Methods Newsletter* from 1968. In Europe, by the early 1980s historians could avail themselves of summer schools offered by the Economic and Social Research Council, Quantum, the Max Planck Institute for History in Göttingen, the University of Bergen, and the Danish Data Archive to name but a few. Journals which disseminate methodological advice are listed in the bibliography section IIIA.

[38] Textbooks and edited compilations are listed in the bibliography sections IA and IB, respectively.

[39] The holdings and catalogues of data archives in Britain, Denmark, Germany, the Netherlands, Norway, Sweden, and the USA are discussed in Ch. 6, pp. 202–3.

funded project to boast the integration of new methods into history.[40] From the mid-1980s institutional support for the promotion of new methods in history literally took off with the confederal, pan-European Association of History and Computing, which currently boasts national branches in a dozen or so countries.[41]

J. Morgan Kousser's survey of articles published in five leading history journals in the USA helps to interpret this seemingly paradoxical trend of diminishing interest in scientific history and expanding interest in computing the measurable. He found evidence that historians were using simple measures in their research but avoiding the complex statistics favoured by the more scientific economic and political historians.[42] A survey of the published proceedings of the first three annual conferences of the European Association for History and Computing held between 1985 and 1987 shows a similar result.[43] Of the fifty-seven papers that touched upon research results only ten used quantitative

[40] A historiographical survey of the European scene has yet to be written. The British story is told in part by R. Floud, 'Quantitative History and People's History: Two Methods in Conflict?', *Social Science History*, 8 (1984), 151–68, and F. O'Gorman, 'Electoral Behaviour in England, 1700–1872', in P. R. Denley *et al.* (eds.), *History and Computing, II* (Manchester, 1989), 220–38. For France see J.-P. Genet, 'L'Historien et l'ordinateur', *Historiens et géographes*, 270 (1978), 133. For Germany, James Harris, 'Computer Analysis in German History', *Computers and the Humanities*, 13 (1979); A. E. Imhof, 'The Computer in Social History: Historical Demography in Germany', *Computers and the Humanities*, 12 (1978), 227–36; E. A. Johnson, 'Counting "How it Really Was"', 61 ff. Other contributions include D. Herlihy, 'Quantification in the 1980s: Numerical and Formal Analysis in European History', *Journal of Interdisciplinary History*, 12 (1981), 115–35; Iggers, *New Directions in European Historiography*; R. C. W. van der Voort, 'The Growth of Historical Information Systems in Historical Sciences', in R. Metz *et al.* (eds.), *Historical Information Systems. Session B–12b. Proceedings, Tenth International Economic History Congress, Leuven, August 1990* (Leuven, 1990), 3–9. Other references to national developments are given in section IVE of the bibliography.

[41] As of summer 1992 national branches exist in Austria, Canada, France, Italy, the 'Nordic Countries' (one branch for Denmark, Norway, and Sweden), Portugal, Spain, Switzerland, the UK, and Canada. Branches are being formed in the CIS, Estonia, Hungary, and Poland.

[42] J. M. Kousser, 'Quantitative Social Science History', in Kammen (ed.), *The Past before Us*, 433–56. The journals included in the survey were *American Historical Review, Journal of American History, Journal of Modern History, Journal of Southern History, William and Mary Quarterly*.

[43] Denley and Hopkin (eds.), *History and Computing*; Denley *et al*, *History and Computing II*; E. Mawdsley *et al.* (eds.), *History and Computing III: Historians, Computers and Data. Applications in Research and Teaching* (Manchester, 1990). Articles of a purely pedagogic and/or methodological nature were excluded from the latter survey.

methods which Kousser classified as 'more advanced'; and here
unlike Kousser's survey the field was made up entirely of papers
resulting from computer-aided research projects. Just as Kousser
discovered that social historians in the USA were willing to use
simple descriptive statistics, the survey of later work conducted in
Europe suggests the computer's principal use in the late 1980s is
for organizing, managing, and summarizing information which
has been hitherto inaccessible to the historian. It is not, on the
whole, used for sophisticated number crunching and mathematical modelling. There is also evidence of relatively 'new' uses
which were not available to the scientific history enthusiasts of
the 1960s and which involve no number crunching at all,
including image processing (art history) and linguistic content
analysis (text-critical studies).[44] In sum, then, the computer was
most certainly a midwife in attendance at the birth of cliometric
and other quantitative attempts at establishing a scientific social
history. But its service to the profession in the intervening thirty
years or so has been far more general and widespread. The computer does not force a scientific perspective onto the historian
even as the scientific historian is likely to be amongst those most
adept in its use.

<br>

'COMPUTERS HANDLE ONLY HIGHLY STRUCTURED
INFORMATION, THE LIKE OF WHICH IS RARELY FOUND IN
HISTORICAL SOURCES'

A third myth assumes that computers can only manage rigidly
structured, unambiguous data and are thus unsuitable for most
historical information, which is inherently woolly. The assump-
tion is accurate when applied to the equipment on which pioneering historians mounted the first computer-aided projects in the
1960s, but ignores the pace of technological advance in subsequent years. Twenty-five years ago there were severe constraints

---

[44] For the latest in image processing see J. Fikfak and G. Jaritz (eds.), *Image
Processing in History: Towards Open Systems* (St Katharinen, 1993); G. Jaritz,
*Images: A Primer of Computer-Supported Research with Kleio IAS* (St Katharinen,
1993); G. Jaritz, 'Medieval Image Databases: Aspects of Cooperation and
Exchange', *Literary and Linguistic Computing*, 6 (1991), 15–19; M. Thaller (ed.),
*Images and Manuscripts in Historical Computing* (St Katharinen, 1992). For textual
analysis see Ch. 5.

on the amount of data that any one project could handle. The media for data storage were primitive and computer processing power, the number of individual transactions conducted in a given period of time, was limited. Data representation on Hollerith or punch cards, however, imposed the most immediate and perhaps the severest limitations. Punch cards, which persisted as data input and storage devices into the 1970s, comprised eighty columns and twelve rows. Any card could contain eighty characters, one per column, and each character could be represented by punching holes in one, two, or three of the twelve rows in its column. Numeric data such as those which might be found in aggregate manufacturing and population censuses, shipping registers, business accounts, and electoral returns were not so much a problem. The numeric data from an account which showed that an 18-year-old male slave sold for $325 dollars in Mudflats, Mississippi, could be represented easily and unambiguously.

With text, only one character could be represented in each column of a punch card, and the natural inclination was to abbreviate wherever possible so as to minimize the tedium of data entry and the number of cards used in any project. Clearly, it was not appropriate to abbreviate the full texts on which early computer-aided content analyses or concordances were being conducted.[45] Studies which attempted systematic characterization of given objects, events, or individuals, however, could economize. Take, for example, a collective biography of a group of parliamentarians. Here, the same variables or kinds of information would be sought for each parliamentarian including, for example, date and place of birth, name of secondary school, name of university, and highest degree obtained. The variables once collected would then be recorded on Hollerith or punch cards in the same order for each person. The person's name would come first, for example, followed by date of birth, place of birth, and so on. When entering data the compulsion would be to restrict to as few cards as possible the information about each individual, preferably by keeping all the data about each individual on one punch card. To do this, the place of birth variable whose value was 'Rochester, Kent' might just as well be represented as a numeric code '196', which could be entered up in far fewer columns than the full text

[45] Hockey, 'An Historical Perspective'.

required. Where textual data needed to be classified anyway for analytical purposes—for example, where Rochester, Kent, needed to be categorized as a city of type 3 indicating that it had a population of between 10,000 and 25,000, and thus permitting analyses of whether parliamentarians tended to be drawn from urban or rural backgrounds—the tendency was to enter the classified value on the punch card rather than the data from which the value was ultimately derived.

Already by the mid-1960s there was concern that the constraints which forced users to seek economies in representing their data wherever possible were distorting the results of computer-aided research. There were two problems. First, the inclination to use the fewest possible punch-card columns for any one variable placed severe restrictions on the schemes that researchers used to classify their variables. Some information was not problematic. Gender, for example, could be classified in one column with numbers representing three possible values: male, female, and unknown. Other information was more difficult to represent in only a small handful of categories without sacrificing its richness and complexity. J. J. McCusker's criticism of T. K. Rabb's study of the British landed class and its role in promoting imperial expansion through investment in foreign trade is indicative of the problem. 'One of [Rabb's] continuing difficulties', McCusker wrote,

concerns the coding of his data. He laments in several places that he was unable to distinguish more than thirty-three trading ventures because of the limitations of the symbols on a keypunch machine (and on an IBM card) to 33 non-numeric punches. There were many more companies which he would have liked to have used but he could only allot one column as his field for this information and he severely feels this restriction.[46]

In retrospect, Rabb could have alleviated the problem to some extent with more sophisticated techniques of which he was apparently unaware. For example, he could have used more than one punch card for every record. But even had he done so, the constraints he felt would only have been somewhat relaxed; they would not have been removed.

Secondly, there was a problem designing classification schemes.

[46] J. J. McCusker's review of T. K. Rabb's *Enterprise and Empire: Merchant and Gentry Investments in the Expansion of England, 1575–1630* (Cambridge, Mass., 1967), in *History Methods Newsletter*, 2 (1969).

For some, historical information was thought to be too richly textured and complex to be easily or neatly classified. The computer, Robert Woods complained, requires 'an uncompromising taxonomy for historical data, which in many cases achieved machine precision only by distorting their complexity and by imposing an artificial certainty on reality'.[47] The more ambiguous the historical evidence was in its original form, the more criticism the coding exercise came in for. It was one thing to categorize place names like 'Rochester, Kent'. It was quite another to classify information whose interpretation was at best subjective. How, for example, was the collective biographer to classify an individual's occupation given simply as 'merchant' in an early nineteenth-century city or business directory? Did the term imply small-time grocer or shipping magnate? Sometimes the ambiguity could be resolved with reference to other sources, for example, to contemporary biographies, personal correspondences, newspapers, or probate inventories. Elsewhere it could be resolved on the basis of contextual information within the directory itself. A merchant whose entry showed a business address near the docks and a residential address in a salubrious part of town might be treated differently from one whose entry showed only one address in an area known to have housed a disproportion of recent immigrants and casual labourers. In either case, however, the researcher was forced to impose an interpretation on the data which was forever lost as soon as the data were entered up onto the punch card.

The imposition of rigid taxonomies on historical events came under even more intense fire as evident in the attacks on Charles Tilly's computer classification of contentious gatherings in industrializing Western Europe.[48] Tilly had collected from literary sources information about the time, place, and outstanding characteristics of hundreds of violent incidents, including material about the issues and participants alleged to be involved. By classifying these data according to pre-defined schemes he hoped to

[47] R. L. Woods, 'Historians, Programmers, and Computer Languages: APL in Historical Research', *Computers and the Humanities*, 16 (1982), 229–43.
[48] C. Tilly, *The Vendée* (Cambridge, Mass., 1964); C., L., and R. Tilly, *The Rebellious Century, 1830–1930* (London, 1975); C. Tilly and E. Shorter, *Strikes in France, 1830–1968* (London, 1974), and the criticisms levelled against their methods as discussed in Stone, 'History and the Social Sciences', 33. The issue is taken up again by Fogel in R. W. Fogel and G. R. Elton, *Which Road to the Past? Two Views of History* (New Haven, Conn., 1983), 53.

determine the objectives, form, timing, and size of contentious gatherings, as well as their underlying social determinants in an era of industrial development.[49] For some, the historical evidence was simply too ambiguous and relied upon too much in the way of subjective interpretation to sustain such analysis. In effect, what Tilly was analysing was not so much hard historical data but his personal reading of them.

For scientific social historians, the exigencies of data representation advanced rather than impeded historical research by forcing scholars to state their research aims and underlying assumptions explicitly.[50] The categories of information which Tilly collected about contentious gatherings were self-consciously defined to answer specific and well-articulated questions. At the same time, the way in which he classified information in any one category, for example the social complexion of the mob's members, explicitly exposed to a critical audience his working assumptions about nineteenth-century social structures. Rabb's classification of trading ventures was likewise an explicit statement of his conception of hierarchy and order amongst late seventeenth-century English commercial traders. For other historians, this practice of cramming historical information into rigidly defined categories only provoked distaste for computer-aided research. It seemed to encapsulate the worst excesses of a scientific history which, in its pursuit of objective results and verifiable models of social change, proved to be less than sympathetic to the ambiguities inherent in the historical record.

The great irony here is that in the past twenty-five years or so technological developments have mitigated the need to impose rigid taxonomies upon historical information. Despite this, doubt and scepticism about computer-aided historical research still

---

[49] For an explanation of his method see C. Tilly and R. A. Schweitzer, 'Enumerating and Coding Contentious Gatherings in Nineteenth-Century Britain', Working Paper, 210, Center for Research on Social Organizations, University of Michigan (Ann Arbor, Mich., 1980) and Tilly's, 'The Web of Contention in Eighteenth Century Cities' in C. Tilly (ed.), *Class Conflict and Collective Action* (Berkeley, Calif., 1981), 48–51.

[50] L. T. Milic, 'The Next Step', *Computers and the Humanities*, 1 (1966), 3–6; C. M. Dollar, 'Innovation in Historical Research: A Computer Approach', *Computers and the Humanities*, 3 (1968), 139–51; K. H. Jarausch's introduction to K. H. Jarausch et al., *Quantitative Methoden in der Geschichtswissenschaft: Eine Einführung in die Forschung, Datenverarbeitung und Statistic* (Darmstadt, 1985); F. Furet, 'Quantitative History', in F. Furet (ed.), *In the Workshop of History* (London, 1984), 44–5.

lingers inhibiting historians from taking full advantage of this increasingly useful tool. Amongst the most significant technological advances are improvements in computer hardware. The magnetic media which store machine-readable information, notably the so-called hard disk, make vast amounts of filestore so readily available and inexpensive as to remove any compunction to economize by abbreviating data. Processing power, too, has increased considerably so that data manipulations which once required days to complete now require only a few seconds. Improvements in data input facilities also have proceeded apace. As any word-processing enthusiast knows, computers are no longer shy or unwieldy where the input of textual information is concerned. Individual characters can be input as quickly as they can be typed from the keyboard; they no longer have to be entered as numeric combinations punched onto Hollerith cards. Editing facilities too have improved. Errant characters may be spotted on the VDT (visual display terminal) and corrected instantaneously. Editing no longer requires the recreation of whole punch cards. And just as the keyboard and the VDT represent a quantum leap over the punch card with respect to the speed, efficiency, and accuracy of data entering and editing, optical character readers, which use a light source to scan whole pages of text in seconds, make further advances of similar magnitude.[51]

A major consequence of these changes is that computers are now far more capable of handling volumes of complex and ambiguous textual information the like of which is central to so much historical research. Information still must be classified before it can be analysed but, as Chapter 3 demonstrates, modern database management systems enable the researcher to enter information as it is found in the original source and store alongside it any number of classification schemes used in its analysis. Classification schemes no longer have to be irrevocably imposed on the data themselves.[52] Likewise, with modern text retrieval and analysis techniques such as those discussed in Chapter 5, Charles Tilly would have been able to capture in machine-readable form the complete running text of the literary sources on which his analysis of contentious gatherings was based. Here,

---

[51] See Ch. 6, pp. 229–34.
[52] See Ch. 3 and D. I. Greenstein, 'Multi-Sourced and Integrated Databases for the Prosopographer' in Mawdsley *et al.*, *History and Computing III*, 60–6.

too, some classification would be a prerequisite of analysis. As with the database exercise, however, classification would take place independently of the raw data, thereby permitting secondary analysts to access the very same information which Tilly had to hand, and to give it a rather different interpretation from Tilly's if they so wished.

### 'COMPUTERS REQUIRE THE CULTIVATION OF VOCATIONAL SKILLS AND THUS IMPEDE THE HISTORIAN FROM ESSENTIAL IMMERSION IN PRIMARY SOURCES'

A fourth myth associated with computer-aided history is that it diminishes the researcher's sensitivity to historical problems and to the vagaries of historical sources through mind-numbing data entry and editing, and through the acquisition of the vocational skills required to operate the machine. Once again we encounter two assumptions which have been largely outmoded by technological advance. In the early 1970s Charles Tilly wrote that computer-aided research projects 'produced important periods when the researchers are so preoccupied with problems of coding, file construction, statistical procedure, computer techniques, and coordination of the whole effort that they practically lose contact with the people, events, places, and times they are studying'.[53] In a 1977 article, Lawrence Stone, another pioneer in computer-aided historical research, agreed, but was somewhat less optimistic than Tilly about the short-term effects that such periods had on the historian. 'Worst of all', Stone wrote, 'is the atrophy of the critical facilities that the mere use of punch cards and computers seems to produce . . . The historian, despite his largely humanistic training, is as liable to this insidiously corrupting mental deformation as are his colleagues in the social sciences.'[54]

Given the computer equipment and processing techniques that were available to Tilly and Stone when they were conducting their work some fifteen and twenty years ago, these sentiments are hardly surprising. Whether they are relevant today is another matter. Quite simply, a great deal of time, patience, assistance, and

[53] C. Tilly, 'Computers in Historical Analysis', *Computers and the Humanities*, 7 (1973), 328.
[54] Stone, 'History and the Social Sciences', 29.

detailed knowledge was required of anyone daring to use a computer well into the 1970s.[55] Powerful yet affordable desktop workstations which allow consenting adults to compute in the privacy of their homes and offices, and 'user-friendly' software which enables non-specialists to perform complex tasks with a minimal understanding of how they actually work, were still in the distant future. Computing took place instead at the university computing centre. There the historian brought 'coding sheets' on which information gathered from the historical record had been transcribed in a form suitable for representation on eighty-column punch cards. Punch cards would be prepared from the sheets by trained keypunch operators and the cards so prepared would be read into the computer and their data output onto magnetic tape (for reuse), and/or printed onto paper so they could be checked by the researcher. Any errors spotted on the print-out could be corrected by replacing offending punch cards or by appending additional punch cards comprising instructions for editing the original ones.

Data entry and editing were labour intensive and would consume years instead of months, especially where projects involved vast quantities of data; and most did. After all, a *raison d'être* of computer-aided research was to make sense of information hitherto thought too voluminous to be at all accessible.[56] Through the years of data entry and verification the historian was removed from the coal-face of day-to-day research, which was left instead to research assistants and computer operators. Given the research environment surrounding a computer-aided project it was impossible for the historian slowly to build his interpretation through total immersion in the literary sources. Historians were at a distance from the research process, too, when a project reached its analytical phase. Here the researcher became almost entirely dependent on highly trained computer programmers who were required to instruct the machine to collate and analyse the data once they were accurately available in machine-readable form.[57] Historical questions once formulated had to be explained to the

---

[55] V. L. Bullough, 'The Computer and the Historian: Some Tentative Beginnings', *Computers and the Humanities*, 1 (1966), 61–4; Dollar, 'Innovation in Historical Research'.

[56] Swierenga, 'Clio and Computers', 1–4.

[57] Although so-called high-level programming languages were available from the mid-1950s, few in the humanities were sufficiently fluent in their use to employ them unassisted in their research.

programmer who would compile the appropriate set of computer instructions so that the questions could be asked of the assembled data. Where analyses were regressive, such that the results of one calculation provoked new questions, the process was by necessity repeated. And there was no guarantee that results could be obtained quickly, especially where data sets were voluminous and/or where the questions asked of them involved complex mathematical or sorting operations.

The absence of much commercial software also impeded the progress of early computer-aided historical research projects. Into the early 1970s there was still very little software from which historians could benefit. Consequently, projects had to develop their own computer programs on an *ad hoc* basis to solve very specific problems. Thus, the data management programs written especially for Aydelotte's parliamentary voting study or for the Library of Congress for that matter, had little to offer other historians with data management problems of a similar nature. Deeply involved in the day-to-day administration of large-scale collaborative research projects and with the development of computer programs for specific data sets, the computer-using historian found less time for traditional archival research. For some, the historian's subordination to the machine was evident in an alleged tendency toward mindless empiricism—a narrowness demonstrated in the published results of computer-aided research and in the so-called SPSS theses.[58]

In the 1990s, the conduct of computer-aided research has been altered radically by technological advance. Improved computer hardware has increased the speed, efficiency, and accuracy with which larger and larger quantities of machine-readable data are created, edited, manipulated, and analysed as indicated above. It also underpins improved computer software which makes computers more accessible to non-specialists whose dependence on computer scientists and trained operators is consequently reduced. The programming and command languages used to instruct computers in their tasks have become simpler to learn and to use as their syntax increasingly approximates that of natural spoken language. They have also become far more powerful, as any one

[58] Kousser, 'Quantitative Social Science History', 444–6; Silbey, 'Delegates from the People?', 603–27; A. G. Bogue, 'The New Political History in the 1970s', in Kammen, *The Past before Us*, 250.

statement now performs functions which would have required tens or even hundreds of individual statements only a decade ago. User-friendly software which can be bought 'off the shelf' and readily adapted to historical research also proliferates and replaces the need for historians to design and create proprietary programs.[59] The word processor is a perfect example. To use it, the user does not need to know how the computer works (or have a hot line to a computer scientist). All that is required is the ability to follow simple on-screen instructions, occasionally choosing between different well-documented options.

In the forthcoming chapters, we shall be examining in a general way several kinds of software including those appropriate for data management (Chapter 3), statistical and graphical analysis, and tabular display (Chapter 4), and for text retrieval and analysis (Chapter 5). All of the software is accessible to anyone with a very basic understanding of computers which includes knowledge of where the on-off switch is, what a keyboard looks like, and perhaps some rudimentary file or disk management procedures. With most of the software that is discussed the novice might be 'up and running' after only a few hours of self-instruction; the assistance of expert computer scientists or trained operators is rarely required. These developments in computer software ensure that computer-aided historical research no longer forces the historian to take up residence at the local computing centre or acquire an expertise in computing science.

Historians have benefited as well from the development and documentation of innovative computational techniques. Computerized nominal record linkage is a particularly good example. Already by the late 1960s historians were experimenting successfully with computer-aided record linkage techniques developed initially for the medical sciences and for business.[60] In five

[59] There is also a tradition of software developed by and for historians. See L. A. Glasco, 'Computerizing the Manuscript Census', *Historical Methods Newsletter*, 3 (1969) 1–4; D. Spaeth, *A Guide to Software for Historians* (Glasgow, 1991), 66; M. Thaller, 'The Historical Workstation Project', *Computers and the Humanities*, 25 (1991), 149–62; M. Thaller (ed.), *Kleio: A Database System* (St Katharinen, 1993). For a general discussion about historians' role in software development see D. I. Greenstein and N. Morgan, 'Software for Historians?', *History and Computing*, 1 (1989), 38–41; J. Olderroll (ed.), *Eden or Babylon? On Future Software for Highly Structured Historical Sources* (St Katharinen, 1992).

[60] See S. W. Baskerville, P. Hudson, and R. J. Morris (eds.), *History and Computing Special Issue: Record Linkage*, 4 (1992) and the bibliography section IID.

months 1,863 of the 2,550 individuals represented in Hamilton, Ontario's 1852 tax assessment were found by hand in the 1851 census. When automated a similar, perhaps even slightly more accurate result was achieved in four machine minutes.[61] This one innovation helped to open up whole new areas to computer-aided investigation by providing an accurate means of building up from several different sources (e.g. city directories, census and census-like lists, probate inventories, parish registers) rudimentary biographies for large numbers of people. Analyses of élites, social mobility, social structures, and historical demography, to name but a few examples, all benefited as a result.[62] Documentation proved as important as innovative developments themselves in so far as it enabled researchers to benefit from their predecessors' experience and free themselves from having to recreate solutions to generic technical and computational problems. Here journals, methodological textbooks, and conferences aimed expressly at historians and devoted in whole or in part to computational methods have been so important.

More powerful hardware, better and more user-friendly software, and better documentation in the techniques most appropriate to historical research have transformed the nature of computer-aided history. Together these developments have helped to populate areas which only ten or fifteen years ago were on the methodological frontier. Admittedly, they detract from the romantic image of pioneering scholarship once associated by some with computer-aided history. At the same time, however, much of the frustration and drudgery that pioneers like Tilly and Stone clearly felt has been eliminated. Despite these developments, however, computer-aided research projects can still absorb an enormous amount of time and money, and require a degree of methodological and technical expertise which is not obtainable in public record offices, libraries, and archives. Consequently, a generation of trained historians is beginning to emerge comprising amongst its number people whose expertise is spread between historical

[61] I. Winchester, 'The Linkage of Historical Records by Man and Computer: Techniques and Problems', *Journal of Interdisciplinary History*, 1 (1970), 112, 123.

[62] Ibid.; K. Schürer, 'Historical Demography, Social Structure and the Computer', in Denley and Hopkin (eds.), *History and Computing*, 33–42; E. A. Wrigley and R. S. Schofield, 'Nominal Record Linkage by Computer and the Logic of Family Reconstitution', in E. A. Wrigley, *Identifying People in the Past* (London, 1973), 64–101.

scholarship as it is normally construed, and computational methods appropriate to history. The regular appearance in educational journals of job advertisements seeking such people for research and/or teaching appointments, demonstrates the extent to which their skills are highly sought after.

Yet there is a conundrum here which only the profession can resolve. To date, the published products of historical scholarship, monographs, and articles in learned journals are still the principal criteria upon which monetary reward and professional recognition are meted out. Other contributions which absorb as much in the way of time and intellectual effort—new methodological or computational techniques, data sets which have some general usefulness—are all but discounted. Until the profession recognizes the merit of less traditional contributions to scholarship it will be unable to secure and promote members whose expertise it clearly requires. Likewise, until we shed the prejudices engendered in a century-long debate about whether history is an art or a science—a prejudice entrenched more deeply by an obsolete image of what using a computer actually entails—we will fail to take full advantage of a technology which is now at a stage of development when it can be harnessed to our work without altering the very individualistic way in which we conduct it.

# 2

# A Daily Diet

Computers are already a part of everyday life—few in humanities disciplines will lack at least some experience in word processing—but they are underutilized. Nor does their greater utilization require advanced knowledge of quantitative methods. This chapter sets out how the computer systems that are available to most historians can be incorporated more fully into the day-to-day tasks of teaching, administration, and research, thereby making those tasks more efficient, more effective, and perhaps even more enjoyable.

## TEACHING MATERIALS

Surely no one will question the benefits of word processing on a desktop computer. For teaching, the word processor is a godsend. Course syllabuses and reading lists once entered into a word processing package can be formatted for printed presentation and altered from year to year reflecting the changes that occur in any course which is offered more than once. Lectures and seminar papers can be modified to incorporate new ideas and information, or amended to take account of a restless or doubting audience when one is encountered the first time a paper is tried. The administration of examination papers and essay assignments is simplified and made more effective if the questions are stored in word-processing files, perhaps adjacent to comments indicating how far each question elicited creative and well-substantiated answers.

Desktop computers can also be used to graph numeric information thereby making it more accessible to a student audience than a recital of the relevant data. A lecture which emphasizes differential rates of nineteenth-century industrial development, for example, is more likely to succeed in getting its message across to students if it confronts them with visual evidence. Figures 2.1 and 2.2 exemplify the point. They make nineteenth-century economic and demographic trends instantly and visibly accessible to the uninitiated. Figure 2.1 compares long-term trends in the gross national product of nineteenth-century European powers.[1] Figure 2.2 shows the pace at which people concentrated in cities in four industrializing nations during the nineteenth century.[2] Lessons in social and economic history will not be the only ones to benefit from graphic material. Pie charts comparing nations' military capabilities (Figure 2.3) and tables showing the proportion of national income spent on defence (Figure 2.4) might be effective in lectures on international diplomacy.[3] Graphs and tables are invaluable to teaching and there are any number of uses to which they can be put. The fact is that historians spend some time counting up or measuring the occurrences of events, and wherever that practice informs their teaching its results may be more effectively presented in a visual than in a spoken form.

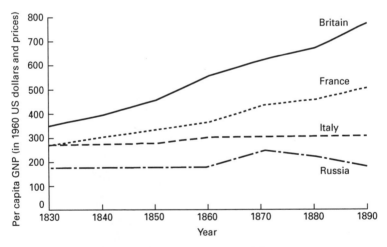

Fig. 2.1 Line graph showing per capita GNP of four European powers, 1830–1899

[1] Figures from P. Kennedy, *The Rise and Fall of the Great Powers: Economic Change and Military Conflict from 1500 to 2000* (London, 1988), 220.

[2] Figures from A. Lees, *Cities Perceived: Urban Society in European and American Thought, 1820–1940* (Manchester, 1985), 4.

[3] Kennedy, *Rise and Fall*, 430, 429.

*A Daily Diet*

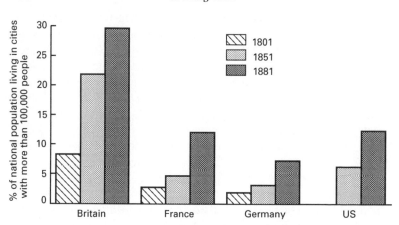

Fig. 2.2 Bar graph showing population growth in large cities in Britain, France, Germany, and the USA, 1801, 1851, and 1881

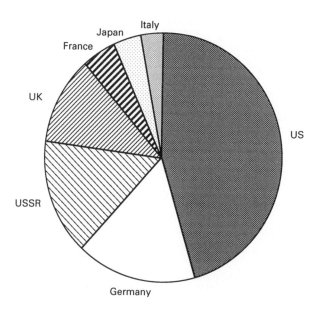

Fig. 2.3 Pie chart showing relative war potential of the powers in 1937

| Country | National income (billions of dollars) | % spent on defence |
|---|---|---|
| United States | 68 | 1.5 |
| British Empire | 22 | 5.7 |
| France | 10 | 9.1 |
| Germany | 17 | 23.5 |
| Italy | 6 | 14.5 |
| USSR | 19 | 26.4 |
| Japan | 4 | 28.2 |

Fig. 2.4 Table showing national income of the powers in 1937, and percentage spent on defence

Visual aids are also useful in focusing the attention of a drifting audience, and most audiences do drift at some point in an hour-long lecture. At least, this is what staff-development and teacher-training officers have us believe; that the lecture or seminar hour does not coincide neatly with the normal attention span of even the brightest and most mature student. The teacher therefore works in the last twenty-five minutes or so of any hour-long class against the diminishing attention of the audience, irrespective of his or her brilliance and charisma. Unsurprisingly, the profession has developed its own presentational devices designed to haul an idly drifting audience back on course at critical junctures. Changes in speech patterns and tone, jokes, and interactive dialogue all help to pull an audience back into the teacher's confidence and argument. To this litany might be added the use of visual aids in the form of graphs and tables which present information effectively while providing a device which breaks up the verbal content of a lecture into more easily digestible bits.

Further illustration of how to prepare graphs and tables with a computer is given in Chapter 4. Suffice it to say here that computational expertise is not required. Figures 2.1 to 2.4 were prepared in a matter of minutes from basic data found in standard textbooks. And the data themselves were used to demonstrate to students the problems inherent in compiling comparative serial or trend information. The data for Figure 2.2, for example, were used to demonstrate the problems involved in compiling comparable population estimates for nineteenth-century nation states with boundaries which were in flux, and with wildly different census-taking techniques.[4] Presenting these problems provides students with a useful starting-point for discussion about the reliability and use of historical sources generally, and the problems of cross-national and serial analysis.

Having gathered the data and drawn the graphs or created the tables appropriate to a lecture, the pictures can be presented in any number of ways. They can be printed for distribution to small seminar groups for closer collective scrutiny. For larger groups it is often more effective to display images on a screen in the front of a lecture theatre or classroom. Graphs and tables can be printed onto acetates and presented onto a screen with an overhead projector. Where a computer is available in the lecture room, the visual aids needn't be printed at all. Instead, they can be displayed on a viewframe or tablet—an alternative computer terminal which is connected to the computer but rests on top of an overhead projector. Alternatively, computer images can be broadcast onto lecture-hall screens through so-called Barco projectors which offer the additional advantage of displaying colour graphics. Once again, none of these techniques requires very much in the way of computational sophistication or financial investment. They rely instead on devices which are relatively affordable, and on computer methods which may be learned in a morning. Despite its overt simplicity, this use of a computer promises to make a greater range of historical information more accessible to students.

## BIBLIOGRAPHIES AND RESEARCH NOTES

Simple computer techniques can also be adopted to the administration of teaching and research materials. Bibliographical references, once stored by necessity on note cards and extensively cross-referenced by author, subject, and/or title, can be computerized for greater and easier accessibility. A computerized bibliography is nothing more than an automated version of what is already available on note cards. The computerized bibliography

---

[4] I wish to thank my first-year students at Glasgow University, whose attempts to reproduce Lee's population estimates for 19th-century European nations proved so instructive.

contains one 'record' or entry for every bibliographic reference
and as many 'fields' or items of information as are required for a
given reference (e.g. author, title). Figure 2.5 shows a sample
record from a computerized bibliography. It contains fields for
author, title, publisher, and for place and date of publication.
Notice, too, that the record contains fields giving supplementary
information including where the item referred to, in this case a
book, can be found in the local library (GUL or Glasgow
University Library), and how it has been used, in this case in a
course called 'USA since 1876'. There are also two fields which
describe the item's contents: a keywords field provides a subject
classification and a description field a rather fuller commentary
about the volume itself.

```
------------------------------BOOK------------------------------
AUTHORS:      Lynd, Robert S.
              Lynd, Helen Merrell

TITLE:        Middletown: A Study in Modern American Culture

PUBLISHER:    Harcourt Brace Jovanovich

PUB LOCATION  San Diego                        DATE: 1929

CALL NUMBER:  Sociology C157 LYN   USE: USA since 1876

LOCATION:     GUL floor 3   KEYWORDS: Sociology - USA - Twentieth Century
------------------------------DESCRIPTION:------------------------------
An early and pioneering community study which examines the structure and
experience of daily life in Muncie, Indiana, in the 1920s.
```

Fig. 2.5 Sample record from a bibliographic database

With these several fields, the computerized bibliography, like
the note-card one, is searchable according to several different criteria. Otherwise, all comparisons cease because the computerized
bibliography is infinitely more flexible than the note-card one. If
the note-card bibliography is to be searched by author's name,
subject keyword, and title, a separate card file has to be prepared
for each of the three search criteria, and each reference copied
onto three separate cards, one for each of the card files. In the
computerized bibliography each reference occurs once and is
accessible according to the information stored in any of its fields.
The reference in Figure 2.5 will be found by searching for either
Helen and/or Robert Lynd, for books published by Harcourt Brace

Jovanovich in 1929, for items used in the course entitled USA since 1876, and for sociological works about Muncie, Indiana.[5]

Computerized bibliographies may be developed with database management or full-text retrieval systems, which are discussed in greater detail in Chapters 3 and 5, respectively.[6] Since such systems are designed to support very general information-management needs, they may not provide the specialist facilities required for bibliographic records. Software designed especially for bibliographies may be more appropriate. In particular it will enable users to deal more easily with the idiosyncratic and varied structure of bibliographic references (references to journal articles and books, for example, are structured very differently), to print bibliographic entries in suitable formats, and to import records from other so-called on-line bibliographic systems.[7] Let us briefly look at each of these three facilities.

Bibliographical references are particularly problematic because their intrinsic structure varies so much from one reference to another. For example, a reference to a monograph is different from a reference to an article in a learned journal, and a reference to an article in a learned journal is different from a reference to an article in an edited book. In a computerized bibliography as in a note-card one, these three references require three different combinations of fields as shown in Figure 2.6. The problem is that database management systems normally permit only one combination of fields for any collection of records.[8] Bibliographic software, on the other hand, will normally permit records in a collection to be structured rather differently. Thus, in one bibliographic database entries for books might use the combination of fields shown in Figure 2.5 while articles in learned journals and in books might possess a slightly different combination of fields as shown in Figure 2.7. There may be facilities as well to handle more eccentric references such as those to audio or visual recordings, to pieces of art, or to items in manuscript collections.

Bibliographic software will also provide the means of printing

[5] For more on selective data retrieval see Ch. 3, pp. 98–104.
[6] For a review of bibliography software written by and for historians see S. Davnall, 'Bibliographic Software for PC's', *History and Computing*, 4 (1992), 139–41.
[7] See pp. 55–8.
[8] Collections of records referring to the same object are commonly known as tables in database parlance. See Ch. 3, p. 64.

| Book | Article in a Learned Journal | Article in an Edited Book |
|---|---|---|
| Authors | Authors | Authors |
|  | Title | Title |
|  | Periodical Title |  |
| Book Title |  | Book Title |
|  |  | Book Editor |
|  | Periodical Volume |  |
|  | Periodical Number |  |
| Edition |  | Edition |
| Publisher |  | Publisher |
| Location |  | Location |
| Date | Date | Date |
|  | Page | Page |

Fig. 2.6 Different structures required for common types of bibliographic citation

records or preparing them for incorporation into a word process-ing file (say, for example, at the end of a journal article, chapter, or book) in an appropriate format and style. Thus, the user should be able to print selected references in an abbreviated or annotated fashion, or as they might be found on a library cata-logue card as shown in Figure 2.8. A range of the most well-known and commonly used 'stylesheets' also should be on offer, for example those recommended by the Modern Language Association, *The Chicago Manual of Style*, or by K. L. Turabian.[9] Bibliography software will also allow users to load records retrieved from other on-line bibliographic databases. For example, it will be possible to search the on-line database *American History and Life* for references to journals and books about the Whig party's performance in South Carolina in the presidential election of 1836, transmit the references to a desktop computer, and load the transmitted references directly into the personal bibliography kept there.[10]

---

[9] *Hart's Rules for Compositors and Readers at the University Press Oxford*, 38th edn. (Oxford, 1978); *The MLA Handbook for Writers of Research Papers*, 3rd edn. (New York, 1988); *The Chicago Manual of Style: For Authors, Editors, and Copywriters*, 13th edn. (Chicago, 1985); K. L. Turabian, *A Manual for Writers of Term Papers, Theses, and Dissertations*, 4th edn. (Chicago, 1973).

[10] See pp. 55–8.

| | JOURNAL ARTICLE |
|---|---|
| **AUTHORS:** | Brunk, Gregory G. |
| **TITLE:** | Freshmen vs. Incumbents: Congressional Voting Patterns on Prohibition Legislation during the Progressive Era |
| **PERIODICAL:** | Journal of American Studies |
| **VOLUME:** 24 | **ISSUE:** 2          **DATE:** August 1990 |
| **PAGES:** 235-242 | |
| **USE:** USA since 1876 | **LOCATION:** GUL floor 5 |
| **KEYWORDS:** Progressive Era - USA - Politics | |
| DESCRIPTION: | |

A compact study of voting volatility amongst freshmen and incumbent US Congressmen.

| | ARTICLE IN BOOK |
|---|---|
| **AUTHORS:** | Fink, Leon |
| **TITLE:** | The Uses of Political Power: Toward a Theory of the Labor Movement in the Era of the Knights of Labor |
| **EDITORS:** | Frisch, Michael H. Walkowitz, Daniel J. |
| **BOOK TITLE:** | Working-Class America: Essays on Labor, Community, and American Society |
| **PUBLISHER:** | University of Illinois Press |
| **PUB LOCATION** Urbana | **DATE:** 1983          **PAGES:** 123-152 |
| **CALL NUMBER:** Economics J3266 FRI | **USE:** USA since 1876 |
| **LOCATION:** GUL floor 5 | **KEYWORDS:** USA - Labor History |
| DESCRIPTION: | |

Analyzes the political outlook and aspirations of the Knights of Labor.

*Note*: The structure of a book citation is shown in Fig. 2.5

Fig. 2.7 Differently structured citations represented in a bibliographic database

    Research notes, like bibliographic references, can also be computerized with software that offers data or text management and retrieval facilities.[11] As with bibliographic references, the structure of research notes will vary. Some notes adhere strictly to the principle of one fact per card; others appear as a list of related facts, for example city-council election results taken from a nineteenth-century newspaper. Still other notes commit to paper the brilliant flashes of imaginative, synthetic insight which occur to the researcher while reading through a particular source.

[11] See Chs. 3 and 5.

Despite this variation it is possible to identify enough common characteristics to design a computerized research-note management system. First, each note is a unique document or record. Secondly, every note makes some reference to its source (e.g. with an abbreviated bibliographic citation and page reference). The structure of a computerized research-note management system reflects these shared characteristics. It will comprise fields for bibliographic information and a field containing the contents of the

**ABBREVIATED:**
**Fink, Leon.** 'The Uses of Political Power: Toward a Theory of the Labor Movement in the Era of the Knights of Labor', in Michael H. Frisch and Daniel J. Walkowitz (ed.), *Working-Class America: Essays on Labor, Community, and American Society*, Urbana: University of Illinois Press, 1983, 123–52.
**Lynd, Robert S. and Helen Merrell Lynd.** *Middletown: A Study in Modern American Culture*, San Diego: Harcourt Brace Jovanovich, 1929.

**ANNOTATED:**
**Fink, Leon.** 'The Uses of Political Power: Toward a Theory of the Labor Movement in the Era of the Knights of Labor', in Michael H. Frisch and Daniel J. Walkowitz (ed.), *Working-Class America: Essays on Labor, Community, and American Society*, Urbana: University of Illinois Press, 1983, 123–52.
   Analyzes the political outlook and aspirations of the Knights of Labor.
**Lynd, Robert S. and Helen Merrell Lynd.** *Middletown: A Study in Modern American Culture*, San Diego: Harcourt Brace Jovanovich, 1929.
   An early and pioneering community study which examines the structure and experience of daily life in Muncie, Indiana, in the 1920s.

**CARD CATALOGUE:**
**Frisch, Michael H. and Daniel J. Walkowitz** (ed.), Economics J3266 FRI *Working-Class America: Essays on Labor, Community, and American Society*, Urbana: University of Illinois Press, 1983
**Lynd, Robert S. and Helen Merrell Lynd.** Sociology C157 LYN *Middletown: A Study in Modern American Culture*, San Diego: Harcourt Brace Jovanovich, 1929.

Fig. 2.8 Selected output formats available with bibliographic software

note itself. Figure 2.9 shows a record from a database constructed to accommodate notes taken for a study of national identity in the USA before 1850. Whereas the information in the bibliographic fields is likely to be abbreviated or at least reasonably brief, that entered up in the note field might be anything from a sentence fragment to an extensive list or commentary.

| RESEARCH NOTE | |
|---|---|
| **AUTHORS:** | Poulson, Charles A. |
| **TITLE:** | Extracts from Various Works of Travel... 1688-1862 |
| **PUBLISHER:** | bound folio, manuscript edition |

| **PUB LOCATION** | Philadelphia | **DATE:** | 1864 | **PAGE:** | no pagination |
|---|---|---|---|---|---|

| **LOCATION:** | Library Company of Philadelphia |
|---|---|

| **KEYWORDS:** | Philadelphia - Independence Hall - Declaration of Independence |
|---|---|

NOTE:

Writes up extracts from Captain Basil Hall's (Royal Navy), Travels in North America (1829) from which one senses a rather limited need amongst Americans for potent symbols of their own identity. After going through the Bank of the United States, Hall came upon the room in which the Declaration of Independence was signed and is astonished by the state of the room: 'all the rich pannelling, cornices, and ornamental work of this room, have been pulled down, and in their place, tame plastering and raw carpentry have been stuck up, on the occasion of some recent festival'. 'The unpleasant truth', according to Hall, is that 'nothing whatsoever, is venerated in America merely on account of its age, or, indeed, on any other account. Neither historical associations, nor high public services, nor talents, nor knowledge, claim any peculiar reverence from the busy generation of the present hour, who are reaping the fruits sown by their ancestors...'

Fig. 2.9 Sample record from a database of research notes collected for a study of emergent US nationalism before 1850

A computerized system for research-note management works along the same lines as a paper-based one. In very sophisticated paper-based systems notes are stored in one place and cross-referenced in card files laid out under logical heads (e.g. names of persons, events, periods, institutions). Notes also may be taken down on loose-leaf paper organized approximately by source, or on cards similarly arranged. These latter organizational methods are less systematic and may require considerable shuffling and reshuffling to find any one particular piece of information. With either system the principal aim is to retrieve selected research notes as required. The computer is particularly well designed to facilitate this operation. Subject keywords indicating the event, person, place, or organization upon which any one research note bears can be entered up in the research-note database to guide computerized retrieval as in the keywords field shown in Figure

2.9. The user might also conduct more comprehensive queries by calling up any note in which 'Declaration of Independence', 'Philadelphia', or 'Travel' appear in the keywords, title, or note fields. The subset of notes, once retrieved, can be arranged alphabetically by source or title, or chronologically by date of publication. Once retrieved and arranged the notes can be perused on screen or printed to paper for further manual refinement of their organization.[12]

There are some problems associated with computerized bibliographies and research-note management systems. First, there is the problem of scale. Anyone who has operated a paper-based system for many years is unlikely to have the time or resources to convert to a computerized one, and there are certainly disadvantages in straddling two systems—one on paper and the other on computer. The size of a computerized system, that is the number and length of its individual records or entries, also impinges on its operating speed. Both bibliographic and research-note databases are likely to grow in time to occupy a considerable amount of filestore and to require powerful computers to conduct standard editing and retrieval operations. Though these problems are likely to be reduced with the declining cost of increasingly powerful desktop computers, they should be considered at the outset of any such project.[13]

A second problem with the research-note database in particular is that the manipulation of research notes in preparation for writing may be a subjective process which some people need to conduct manually at least in the last instance. The computer is good at making aggregate retrievals (e.g. references to Independence Hall). More refined, highly context-sensitive, and inference-driven queries are not so easily conducted. The values entered in a keywords field, for example, may not meet the requirements of a particular retrieval. Nor is it possible to ensure that the research notes containing 'Declaration of Independence', 'Philadelphia', or 'Independence Hall' in their title, keywords, or notes fields are the ones which are most relevant to an enquiry about potent symbols of American identity in the early national period. Other records in

---

[12] A. MacFarlane, *Reconstructing Historical Communities* (Cambridge, 1977) describes a paper-based system, D. A. Spaeth, 'Computerizing the Godly: The Application of Small Databases to Anecdotal History', in E. Mawdsley *et al.* (eds.), *History and Computing III* (Manchester, 1991), 156–62, a computerized one.

[13] See Ch. 6, pp. 210–13.

which these words and phrases are absent may be more relevant. Some of these problems may be overcome in the database design stage when the field structure and the list of keywords, for example, are considered. Others may be overcome as experience is gained in searching a given system—retrievals made on the basis of narrowly defined criteria may not yield the best results. Where these shortcomings can be overcome, the computer can be a valuable aid in storing, organizing, and selectively retrieving research notes.

## ADMINISTERING COMPUTERIZED INFORMATION

Using a computer to organize lecture and seminar papers, course outlines, research and teaching bibliographies, and research notes will inevitably create an entirely new set of administrative problems—that is, how to administer the voluminous information which rapidly begins to take over a computer's filestore.[14] Like any paper-based system for organizing and storing information, the computer-based system will require some attention to the routine matters of file management. Paper-based information is normally organized in hierarchically arranged systems of which the filing cabinet is the best example. At the top of the hierarchy is the filing cabinet which is designated, for example, to store teaching materials. At another level of the hierarchy are the labelled drawers, two in this case, one each for a course entitled 'USA since 1876' and another entitled 'History and Computing'. At yet a third level of the hierarchy, the files in each of the drawers are subdivided into three areas, one each for bibliography, lecture notes, and course administration materials.

Information stored on a computer's hard disk is also normally arranged in a hierarchical fashion. Hard disks are subdivided into named or labelled directories where related computer files are stored, just as the filing cabinet is divided into labelled drawers into which related paper files are placed. The advantage with a computer is that each directory can be subdivided into one or several additional sub-directories. Take as an example a 30 megabyte hard disk (the machine-readable version of a 100,000-

---

[14] The discussion is directly relevant to PCs but also to Unix-based systems and to Apple Macs which store their files hierarchically.

word Ph.D. thesis might take up 0.3 or 0.4 megabytes by way of comparison) divided into three principal directories as shown in Figure 2.10, one each for computer software (programs), teaching materials, and research materials. The directories are further

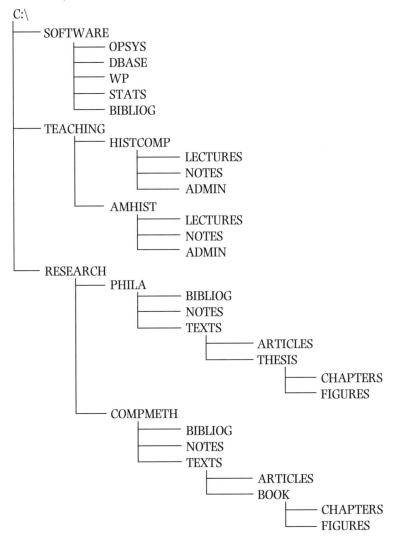

*Note*: C:\ represents an unnamed top-level or root directory

Fig. 2.10 Schematic diagram of directories on a PC's hard disk

divided into a number of subdirectories. The software directory, for example, is divided into five subdirectories, one each for the operating system, databases, word-processing packages, statistics, and bibliography software. The teaching directory is divided into two subdirectories, one for each of two courses. Notice that these directories are themselves subdivided into three subdirectories for lectures, lecture notes, and course administration materials, respectively. Lastly, the research directory is divided into two sub-directories, one for each of two lines of research on Philadelphia's political history and on computer methodology, respectively. Computer files may appear in any of the directories and subdirec-tories but most are likely to be bunched in the subdirectories at the lowest level in the hierarchy (those listed on the right-most side of Figure 2.10). As capacious hard disks become common on personal computers, software applications designed to help admin-ister a disk's filestore (so-called disk management tools), become more affordable and easier to use.[15] Such tools enable users to navigate more easily through the hundreds or even thousands of files contained on any hard disk by providing, for example, dia-grams of a disk's directory structure (Figure 2.10), alphabetical lists of files within a directory or combination of directories, and tools to search the entire disk for a file with a given name or for files in which the phrase 'Civil War' appears.

A rationally organized hard disk is not alone sufficient to ensure sound computer-aided information management, however. Magnetic filestore is volatile. That means it can become corrupt or rendered unusable. Most commonly, corruption occurs as the result of human error. It is all too easy to delete a file mistakenly. It is as easy to 'overwrite' the most up-to-date version of a file by copying onto it an older version with the same name and stored in a different hard-disk directory or on a floppy disk or diskette.[16] To protect against such disasters, it is absolutely essential to make 'back-up' copies of files whose loss would be intolerable. In the words of the ever-helpful David Cooper, 'save early, save often'.[17] Unfortunately, one suspects that this simple lesson is only ever

---

[15] See J. Wilkes, 'Disk Utilities Software: PC Tools and Norton Utilities', *History and Computing*, 4 (1992), 142–4.

[16] Some disk management tools can 'unerase' mistakenly deleted files. Overwritten files are, however, irretrievably lost.

[17] The Librarian at Corpus Christi College, Oxford, who guided me when com-puters were still unfamiliar.

learned through the bitter experience of erasing, overwriting, or corrupting a file which is absolutely essential, and for which there is no back-up copy. It may be some consolation to know that such a trauma is normally experienced only once. Thereafter, file management techniques improve considerably! With a desktop computer, back-up copies can be taken onto floppy disks or diskettes or onto magnetic tapes.[18] Files which are stored on remote computers but accessed via a desktop (as in a network) may be managed by people with responsibility for periodically backing up the entire system. When using such a system, however, it is essential that you check with its managers to ascertain whether their normal back-up routines furnish sufficient protection.

## COMPUTER NETWORKS

So far, we have only looked at how the personal computer can add value and efficiency when managing information stored in the historian's office. Another advantage is that a personal computer, if it is 'networked' together with other computers and/or connected to appropriate telecommunication systems, gives the historian access to an enormous amount of information stored at other locations within a given institution, the nation, or even the world. Across so-called local and wide area networks (LANS and WANS, respectively) computers can 'share' their resources including their data files, software, and processing power. LAN and WAN users also will be able to send messages to people whose computers are linked to the same network. The term network simply refers to a group of computers which can communicate with each other either because they are connected through specially installed local cables (for example, with LANS of Macs and PCs residing in close proximity and wired together), or through a nation's or region's telecommunications infrastructure (e.g. with WANS). The two kinds of networks are not mutually exclusive because networks can communicate with one another thereby allowing computers on different networks to share each other's resources.

---

[18] Magnetic tapes which look like audio cassette tapes require a so-called tape-drive. They are becoming increasingly affordable and reliable.

The environment that a university member is most likely to encounter is one in which several computer networks are themselves networked together. Thus, access to one network will often provide access to others through so-called bridges and gateways. For example, the personal computer which sits in my office can act as a so-called stand-alone relying on its own programs, data files, and processing power. To use it, one needs to be sitting in front of it. At the same time, the computer is linked with local cabling to a more powerful computer (generically called a server) which provides the processing power, filestore, and software for a cluster of twenty-eight computers housed two floors beneath my office. 'Communications' software resident on my own computer enables me to call the server much as a telephone enables me to call an associate. Once communications have been established with the server, I need to specify my username and password to prove that I am allowed to use it. Usernames and passwords are essential to protect networked machines against interference from unauthorized users known as 'hackers'.[19]

Having logged onto the server, I can obtain access to the server's software, data files, and processing power. I also have access to more remote computers since the server acts as a so-called gateway to a number of wide area networks. From within the UK the two most important wide area networks are JANET and Internet. JANET (the Joint Academic NETwork) links together computing installations housed at the universities and research institutes in the UK. Internet links together several underlying academic and related networks, and provides access to computer installations in Europe and North America, and elsewhere. Both networks offer the same three facilities: electronic mail (e-mail), remote log-ins, and anonymous file transfer protocol (ftp).[20] None of these networks is free to install and run although at present their use is free of charge to people with accounts on connected computer installations.[21]

---

[19] A good password keeps unwanted and unauthorized users off a computer. It should comprise at least six alphanumeric characters and avoid the names of Star Trek characters and loved ones. Change passwords every few months and immediately if there is evidence of tampering.

[20] Users are also likely to come into contact with BITNET (Because It's There NETwork) which connects over 2,300 computers mostly in North America, Europe, and Asia through its network affiliations, and with EARN (European Academic Research Network).

[21] BITNET and EARN offer electronic mail but not remote log-in or ftp. For

*Electronic mail*

Electronic mail is very much the late twentieth-century equivalent of the post office. With it people send machine-readable information back and forth between different computers which are associated together on the same network or on different but interlinked networks. All they need to know about one another is their electronic mail address.[22] Electronic mail addresses consist of a username and the address of a networked computer where mail is received and from which it is sent. Usernames are normally assigned (perhaps with some negotiation) by the managers of the local networked computer installation to which the user has applied for authorized access. My username on the networked server which resides two floors beneath my office is a rather informal one, 'DIGGER'. Computer addresses, on the other hand, are normally assigned by the wide area network managers and will contain some abbreviated name for the computer installation and perhaps some indication of its network affiliation as well. Variation in computer addresses occur because different networks seem unable to agree how to structure them. Confusion is compounded where the same computer installation is accessible via different networks, each of which assigns it a slightly different name. The address of the server on which DIGGER is located is UK.AC.GLASGOW.DISH. That is, if you happen to be mailing the server from another computer linked to JANET. Internet knows the server rather differently as DISH.GLASGOW.AC.UK. Combining username and computer address produces an electronic mail address making my JANET-accessible Glasgow addresses DIGGER@UK.AC.GLASGOW.DISH (DIGGER@DISH.GLASGOW.AC.UK via Internet).

more information about BITNET, EARN, JANET, Internet, and other networks and network services see M. Gregson, 'Electronic Communication in the Social Sciences', in R. Welford (ed.), *Information Technology for Social Scientists* (Shipley, 1990), 87–116; I. Lancashire (ed.), *The Humanities Computing Yearbook 1989/90: A Comprehensive Guide to Software and other Resources* (Oxford, 1991), 567–8; S. Fisher, 'Whither NREN?', *BYTE* (July, 1991), 181–9; T. L. La Quey, *User's Directory of Computer Networks* (Bedford, Mass., 1990); J. S. Quarterman, *The Matrix: Computer Networks and Conferencing Systems Worldwide* (Bedford, Mass., 1990).

[22] Electronic mail addresses are highly unstandardized making any more than the most general discussion impossible.

Electronic mail is put to many uses. Brief messages composed interactively with an electronic mail editor are useful for 'staying in touch' with friends and colleagues located at other universities and research institutes. Much longer files comprising anything from word-processed documents (draft chapters or journal articles) to database records also can be exchanged. Electronic mail recently proved invaluable when editing a book on computer methods. Machine-readable drafts were sent to me electronically from contributors located in Austria, Denmark, England, Germany, and Norway. Once received the contributions were loaded into a word processor for revision and the revised documents returned electronically to their authors for approval and further revision. Similarly, electronic mail can be useful when organizing international conferences whose participants can be sent information about travel, accommodation, conference schedules, and paper abstracts without impinging greatly on the world's rain forests.

Electronic mail software varies considerably and therefore defies description in any but the most general terms. Central to any mailer will be an editor—a very basic word processor of sorts—in which out-going messages can be composed and both in-coming and out-going messages can be read and edited. With the editor, the user will be able to scroll through a message, insert text, and delete words and lines. More sophisticated text-editing facilities, including page and character formatting, deleting, and moving blocks of text, are unlikely to be available. Consequently, where messages require more rigorously considered prose, one might as well use a desktop computer's word processor, save the finished texts as an ASCII file, and use the mailer to send the entire file to the appropriate recipient.[23] Mailers will also offer a range of message-administration facilities, for example, to delete received messages or to save them as permanent files. The user may also be able to define abbreviated addresses which save typing the long-hand version. Similarly, abbreviations might be defined to consist of several addresses, for example, those belonging to each of the colleagues participating in a collaborative venture. Using such abbreviations, it is possible with one address to mail the same document or message to several people simultaneously.

---

[23] For more about line editors, word processors, and ASCII files see Ch. 5.

*Electronic discussion lists*

Electronic discussion lists, also called distribution lists, extend the possibilities offered by electronic mail. They comprise a collection of members or users who will receive all of the messages sent by other users to the discussion list's electronic address. They are either moderated (incoming messages are edited by a controller before being sent to participating users) or unmoderated (messages are automatically sent out to subscribers). Electronic discussion lists can be an invaluable source of information and assistance. My first and perhaps best experience was in 1987 with HUMANIST, a list whose members share an interest in humanities computing. A much-needed Christmas holiday in New York threatened to interrupt on-going collaboration between colleagues in three UK universities who were compiling a funding application that was due at the end of January. The drafting process had already relied extensively on electronic mail as sections of the document were sent electronically between collaborators for their review and amendment. To ensure my continued involvement in the process even from distant shores, a message was posted on HUMANIST explaining the problem, and requesting access to a BIT-NET affiliated computer with which I could stay in touch with colleagues in the UK.[24] Within five or six hours I had three offers and was ultimately able to continue my work amidst the merriment from a room at Hunter College in New York City. Hundreds of discussion lists have been established to facilitate communications between like-minded users, and between users in cognate disciplines interested in subjects ranging from very specific computer applications to anthropology, philosophy, science fiction, sexual politics, and the rock group, the Grateful Dead.[25] The electronic addresses and subjects of some of the lists likely to be of interest to historians are given in the bibliography.[26]

*Remote log-in*

Remote log-in facilities enable users to take advantage of the filestore, processing power, and software of computers which are

---

[24] In 1987, BITNET-affiliated computers could send electronic mail to JANET-affiliated ones.

[25] Available via Internet at: DEAD-FLAMES@MC.LCS.MIT.EDU.

[26] See bibliography, section IID.

physically distant from them but to which they have authorized access. A database comprising biographical information on Oxford University's twentieth-century students, which furnishes some of the examples used in the forthcoming chapters, is mounted on a computer housed at Oxford University. With remote log-in, however, the database's physical location did not matter. Much of the work involved in compiling and analysing the data was done from a desktop computer at Glasgow University some 350 miles north using the remote log-in facilities available over JANET. More recently, Internet has enabled transcontinental remote log-in. Consequently, on a recent sabbatical in Philadelphia it was possible to log onto Glasgow's history server to read and respond to electronic mail.

More common usage of remote log-in involves publicly accessible on-line databases and electronic bulletin boards. These are information stores which are mounted and managed on one computer and are accessible to authorized users over one or other network. Having logged onto an on-line database or bulletin board the user may browse through its information and, depending on the on-line database, transmit information back to a local computer. Information thus transmitted can then be printed locally, incorporated into a word-processing file for modification (and then printing), and perhaps loaded into personal bibliographic or database software.[27] A session on BIRON, the on-line catalogue of machine-readable data held by the UK's Economic and Social Research Council's data archive, provides a typical example.[28]

Loading the appropriate communications software from my desktop (and JANET-networked) computer, it is only necessary to call the JANET-linked machine in Essex which hosts the computerized catalogue (JANET address is UK.AC.SX.SOLB1). When a connection with the Essex machine is established, I am prompted for a username (in this case 'biron') and a password ('norib'). Within seconds, a welcoming screen appears offering helpful information and an invitation to continue browsing the catalogue. A second screen, invoked by hitting the 'Enter' key, asks me to refine my

---

[27] Users should check with their software vendors or computer advisers whether their personal bibliographic and database software can import information from commercial on-line databases.

[28] The results were obtained from a search conducted in July 1992.

search of the archive catalogue by indicating the subject, geo-graphical area, or date in which I am particularly interested. Always interested in discovering historical databases I enter '1700–1750' and find that the archive holds nine datasets comprising information on that period. There are three on career mobility in two British Regiments, 1690–1930, three on English demography, one on insurance policies, one on the urban population of eighteenth-century Denmark, and one on the Huguenot influx to Britain, 1680–1709. The search is not at all dissimilar to a session on a computerized library catalogue, only in this case the catalogue contains references to machine-readable data rather than books, and the catalogue is stored on a computer which is several hundred miles away from my computer.

To my mind anyway, the many on-line services, amongst which the computerized library catalogue is probably the best known, represent the greatest benefit that computer networks can offer students and scholars. Many bibliographic searches which once took hours, days, and even weeks, and which were costly whenever the appropriate library catalogue was not available locally, are now possible from the user's office. At the same time, the searches themselves are far more effective than manual ones ever could be. Users have access to bibliographic citations by their author(s), title, and subject, as with non-computerized catalogues, but also by date of publication, by author, title, or subject key-word, by any combination of the above, and by many other criteria as well. The advantages that on-line data services offer to the academic and non-academic communities account in part for their recent proliferation. In the early 1970s there were only about 100 such services. By 1989 the number had increased to 4,250 databases compiled by nearly 2,000 separate producers and available on more than 600 networks.[29]

The computerized library catalogues of most UK universities are accessible freely over JANET. In the USA the Research Libraries Group provides access through RLIN to the on-line catalogues of affiliated academic institutions and thus to over 30 million library holdings. Other on-line database services available from commer-

[29] P. K. Doorn and H. Tjalsma, 'Online or Offline? Providing Access to Databases and the Netherlands Historical Data Archive' (unpublished paper presented at 'Social History: The Challenge of Technology Workshop', University of Essex, 1 June 1991), 5.

cial vendors such as DIALOG, BRS, and the British Library's BLAISE-LINE are only accessible to members and/or institutions who have paid a subscription fee. These will not, on the whole, reside on computers linked to academic networks. Access to these commercial databases is gained instead through telecommunication lines. Consequently, the subscription fee for a commercial on-line database only represents a portion of the total cost to the user who will also incur charges for the time spent connected to the service.

Because connection fees can be costly (especially where long-distance calls are made during peak weekday periods), it is essential to plan the aims and objectives of a commercial database search carefully before connecting to the service. A user hoping to find in a vast on-line bibliographic database references to articles and books on the origins of the Thanksgiving feast in the USA would not, for example, be advised to begin the search by looking for entries with the abbreviation 'US' in their title or subject fields. Such a general query would locate thousands of citations. It would consequently take up a considerable amount of time and be very costly. The user would be better advised to narrow the search by requesting references which contain the term US as well as Thanksgiving, feasts, or holidays. Transmitting the results of an on-line session back to a local computer will also take time in direct proportion to the amount of information that is sent. Consequently, the results of a very general query containing hundreds of redundant references will incur unnecessary costs. Because of the high cost involved in using commercial on-line databases, interested users should consult local librarians who are likely to be skilled in their efficient use. They also will be adept with the database command languages which are by no means the same for all commercial services. A partial list of the on-line databases (including vendors) in which historians are most likely to be interested is given in the bibliography.[30]

### Anonymous file transfer (ftp)

Anonymous file transfer protocol (ftp) is not dissimilar to remote log-in and has become increasingly available to academic institu-

[30] See section IIIc. For more on commercial on-line services see Lancashire, *Humanities Computing Yearbook, 1989–90*, 384–93.

tions as more academic networks (and thus more computers) are linked to the Internet. Ftp enables the managers of a networked computer installation to establish a 'guest' username in which to place files and programs that the managers wish to give away freely.[31] Users at other networked sites can then log onto the guest username as if it were their own, browse through its contents (normally organized into directories and subdirectories) and transfer to their own local computers whatever files are of interest. Free software (also known as shareware or public domain software) and data files may be available. With ftp a machine-readable version of the *Federalist Papers* which was used to provide examples of text processing and linguistic content analysis in Chapter 5, was transferred to Glasgow from a computer in Urbana, Illinois. The transaction was virtually instantaneous. As with remote log-in, all that one needs for ftp is the address of the computer installation which permits ftp and the username and password of its guest account (normally 'anonymous' and anything, respectively).[32] Having logged onto my Internet-linked server at Glasgow, all that was required to get the *Federalist Papers*, for example, was the ftp command, 'ftp', and the address of the computer installation in Illinois where the *Federalist Papers* were stored. Within seconds a connection was established and a username and password requested by the remote site. With these supplied, the contents of the ftp account were mine for the taking, and the 'get' command brought the nearly 19,000 lines of the *Federalist Papers* onto my own computer in the UK.[33]

Less straightforward than conducting file transfer is discovering the sites where useful shareware and data files are located. As with discussion lists, ftp sites seem to come and go, and to change their addresses from time to time, and I have yet to discover a comprehensive catalogue. Still, the electronic grapevine is ripe for picking. Discussion lists frequently carry messages about on-line databases and publicly accessible files stored on ftp sites. Where a discussion list is quiet on the subject, a request for information can produce helpful suggestions.

[31] Where users are willing to give away their own usernames and passwords, ftp can draw on data held in personal accounts.

[32] Hence the designation, 'anonymous ftp'.

[33] The account is maintained by Project Gutenberg, see bibliography, section IIв2.

With electronic mail, remote log-in, and ftp, the desktop computer which already promises enormous efficiencies in organizing information and preparing printed materials, can serve as a gateway onto what is quite literally a world of information. The user needs to beware, however, as that information is simply too voluminous to comprehend. Despite this, the naturally curious will be all too tempted to try and may, as a result, end up losing sight of the aims associated with a particular enquiry. In the late twentieth-century, computer networks provide better and more direct access to more information. They also permit the ambling, uncritical search for any information that is sometimes associated with the nineteenth-century antiquarian historian.

# 3

# Historical Data and Databases

HISTORIANS, by necessity, are constantly developing systems for collecting, organizing, and selectively retrieving information. Whether computerized or not, such systems are database management systems or, more simply, databases. Lecture notes stored in labelled folders and organized sequentially by course in the top drawer of a filing cabinet comprise a database capable of delivering up the third lecture given in a 'History and Computing' course. A collection of bibliographic references written onto $3'' \times 5''$ note cards and arranged alphabetically by author is another kind of database, this one constructed to find works written by Sperberg-McQueen and by Burnard. More research-oriented databases will normally comprise notes—'one note card, one fact'—which are selectively retrieved, classified, grouped, and counted to answer specific questions. The reason that computerized databases are so popular with historians, and social scientists for that matter, is that they automate well-tried, manual information management systems. They are in effect, familiar, and it is with this familiar ground—why we use manual databases and how they work—that this chapter launches out. Having examined the basic characteristics of a manual system, the chapter goes on to demonstrate how and where computerized systems are better than manual ones, looking initially at a simple census database, before considering the additional advantages of more sophisticated multi-table systems. The chapter concludes with a brief review of the facilities found in most database software, and with a discussion of some of the constraints inherent in computerized database management.

## INFORMATION MANAGEMENT: THE MANUAL SYSTEM

Let us begin, then, with the manual information management system. Manual database systems are built up from individual records about some pre-defined class of object.[1] The objects may be physical ones, as is the case with lecture notes that are tucked in labelled folders and stored in a filing cabinet. Most database records, however, simply describe objects just as bibliographic references describe books. Research-oriented databases, for example, contain records describing people (e.g. state assemblymen in *ante bellum* Georgia), property (e.g. grand villas in ancient Rome), or events (e.g. British parliamentary elections).

A second property common to all databases is that their records comprise fields of information.[2] Thus, a record pertaining to a book and stored in a note-card bibliography has fields for the book's author(s), title, publisher, and date and place of publication. A biographical record for a Georgia state assemblyman might have fields giving the assemblyman's date and place of birth, the date of his first election to the Georgia state legislature, and his party affiliation, occupation, and number of slaves owned at that date. A psephological record collected for a study of late twentieth-century British parliamentary elections might have fields giving an election's date, a constituency name, and the vote returned for each party contesting the election on that date in that constituency.

The fields associated with each record in a database determine how records can be retrieved and classified, making up a third property common to all databases. Lecture notes can be retrieved from a filing cabinet by their title but not by their word length because the lecture title and not the word length is printed on the folder containing each set of notes. Where records are collected for research purposes, their component fields impinge on analysis as well as retrieval. The psephological records described above sustain analysis of party balance in particular constituencies. They do not reveal men's and women's voting preferences. Because the range of fields associated with each record in a database determines how the records can be analysed, it is essential to define very precisely what fields of information should be collected before data gathering is begun. At this stage the issue is never

[1] Database enthusiasts prefer the term 'entities' to 'records'.
[2] Database enthusiasts prefer 'entities have attributes' to 'records have fields'. See D. Andrews and M. Greenhalgh, *Computing for Non-Scientific Applications* (Leicester, 1987), 77, who claim that if 'entities' is a noun, then 'attributes' is an adjective.

whether a particular field is interesting or relevant in the abstract, but whether it is interesting and relevant given a database project's aims. And there is never a 'correct' range of fields. Two historians compiling biographical records about Georgia state assemblymen might choose to collect very different fields of information depending on what questions they had in mind to ask.

Where the same range of pre-defined fields is supplied for every record in a particular database, the records can be analysed systematically. A bibliographic reference which excludes an author's name cannot be entered into the note-card bibliography. If it was entered anywhere in the stack of note cards, it would be lost to the system. Where research notes are concerned, the same range of fields must be provided for each record if the records are to sustain meaningful analysis. The relative propensity for slave owning amongst Georgia's Democrat and Whig state assemblymen could not be compared if the actual number of slaves owned was gathered for some legislators and not for others. Neither could it be compared if some records gave the number of slaves owned while others indicated slave-owning status with a simple yes or no.

Fourthly, in order for a database to function consistently, no two records can be identical. The lecture's uniqueness is determined by its course affiliation and sequence number; the bibliographic reference's by its author and title. When the uniqueness of each record is not preserved, the database becomes corrupt and begins to return inaccurate or ambiguous results. If two folders in the filing cabinet share the same lecture title, course name, and sequence number, for example, how would the lecturer choose between them? Similarly, if the biographical record of some Whig assemblymen appears twice in the database of Georgia state assemblymen, analyses, for example, of the number of sexagenarian Whig assemblymen would be inaccurate—some of the assemblymen could be counted twice.

Fifthly, the rules which govern a database's consistency and which therefore facilitate data retrieval must also govern the process by which the database is updated. When each new lecture is added to the filing cabinet, its lecture title, course title, and sequence number are entered onto the folder label so the record can be retrieved at some later date. When records about Georgia's *post bellum* state legislators are added to those already collected for pre-war assemblymen, they must provide information in each of the pre-defined fields if comparative or serial analysis is to be sustained.

## COMPUTERIZED DATABASES: THE SIMPLE ONE-TABLE SYSTEM

*Database definition: tables, fields, data types, and values*

Computerized databases are identical to the manual ones described above with two exceptions. First, with the computerized database, records and fields are represented as rows and columns in a so-called database table and not on hundreds of note cards or scraps of paper. Figure 3.1 shows a database table with records drawn from Britain's 1881 manuscript census.[3] The table possesses the five properties outlined above. It contains records about a pre-defined class of object. In this case, the records refer to people living in the Gorbals, a built-up working-class area adjacent to Glasgow in 1881. Each record makes up a row in the table—there are as many rows in the table as there are records. Here there are 396 records, one for each person recorded as residing on Norfolk Street, Gorbals, on census Sunday 1881. Notice, too, that each record has the same fields just as in the manual systems described above. The twelve fields in the Gorbals database table are fully described in Figure 3.2.

As with the manual database, the range of fields defined for the computerized database table determines how information can be retrieved from the table and analysed. With the Gorbals database table we can display all of the records pertaining to people who gave their occupation as 'Seamstress', count the Glasgow-born household heads (where the so-called value or piece of information in the *Relation* field was given as 'Head' and that in the *TBirth* field as 'Glasgow'), and arrange the records in descending order of age. We could not order the records in ascending order of income because income data are not provided. Note, too, that every record in the database table is unique thanks to the values

---

[3] Example data are based on the 'Gorbals Census Datafile', prepared by the Strathclyde Regional Archives together with the Glasgow Division of Strathclyde Region's Education Department; see Glasgow's Department of Education, 'Using Quest: Gorbals Census Datafile' (Glasgow, 1984).

| HNo | PNo | Surname | Forename | Address | Relation | Sex | Age | Occupation | TBirth | Rooms | HSize |
|---|---|---|---|---|---|---|---|---|---|---|---|
| 1 | 1 | Fletcher | John | 28 Norfolk St | Head | M | 28 | Iron worker | Ayr | 3 | 4 |
| 1 | 2 | Fletcher | Eliza | 28 Norfolk St | Wife | F | 28 | Seamstress | Edinburgh | 3 | 4 |
| 1 | 3 | Fletcher | John | 28 Norfolk St | Son | M | 8 | Scholar | Glasgow | 3 | 4 |
| 1 | 4 | Fletcher | James | 28 Norfolk St | Son | M | 6 | Scholar | Glasgow | 3 | 4 |
| 2 | 1 | Hepburn | Robert | 28 Norfolk St | Head | M | 44 | Grocer | Kilmarnock | 5 | 4 |
| 2 | 2 | Hepburn | Janet | 28 Norfolk St | Wife | F | 29 | None | Kilmarnock | 5 | 4 |
| 2 | 3 | Hepburn | Mary | 28 Norfolk St | Daughter | F | 2 | None | Glasgow | 5 | 4 |
| 2 | 4 | Cameron | Margaret | 28 Norfolk St | Servant | F | 17 | Domestic | Ayrshire | 5 | 4 |

Fig. 3.1 The first eight records in the Gorbals census database table

| Field Name | Data type | Brief description (where necessary) |
|---|---|---|
| HNo | Number | Household number – sequential number assigned by the database creator to each household. |
| PNo | Number | Person number – sequential number assigned by the database creator to the people enumerated in each household. |
| Surname | c20 | |
| Forename | c16 | |
| Address | c20 | Street address. |
| Relation | c12 | Relationship to head of household. |
| Sex | c1 | Male or female. |
| Age | Number | |
| Occupation | c20 | |
| TBirth | c20 | Town of birth. |
| Rooms | Number | Number of rooms in household. |
| HSize | Number | Number of people in household as calculated by the database creator. |

*Note*: Fields which accept character data are indicated with a 'c' followed by a number giving their permitted maximum length.

Fig. 3.2 Field structure of the Gorbals database table, showing for each field its name, data type (e.g. textual or numeric data), and a description of the information it contains

in the *HNo* and *PNo* fields, which give sequential numbers to households and to the people within them, respectively. Finally, if the database is to remain consistent, records which are added or amended must preserve the field structure already adopted by others in the table.

Computerized databases differ from manual ones because they demand more precise field definition. With a computerized database, each field must be assigned a formal name. On a note card, fields may be indicated typographically (book titles which are underlined), spatially (the names of Georgia state assemblymen always written in the upper-left-hand corner of each note card with surname preceding first names), or not at all (notes given in running prose with fields of information supplied in no fixed place or order). The computerized database also requires the user to define the data type—that is a description of the values (e.g.

numbers, text) permitted in each field. Most computerized databases will support at least some of the following data types: inte-
gers (also called counting or whole numbers); real numbers
(numbers with decimal points); variable-length character strings
(which may consist either of numbers and/or text up to a maximum specified number of characters); and calendar dates. The
data-type definition of the fields in the Gorbals database table are
shown in Figure 3.2.

This more precise approach to field definition is beneficial for a
number of slightly different reasons, some of them technical—
most databases simply will not work unless data types are supplied for each field. At a non-technical level, the need for precise
field definition forces the database designer to think very carefully
about how the information contained within a field is likely to be
used. The occupational information shown in Figure 3.1 provides
an ideal example. Censuses are notorious for their ambiguous
one-word occupational descriptions. 'Merchant', 'Businessman',
'Seamstress', and 'Labourer' are far more likely to appear on the
enumerator's manuscripts than 'Assistant Headmaster, Glasgow
Academy, Glasgow' or 'Accounts clerk, Glasgow Textile
Manufacturing Co., Anderston'. Still, fuller entries will occasionally appear. The problem for the database designer in this case is
to accommodate both full and abbreviated occupational information. One option is to put occupational information into one field,
perhaps abbreviating the lengthier references, for example, as
'Teacher' and 'Accounts clerk'. Another option is to define fields
for each of the distinct components that might be encountered,
notably job title ('Seamstress', 'Assistant Master', 'Accounts
clerk'), employer ('Glasgow Academy', 'Glasgow Textile
Manufacturing Co.'), and place of employment ('Glasgow',
'Anderston'). With these several fields the researcher could ask
more questions of the assembled data, for example, do any firms
seem to employ a disproportionate number of people living in the
Gorbals? How many residents commute outside the Gorbals to
work and where do they commute to? At the same time, if fields
are allowed to proliferate unduly, data entry may take longer and
thus become more expensive. Consequently, it is important to
supply only those fields which have some analytical value.

Data-type definition is also important because it forces
the researcher to define very precisely what information in a

particular field actually means and how it can be distinguished from other, perhaps very similar kinds of information. How, for example, would we handle a census record in which a house-holder's occupation is given as 'MA Glasgow University'? Are we satisfied that university degrees qualify as occupational descrip-tions? Or do we need to include a new field or fields in our data-base table to handle such idiosyncratic census entries? There are no correct answers to these so-called data-modelling questions. Rather, correct answers will be contingent upon a project's particular aims, and on the richness of its data. With the Gorbals census data, most occupational descriptions are highly abbreviated and refer to householders' gainful employment. Consequently, one field is suitable for occupational information. As a general rule of thumb, however, a distinct field should be provided for information which is likely to be the subject of some future analysis and which is available for enough records to make the analysis meaningful.

*Data retrieval, analysis, and manipulation*

Another major difference between a manual and a computerized database system is that with the manual system the physical order in which records are stored determines how they can be retrieved. In a note-card bibliography references can be retrieved by author when the cards are arranged alphabetically by authors' names. Title searches are possible but they involve thumbing sequentially through every note card in the hopes of stumbling across the desired reference. Alternatively, it is possible to create a duplicate set of note cards organized alphabetically by title. With the manual research-oriented database it is necessary to shuffle and reshuffle the note cards every time a new question is asked. To see whether Whigs or Democrats dominated the Georgia state assembly, the note cards have to be sorted into two piles—one for Whigs and one for Democrats. Two entirely different piles are required to determine the proportion of assemblymen born outside the state of Georgia, and two different piles have to be created again to determine the proportion of slave-owning Whigs. With a computerized database the records' physical order does not impinge upon their retrieval. Consequently, records can be selec-tively retrieved, ordered, grouped, and counted automatically and in an instant. Look more closely at each of these facilities with particular reference to the Gorbals database table.

First, we can selectively retrieve records and fields from a computerized database table. The result which is achieved instantly looks like another database table when displayed on the computer screen. Having conducted one retrieval, selection criteria can be radically altered and an entirely new result obtained again within seconds. There is no need to reorganize the records physically as is the case with a manual database whenever a new search with different criteria is required. By way of example, imagine a session with the Gorbals database table designed to form some impressionistic sense of the social-class complexion of Gorbals residents in 1881. As a first step we might retrieve a simple list of male household heads' occupations and birthplaces. The result, shown in Figure 3.3, looks like a portion of the original table. It has four fields (*HNo*, *PNo*, *Occupation*, and *TBirth*) and those records from the Gorbals table pertaining to male household heads (where the value in the *Relation* field is given as 'Head' and that in the *Sex* field as 'M'). Continuing along this analytical line the search might be refined to include only male household heads born in Glasgow (*Relation* given as 'Head', *Sex* as 'M', and *TBirth* as 'Glasgow'). Still a third retrieval might look at the occupations and birthplaces given by the sons of all household heads (*Relation* given as 'Son'). Partial results of these two additional retrievals are displayed in Figures 3.4 and 3.5, respectively.

| HNo | PNo | Occupation | TBirth |
|-----|-----|------------|--------|
| 1 | 1 | Ironworker | Ayr |
| 2 | 1 | Grocer | Kilmarnock |
| 3 | 1 | Cutler's shopman | Glasgow |
| 4 | 1 | Fishmonger | Glasgow |
| 5 | 1 | Flesher | Berwick on Tweed |
| 6 | 1 | Bank watchman | Edinburgh |
| 7 | 1 | Glasscutter | Glasgow |
| 8 | 1 | Paper ruler | Kinnigaff |
| 9 | 1 | Engine fitter | Carnoustie |

Fig. 3.3 Simple retrieval from the Gorbals database table showing the occupations and birthplaces of male household heads residing on Norfolk Street in 1881

| HNo | PNo | Occupation | TBirth |
| --- | --- | --- | --- |
| 3 | 1 | Cutler's shopman | Glasgow |
| 4 | 1 | Fishmonger | Glasgow |
| 7 | 1 | Glasscutter | Glasgow |
| 10 | 1 | Butcher | Glasgow |
| 17 | 1 | Tailor | Glasgow |
| 20 | 1 | Letter carrier | Glasgow |
| 23 | 1 | Stationer | Glasgow |

Fig. 3.4 Another simple retrieval from the Gorbals database table showing the occupations and birthplaces of Glasgow-born male household
heads residing on Norfolk Street in 1881

| HNo | PNo | Occupation | TBirth |
| --- | --- | --- | --- |
| 1 | 3 | Scholar | Glasgow |
| 1 | 4 | Scholar | Glasgow |
| 3 | 3 | Shoemaker | Glasgow |
| 6 | 3 | Publican's shopman | Glasgow |
| 6 | 4 | Apprentice tailor | Coatbridge |
| 7 | 4 | None | Glasgow |
| 9 | 5 | Scholar | Aberdeen |

Fig. 3.5 Complex retrieval from the Gorbals database table showing the
occupations and birthplaces of the sons of all male household heads
residing on Norfolk Street in 1881

Had the Gorbals records been stored on 396 note cards sequentially arranged by house and person numbers, respectively, the
same three retrievals would require thumbing through the cards
three times and could take an hour or more to conduct. With the
computer the results are available instantaneously. The speed of
automated selective retrieval encourages reiterative exploration of
one's data. The results thrown up by preliminary questions stimu-
late new questions. With a manual system the same kind of
analysis is possible but tedious. The manual system also may be
prone to error in a way that the computerized system is not especially where search criteria are complex and need to be applied to
each note card. Imagine a single manual search for records referring to Glasgow-born, male, household heads between the ages of

25 and 50, in households with one or two rooms and no servants, and those pertaining to Irish-born female household heads in households with three or more children under the age of 6!

Wherever our retrievals produce more than one record, it is possible to determine the alphabetical and/or numerical order or sequence in which the records are displayed. Returned records can be organized in ascending or descending order of the values in any one or more fields. Figure 3.6 shows a partial result of a retrieval designed to display the names and ages of Norfolk Street residents ordered in ascending alphabetical order by surname and forename, respectively. Figure 3.7 shows a partial result of the same query, only this time, ordered by descending order of age and within age, by ascending order of surname and forename, respectively. Once again, had the records been stored on note cards rather than in a computerized database table, the same two retrievals might have required hours whereas with the database they are both conducted in seconds.

| Surname | Forename | Age |
| --- | --- | --- |
| Abrahams | Annie | 30 |
| Abrahams | Eva | 3 |
| Abrahams | Joseph | 5 |
| Abrahams | Katherine | 10 |
| Abrahams | Nathan | 31 |
| Adie | Annie | 10 |
| Adie | Helen | 8 |
| Adie | James W | 5 |
| Adie | John | 30 |
| Aitken | Jane K | 60 |
| Bannister | Samuel | 22 |
| Beverley | Ann | 25 |
| Beverley | Catherine | 0 |
| Beverley | Mary A | 6 |
| Beverley | William | 27 |
| Beverley | William | 3 |

*Note*: The names and ages of Norfolk Street residents are listed in alphabetical order of surname and forename.

Fig. 3.6 Retrieval from the Gorbals database table demonstrating simple sorting facilities

| Surname | Forename | Age |
| --- | --- | --- |
| Morrison | Christina | 78 |
| McDonald | Margaret | 75 |
| Steven | James | 74 |
| Steven | Mary | 74 |
| McColl | Margaret | 73 |
| Duncan | Henry | 70 |
| McPhail | Marion | 70 |
| Blackley | John | 64 |
| Campbell | Elizabeth | 64 |
| Hart | Elizabeth | 63 |
| Hart | John | 62 |
| Leslie | George | 61 |

*Note*: The names and ages of Norfolk Street residents are listed by descending order of age, and within age by ascending order of surname and forename.

Fig. 3.7 Retrieval from the Gorbals database table demonstrating complex sorting facilities

More quantitative measures which summarize the results of selective retrievals are also available with the computerized database. Thus, within seconds the Gorbals database can produce a count of all Glaswegian-born residents living in Norfolk Street in 1881 (142), an average age for all household heads (40), and an average number of rooms per Gorbals household (2.9). The database also can be enlisted to transform some of the data stored within it. It can, for example, create new variables from existing ones, thereby giving further scope for analysis. The Gorbals database table contains two fields, *Rooms* and *HSize*, which respectively give the number of rooms and the number of people in each household. The fields are useful in their own right because they provide some indication of living space and household size in the Gorbals. They also can be combined mathematically to create a further indication of living conditions, notably the average number of people per room in a household. Figure 3.8 shows the partial result of a retrieval which divided the value of *Rooms* into the value for *HSize* for every record in the database and entered the result into a new field named *Person/Room*.

| HNo | PNo | Surname | Forename | Address | Relation | Sex | Age | Occupation | TBirth | Rooms | HSize | Person/Room |
|---|---|---|---|---|---|---|---|---|---|---|---|---|
| 1 | 1 | Fletcher | John | 28 Norfolk St | Head | M | 28 | Ironworker | Ayr | 3 | 4 | 1.33 |
| 1 | 2 | Fletcher | Eliza | 28 Norfolk St | Wife | F | 28 | Seamstress | Edinburgh | 3 | 4 | 1.33 |
| 1 | 3 | Fletcher | John | 28 Norfolk St | Son | M | 8 | Scholar | Glasgow | 3 | 4 | 1.33 |
| 1 | 4 | Fletcher | James | 28 Norfolk St | Son | M | 6 | Scholar | Glasgow | 3 | 4 | 1.33 |
| 2 | 1 | Hepburn | Robert | 28 Norfolk St | Head | M | 44 | Grocer | Kilmarnock | 5 | 4 | 0.80 |
| 2 | 2 | Hepburn | Janet | 28 Norfolk St | Wife | F | 29 | None | Kilmarnock | 5 | 4 | 0.80 |
| 2 | 3 | Hepburn | Mary | 28 Norfolk St | Daughter | F | 2 | None | Glasgow | 5 | 4 | 0.80 |
| 2 | 4 | Cameron | Margaret | 28 Norfolk St | Servant | F | 17 | Domestic | Ayrshire | 5 | 4 | 0.80 |

Fig. 3.8 Retrieval from the Gorbals database table demonstrating a mathematical function which adds a new field to each record

COMPUTERIZED DATABASES: THE MULTI-TABLE SYSTEM

*Accommodating complex data structures*

So far we have looked at a database which contains only a single table. Single-table databases have their uses but these may be limited for the historian whose information does not fit neatly into one table. To demonstrate the point try to design a one-table database for a study of early nineteenth-century British convict labour and how it was deployed in the colonies through the administration of criminal justice.[4] The study is based on the colonial administration's *Convict Description* and *Offence Registers*, which provide both biographical characteristics and the criminal records of transported convicts.

**CONVICTS**

| Pid | Surname | Forenames | Place | Age | Religion | Sex |
|-----|---------|-----------|-------|-----|----------|-----|
| D1256 | MacDonald | John | Born at sea | 37 | P | M |
| B349 | O'Brien | Ellen | Co Wicklow | 25 | RC | F |
| . . . | | | | | | |

*Note*: The table contains rudimentary biographical information about the convicts.

Fig. 3.9 A table from the multi-table database of British convicts transported to the colonies in the nineteenth century

The database table constructed for the study needs to accommodate some biographical information about the convicts. It also needs to chart their course through the British criminal justice system focusing in particular on criminal hearings where they were tried and penalized for their reported offences. Some of the biographical categories are easily housed in a single CONVICTS table shown in Figure 3.9. The table includes fields for convicts' names, place of birth, age, religion, and sex. Each record in the table is

[4] I am grateful to Dr Hamish Maxwell-Stewart, History of Medicine, Glasgow University, who kindly furnished this database example from his study of the management of convict labour, 'Bushrangers and the Convict System in Van Dieman's Land, 1807–1846' (Edinburgh Ph.D. thesis, 1991). The example data are based on Tasmanian State Archives, *Description Registers of Male and Female Convicts* and *Colonial Offence Registers for Convicts Arriving in the Assignment Period*.

also unique thanks to the colonial administration's record-keeping practices which assigned unique identifying tags to each convict. These tags are entered into the table's *Pid* field.

Other information given in the convict records is essential to the study but more difficult to manage within the confines of the table. How, for example, do we represent criminal hearings especially for convicts who were tried several times? Do we record information only for that hearing which resulted in a convict's transportation to the colonies? If so, what do we do with the male convict who had several hearings in Britain before being transported and several more after his arrival in Van Dieman's Land (Tasmania)? Selecting one value where several are available for a particular field of information can cause problems. First, it can introduce unwarranted or inaccurate assumptions into the investigation. Omitting references to British hearings which did not result in transportation assumes that magistrates or judges took no account of offenders' criminal records when determining their penalties at any one hearing. Secondly, interesting lines of enquiry can be cut off unnecessarily. Excluding references to hearings in Van Dieman's Land after a convict had been transported from Britain prohibits analyses of how the colonial authorities dealt with secondary offenders. Thirdly, rules for selectivity are not always so easy to apply consistently when data are being collected.[5] How, for example, would the researcher record the fact that at a hearing held on 4 June 1828, Donald McGee was sentenced to seven years' transportation for several offences some of which had already been tried three months before? In this case, selectivity may actually threaten the veracity and representativeness of the machine-readable data.

Accommodating multiple hearings in our database table is another possibility. But then, how many fields do we need to provide? How many hearings will we allow any one convict to have? What happens to the particularly wayward Englishmen whose litany of offences resulted in several hearings in both Britain and the colonies? The problems caused when some records have far more information associated with them than others are inherent in any collective biography. People simply have a habit of leading

---

[5] Consistent application of data-collection rules is particularly difficult where several researchers and/or assistants are collecting the data over a long period of time.

irregularly patterned lives. Some will have more jobs, spouses, and children, and will be tried more often than others. And the problem is not unique to collective biography. It crops up in any study where a given field of information can have more than one value for any one record.

To accommodate both richly and scarcely textured records, one can use a multi-table database.[6] Here fields which can have multiple values (hearings, jobs) are stored separately as the records of altogether different tables which are joined up with the parent record by values stored in common fields. Take the problem of recording multiple entries for convicts' hearings as discussed above. One solution is to treat information on transported convicts and on the hearings they attended in two independent tables shown in Figure 3.10 as CONVICTS and HEARINGS, respectively. The CONVICTS table contains rudimentary biographical data as already seen. The HEARINGS table holds information about hearings at

**CONVICTS**

| Pid | Surname | Forenames | Place | Age | Religion | Sex |
|-----|---------|-----------|-------|-----|----------|-----|
| D1256 | MacDonald | John | Born at sea | 37 | P | M |
| B349 | O'Brien | Ellen | Co Wicklow | 25 | RC | F |
| . . . |  |  |  |  |  |  |

**HEARINGS**

| Pid | HNo | Day | Month | Year | Place |
|-----|-----|-----|-------|------|-------|
| D1256 | E08062104 | 8 | Jun | 1821 | Edinburgh |
| D1256 | V01012601 | 1 | Jan | 1826 | VDL |
| D1256 | V03012601 | 3 | Jan | 1826 | VDL |
| >>D1256 | V26022602 | 26 | Feb | 1826 | VDL |
| B349 | D18052203 | 18 | May | 1822 | Dublin |

*Note*: The arrow shows how records in the two tables are joined by the values stored in the common *Pid* field. The arrow's double head indicates that any one record in the CONVICTS table may be associated with more than one record in the HEARINGS table.

Fig. 3.10 Two joined tables from the convicts database

[6] For extensive references to databases and their use in historical research see the bibliography section IIA.

which convicts appeared in both Britain and the colonies. The records give the date and place of the hearing and a tag, *HNo*, which uniquely identifies each hearing (the tag is especially important where any one person had two or more hearings).[7] The hearing records are joined to the convicts to whom they pertain by shared values stored in the tables' respective *Pid* fields. Thus, we see that John MacDonald whose *Pid* is given in the CONVICTS table as D1256 was tried once in Edinburgh in June 1821 and three times in Van Dieman's Land in January and February 1826. Ellen O'Brien (*Pid* B349), on the other hand, had only one hearing in Dublin in 1822. One of the greatest advantages of the multi-table database is that it allows the researcher to postpone decisions about what to do where multiple values occur for a particular field of information. In this case, it was not necessary to decide how many hearings to allow for each convict. As more hearings were discovered, they were added as additional records to the HEARINGS table.

In the convicts study many categories of information supplied in the *Offence* and *Convict Description Registers* were treated in this multi-table fashion because many had recurring or multiple values. Hearings could involve one or more reported criminal offences and/or result in multiple penalties. Consequently, the database required two additional tables shown in Figure 3.11, notably OFFENCES and PENALTIES. The records in these tables were linked to those in HEARINGS which had the same value in their respective *HNo* fields. In the OFFENCES table the sequential numbers in the *ONo* field distinguish between offences where more than one was tried at any one hearing. Thus we see in Figure 3.11 that hearing number D18052203 involved two offences, theft and prostitution. In the PENALTIES table, the values in the *PNo* field serve a similar purpose—they distinguish between penalties where more than one was meted out at a given hearing. Hearing number V03012601, for example, resulted in two penalties for the defendant including one hundred lashes and a year's hard labour on the roads. An OCCUPATIONS table was also created to record convicts' British employment experiences as set down in the *Convict Description Register*. The employment records in the OCCUPATIONS table are linked to the records in the CONVICTS table by

---

[7] The value is assigned by the database creator and is based on those in the place and date fields.

**CONVICTS**

| Pid | Surname | Forenames | Place | Age | Religion | Sex |
|---|---|---|---|---|---|---|
| D1256 | MacDonald | John | Born at sea | 37 | P | M |
| B349 | O'Brien | Ellen | Co Wicklow | 25 | RC | F |
| ... | | | | | | |

**OCCUPATIONS**

| Pid | OccNo | Occupation | Employer | Place |
|---|---|---|---|---|
| D1256 | 1 | Stonemason | Mr Hudson | Anderston |
| >>D1256 | 2 | Labourer | | |
| B349 | 1 | Washerwoman | | |
| ... | | | | |

**HEARINGS**

| Pid | HNo | Day | Month | Year | Place |
|---|---|---|---|---|---|
| D1256 | E08062104 | 8 | Jun | 1821 | Edinburgh |
| D1256 | V01012601 | 1 | Jan | 1826 | VDL |
| D1256 | V03012601 | 3 | Jan | 1826 | VDL |
| >>D1256 | V26022602 | 26 | Feb | 1826 | VDL |
| B349 | D18052203 | 18 | May | 1822 | Dublin |
| ... | | | | | |

**PENALTIES**

| HNo | PNo | Penalty |
|---|---|---|
| E08062104 | 1 | 14 years' transportation |
| V01012601 | 1 | Admonished |
| V03012601 | 1 | 100 lashes |
| >>V03012601 | 2 | Hard labour on the roads for 12 months |
| V26022602 | 1 | Solitary confinement for three days |
| D18052203 | 1 | 7 years' transportation |

**OFFENCES**

| HNo | ONo | Inf_Site | Infraction | Place |
|---|---|---|---|---|
| E08062104 | 1 | Near Edinburgh | Highway robbery | Edinburgh |
| V01012601 | 1 | Stonemason's yard | Refusing to work | VDL |
| V03012601 | 1 | Stonemason's yard | Striking overseer with hammer | VDL |
| >>V26022602 | 1 | Notman's chain gang | Not emptying wheelbarrow | VDL |
| V26022602 | 2 | Notman's chain gang | Relieving himself vs orders | VDL |
| D18052203 | 1 | | Stealing trousers from line | Dublin |
| D18052203 | 2 | | On the town for three years | Dublin |

*Note:* The arrows show how records in the tables are joined by values stored in common fields.

Fig. 3.11 Five joined tables from the convicts database

the values in their respective *Pid* fields. Where several employment experiences were given for a convict, these were distinguished by sequential values in the table's *OccNo* field.

The five tables of the convicts database are shown together in Figure 3.11 with arrows indicating how their respective records are joined. There we see that John MacDonald, a stonemason and labourer, was transported to Van Dieman's Land in 1821 for highway robbery. On 1 January 1826 he turned up at a hearing in Van Dieman's Land and was admonished for refusing to work at the stonemason's yard where he was employed. A second hearing took place two days later after MacDonald allegedly struck his overseer with a hammer for which offence MacDonald was given 100 lashes and a year's hard labour on the roads. MacDonald was prosecuted once again in February 1826, this time for two acts of insubordination while on the job. Ellen O'Brien's record is simpler than MacDonald's but just as easily stored in the same database. Initially a washerwoman in Dublin, O'Brien was transported for seven years for theft (prostitution was not a transportable offence). Thereafter, she disappears from the *Colonial Offence Register*.

Referring to the convicts database we can see that multi-table databases operate on the same principles as single-table ones, even as they are more sophisticated and better suited to the management of complex data. First, the multi-table database consists of tables. Secondly, each table is used to store information about a certain class of object; in this case convicts, occupations, hearings, offences, and penalties. Records in any one table share the same range of pre-defined fields, and each record in a table is somehow unique.[8] Even retrievals are similar to those conducted with single-table databases, only here it is possible to join together related records stored in two or more tables. Figure 3.12 shows the partial result of retrievals which draw on records stored in two or more tables in the convicts database.[9]

---

[8] In some tables, a record's uniqueness is preserved by the values stored in two or more fields. In the HEARINGS table, for example, each record has a unique combination of values in its *Pid* and *HNo* fields. This enables one person, D1256 for example, to have several different hearings, in this case EO8062104, V01012601, V03012601, and V26022602.

[9] Also see pp. 98–100 and Figure 3.25.

(*a*) **This retrieval displays the unique convict-identification tags (*Pid*) and penalties meted out in Van Dieman's Land (with dates) to transported convicts who were once employed in Britain as stonemasons and were tried for offences in the colony. It draws upon data stored in selected tables.**

| | |
|---|---|
| **OCCUPATIONS** | the *Pids* of convicts who worked as stonemasons; |
| **HEARINGS** | the dates on which hearings were held in Van Dieman's Land for stonemason convicts (records with the same *Pid* as those retrieved from the OCCUPATIONS table and with a value in the *Place* field of 'VDL'); |
| **PENALTIES** | the punishments meted out in the selected hearings (records with the same *HNo* as those retrieved from the HEARINGS table). |

| Pid | Day | Month | Year | Penalty |
|---|---|---|---|---|
| D1256 | 1 | Jan | 1826 | Admonished |
| D1256 | 3 | Jan | 1826 | 100 lashes |
| D1256 | 3 | Jan | 1826 | Hard labour on the roads for 12 months |
| D1256 | 26 | Feb | 1826 | Solitary confinement for three days |
| F1483 | 9 | Sep | 1828 | 50 lashes |
| F1483 | 17 | Oct | 1828 | 100 lashes |

(*b*) **The retrieval shows the place of birth and religion for female convicts who did not have any further hearings after arriving in Van Dieman's Land. It draws upon data stored in selected tables.**

| | |
|---|---|
| **HEARINGS** | the *Pids* for all hearings held in Van Dieman's Land (*Place* = 'VDL'); |
| **CONVICTS** | the place of birth (*Place*) and religion (*Religion*) of female convicts (*Sex* is 'F') whose *Pid* is not located in the list retrieved from HEARINGS. |

| Place | Religion |
|---|---|
| Co Wicklow | RC |
| Co Cork | RC |
| Lancashire | RC |
| Glasgow | P |

Fig. 3.12 Simple retrievals from the multi-table convicts database

*Editing machine-readable data with a multi-table system*

The results of computer-aided research projects will rely to a large extent on the accuracy of the underlying information. Accurate data entry is therefore terribly important, so much so that it is given extensive consideration in Chapter 6.[10] Even where every precaution is taken with data entry, however, the researcher will still want to verify the machine-readable data that result. Where database projects involve thousands or hundreds of thousands of records, constraints of time and money may prohibit browsing through every record for possible sources of error. Here the multi-table database can point a more economical way forward.

Take the tables in the convicts database again as an example. As the number of records in them increases many of their fields will contain values which are repeated time and again. Consequently, where tables are edited one record at a time, the researcher will be checking the same geographical place names, for example, which in this case crop up in four of the tables (CON-VICTS, OCCUPATIONS, HEARINGS, and OFFENCES). To minimize the editing task, a secondary table, called CHECKPLACE is created as shown in Figure 3.13. The table has two fields, *Place* and *Check*, both of them identical (i.e. with the same datatype definition) to the *Place* fields in the CONVICTS, OCCUPATIONS, HEARINGS, and OFFENCES tables, respectively. Once created the CHECKPLACE table is loaded with the distinct place names in the other four tables.[11] If the value 'Edinburgh' occurs 56 times in the *Place* field of the CONVICTS table and another 157 times in the *Place* field of the hearings table, it would occur only once in CHECKPLACE.

By eliminating duplicate values the number of place names associated with the convict records is reduced considerably.[12] Thereafter it is only a matter of looking through the place names in the CHECKPLACE table for possible sources of error, for example,

[10] See pp. 216–25.

[11] Multi-table databases allow users to save retrieval results as new tables. They also allow retrieval results to be inserted into existing tables. In the latter case, it is important to ensure that the fields of the receiving table are able to accommodate the records being inserted. Inserting data from a twenty-character text field into a ten-character text field, for example, would have the potentially disastrous consequences of truncating the inserted field values.

[12] The amount of reduction is contingent on the degree of repetition in the data.

|  | | **CHECKPLACE** | |
|--|--|------------|-------|
|  | | Place | Check |
| **CONVICTS** | <<——————— | 50 lashes | x |
|  | | Anderston | |
| **OCCUPATIONS** | <<——————— | Born at sea | |
|  | | Co Wicklow | |
| **HEARINGS** | <<——————— | Dublin | |
|  | | Edinburgh | |
|  | | Edinburgn | x |
| **OFFENCES** | <<——————— | VDL | |
|  | | Williamson | x |
|  | | . . . | |

*Note*: The double-headed arrows indicate that the place names in the CHECKPLACE table are joined to those in the *Place* fields in four of the database's other tables. Records which have an 'x' in their *Check* field are deemed to be inaccurate.

Fig. 3.13 Editing data in the multi-table convicts database

place names given as '50 lashes', 'Williamson', or 'Edinburgn'. Where such records are located, an 'x' is placed in their *Check* fields as shown in Figure 3.13. Since the records in CHECKPLACE are joined to those in CONVICTS, OCCUPATIONS, HEARINGS, and OFFENCES which share the same value in their respective *Place* fields, it is possible to selectively retrieve and edit those records from CONVICTS, OCCUPATIONS, HEARINGS, and OFFENCES which contain a dubious place name. The method is particularly effective because records which have inaccurate values in one field (in this case the *Place* field) are likely to have inaccuracies in other fields as well. After editing the records with incorrect place names, additional editing tables could be created to minimize the search for erroneous values in other fields.

### Coding data for analyses with a multi-table system

Using a method similar to that described above for editing, data may be coded or classified for analytical purposes. To exemplify the point, look at another multi-table database, this one developed for a study of early-nineteenth-century Scottish psychiatric practices.[13] The data, drawn from the Gartnavel Royal Hospital's admission records and from its patient case notes are stored in three tables as shown in Figure 3.14. The ADMISSIONS table is based on the hospital's admission register. It provides rudimentary socio-economic data pertaining to the patients who were admitted to the hospital, the date of their admission, and the admitting medical attendant's summary diagnosis of their condition. The records shown in Figure 3.14 refer to a manic 39-year-old schoolteacher, admitted to Gartnavel as a private patient in March 1841, and to a 52-year-old widowed domestic admitted as a pauper and diagnosed as suffering from melia (melancholia).

A HISTORY table is based on a questionnaire filled in at or prior to admission by a patient's relatives or guardians, normally with the aid of the admitting medical attendant. The information on the questionnaire gives a patient's case history and summarizes his or her symptoms. In the HISTORY table, the two values in the *Occurrence* field distinguish between those symptoms reported as antecedents to admission and those manifest in the patient at the time he or she was admitted to hospital. The values in the *HNo* field reconstruct the order in which items in the case history were taken down on the admissions form. The values in the *Adid* field ensures that symptoms are linked to the appropriate patients about whom rudimentary biographical data are recorded in the ADMISSIONS table. The data in Figure 3.14 show that the manic teacher had recently suffered dysentery with discharge of blood, was prone to raving on various religious subjects, had occasionally required physical restraint, and appeared violent and threatening upon admission to hospital. The melancholic widow, on the other hand, laboured under depression of spirits for more than a year, had threatened to destroy herself, and appeared upon admission as being mindless, silly, and idiotic.

A third table called TREATMENTS summarizes the treatments that were prescribed for patients as documented in their case notes. The table's *Month* and *Year* fields indicate approximately when a

[13] I am grateful to Dr Jonathan Andrews, History of Medicine, Glasgow University, who kindly furnished this database example from his study of the Gartnavel Royal Hospital, *Mad People and Mad Patients: A History of Gartnavel Royal Hospital and Psychiatry in the West of Scotland, 1814–1994* (forthcoming). The example data are based on clinical and administrative records of the Gartnavel Royal Hospital stored at Glasgow Greater Health Board Archive Repository at Ruchill Hospital under the listing HB13.

**ADMISSIONS**

| Adid | Month | Year | Age | Sex | Employment | Abode | Status | Marital | Religion | Diagnosis |
|---|---|---|---|---|---|---|---|---|---|---|
| M1841145 | March | 1841 | 39 | M | School teacher | Kelvinside | Private | Married | Free church | Mania |
| A1841356 | August | 1841 | 52 | F | Domestic | Partick | Pauper | Widowed | RC | Melia |

**HISTORY**

| Adid | HNo | Occurrence | Symptom |
|---|---|---|---|
| M1841145 | 1 | Antecedent | Has recently suffered dysentery with discharge of blood |
| M1841145 | 2 | Antecedent | Prone to raving on religious subjects too numerous to mention |
| M1841145 | 3 | Antecedent | Occasionally requiring physical restraint |
| >>M1841145 | 4 | Current | Violent and threatening disposition |
| A1841356 | 1 | Antecedent | Laboured under depression of spirits for more than a year |
| A1841356 | 2 | Antecedent | Threatened to destroy herself |
| A1841356 | 3 | Current | Appeared mindless with a silly and idiotic expression |
| ... | | | |

**TREATMENTS**

| Adid | Month | Year | TNo | Treatment |
|---|---|---|---|---|
| M1841145 | Apr | 1841 | 1 | Cold bath |
| M1841145 | Apr | 1841 | 2 | Head shaved |
| >>M1841145 | Sep | 1841 | 3 | Cream of tartar |
| A1841356 | Aug | 1841 | 1 | Accompanied to chapel |
| ... | | | |

Fig. 3.14 Three joined tables from a multi-table database of nineteenth-century Scottish psychiatric cases

treatment first appeared in the case notes; the *TNo* field distinguishes treatments from one another and preserves the sequential order in which they were prescribed.[14] The value in the *Adid* field ensures that treatments are linked with the appropriate patients and case histories stored in the ADMISSIONS and HISTORY tables, respectively. Here we see that the manic teacher was prescribed a variety of treatments including cold baths and cream of tartar while the melancholic widow was only accompanied to chapel.

The information in the database is a rich source for medical historians and psychiatrists who are interested in the etiology and treatment of psychiatric disorders and in the medical professions' changing understanding of them. In certain cases, however, it is almost too precise. Only some analyses of the treatments given to manic patients, for example, will be interested in the proportion receiving cold baths, cream of tartar, or religious instruction and ministration. Others will be satisfied to know the relative extent to which physical, medicinal, or moral prescriptions were employed, or whether patients received any treatment at all. Coding the symptoms given in the HISTORY table might be as beneficial. How psychiatrists understood the etiology of the disorders they were treating, for example, might be illuminated by coding individual symptoms as either physical (dysentery) or temperamental (violent, raving, depressed).

The multi-table database is ideally suited to the coding task. Take the treatment data as an example. To implement the simple coding scheme outlined above a new table called TREATCODE is created with two fields. The first of these, *Treatment*, contains the distinct treatment descriptions given in the TREATMENTS table. The second field, *TCode*, codes each treatment as being 'Physical', 'Medicinal', or 'Moral'. In this way, the single record in TREATCODE which classifies 'Cold bath' as 'Physical', classifies all records in the TREATMENT table where the value in the *Treatment* field is 'Cold bath'—records in the two tables are joined where they have the same value in their respective *Treatment* fields. With the coding table in place, more meaningful analyses of psychiatric treatments can be conducted. And analyses need not rely solely on the data stored in the linked TREATMENTS and TREATCODE tables. In this data-

---

[14] This is particularly important as dates are not always available or sufficiently precise in the case notes.

base, treatments (and thus their coded values stored in the TREAT-
CODE table) and case histories are all joined to particular patients as
shown in Figure 3.15. Thus, it is possible, for example, to calculate the number of pauper and private patients, respectively, who
received some medicinal treatment, to determine whether moral
suasion was used more frequently with male or female patients,
and to analyse the extent to which physical treatment was prescribed to patients exhibiting violent symptoms at admission.
Using this same multi-table approach to data classification, the
convict study could code offence, penalty, and biographical data to
determine the social complexion of transported convicts, and
whether particular biographical characteristics (place of origin,
religion, work experience, or skill), had any bearing on the kinds
of penalties that were incurred for given categories of offences.

The multi-table approach to data classification is useful, indeed
highly desirable for at least five reasons. First, it can reduce the
amount of editing involved when implementing a coding scheme.
A TREATMENT table with thousands of records is likely to contain
far fewer distinct treatment descriptions to which codes have to
be assigned. Coding only the distinct references in the independent TREATCODE table will be far quicker than assigning a code to
every record in the TREATMENT table. Secondly, it simplifies the
process by which a coding scheme, once implemented, is refined
or altered to suit different research aims. Preliminary analyses of
treatments coded according to the simple scheme outlined above
may indicate that a more refined scheme is necessary, for example, to distinguish between different physical, medicinal, and
moral treatments, respectively. Thus, medicinal treatments might
be recoded to identify those which operate internally (e.g. cream
of tartar and other ingested concoctions) and those which operate
externally (e.g. applications which cause blistering). Physical
treatments might be recoded to distinguish between restraint
(jacketing, manacling), exercise (walking), sensory stimulation
with cold (cold bath, nakedness), sensory stimulation with heat
(hot bath), sensory stimulation with shocks to the body (whirling
chair). The new coding scheme could be implemented by creating
a new TREATCODE table, this one perhaps with three fields, one for
the treatment descriptions and one for each of the coding
schemes used in their analysis. Had the treatment descriptions
been classified according to the initial scheme before they were

**ADMISSIONS**

| Adid | Month | Year | Age | Sex | Employment | Abode | Status | Marital | Religion | Diagnosis |
|------|-------|------|-----|-----|------------|-------|--------|---------|----------|-----------|
| M1841145 | March | 1841 | 39 | M | School teacher | Kelvinside | Private | Married | Free church | Mania |
| A1841356 | August | 1841 | 52 | F | Domestic | Partick | Pauper | Widowed | RC | Melia |

**HISTORY**

| Adid | HNo | Occurrence | Symptom |
|------|-----|------------|---------|
| M1841145 | 1 | Antecedent | Has recently suffered dysentery with discharge of blood |
| M1841145 | 2 | Antecedent | Prone to raving on religious subjects too numerous to mention |
| M1841145 | 3 | Antecedent | Occasionally requiring physical restraint |
| >>M1841145 | 4 | Current | Violent and threatening disposition |
| A1841356 | 1 | Antecedent | Laboured under depression of spirits for more than a year |
| A1841356 | 2 | Antecedent | Threatened to destroy herself |
| A1841356 | 3 | Current | Appeared mindless with a silly and idiotic expression |
| ... | | | |

**TREATMENTS**

| Adid | Month | Year | TNo | Treatment |
|---|---|---|---|---|
| M1841145 | Apr | 1841 | 1 | Cold bath |
| M1841145 | Apr | 1841 | 2 | Head shaved |
| >>M1841145 | Sep | 1841 | 3 | Cream of tartar |
| A1841356 | Aug | 1841 | 1 | Accompanied to chapel |
| . . . | | | | |

**TREATCODE**

| Treatment | TCode |
|---|---|
| Cold bath | Physical |
| >>Head shaved | Physical |
| Cream of tartar | Medicinal |
| Accompanied to chapel | Moral |
| . . . | |

Fig. 3.15 Coding data in the multi-table psychiatric database

entered into the computer, subsequent analyses would be much more constrained.[15]

The ability to implement multiple coding schemes is especially important with respect to databases which will be used by researchers with very different interests. Modern psychiatrists, for example, might prefer recasting nineteenth-century diagnoses and symptom descriptions in late twentieth-century terms in an attempt to chart the incidence of disorders known to the modern medical establishment. The medical historian, on the other hand, might prefer to code the same diagnoses and symptoms data with the categories that nineteenth-century practitioners employed in order to illuminate how psychological disorders were understood by contemporaries.

Thirdly, coding data in independent tables is useful where coding schemes are essentially contestable either because the data underlying them are ambiguous or because the coding schemes themselves are contingent upon contestable assumptions. The problems inherent in coding occupational data provide the most obvious examples.[16] The psychiatric case notes can help illuminate the extent to which diagnoses and treatments were related to individuals' social or economic standing. Such analyses require that individuals' economic or social standing be inferred from the occupational descriptions given on the admissions register. One problem is that the occupational descriptions are rather vague. Surely, any assessment of individuals' social or economic standing requires information about their income and level of education, and about the income and occupations of their parents, spouses, and spouses' parents, for example. Another problem is that irrespective of the socio-economic data's comprehensiveness, disagreement is likely to emerge over how best to classify them. Analysts will create different coding schemes based upon their particular understanding of the socio-economic composition of early nineteenth-century Scotland. Multi-table databases will not make the task of coding occupational and other data any less

[15] The praises of so-called post coding were already being sung in 1975 by J. H. Levitt and C. E. Labarre, 'Building a Data File From Historical Archives', *Computers and the Humanities*, 9 (1975), 77–82.

[16] D. I. Greenstein, 'Standard, Meta-Standard: A Framework for Coding Occupational Data', *Historical Social Research*, 16 (1991), 3–22; K. Schürer and H. Diederiks (eds.), *The Use of Occupations in Historical Analysis* (St Katharinen, 1993), and section IIE of the bibliography.

contentious. They will, at least, permit several competing coding schemes to be implemented simultaneously as the underlying data are never lost to secondary analysts. The multi-table database is particularly useful in this respect because so many categories of historical information can be as difficult to code as occupational data.[17]

Fourthly, by classifying data in separate coding tables, the researcher is able to see all of the values from a particular field together in a condensed form. Here, values whose meaning would be ambiguous if they were encountered in isolation may become clearer. Take the treatment data again as an example. When entered into an independent TREATCODE table there may be several slightly different records all referring to 'Cold bath' simply because to the computer, the values 'Cold bath', 'Cold bathe', and 'Immerse in cold water' are all different. If the same list contained a reference to 'Bath' as well, the researcher using the more refined coding scheme outlined above would be tempted to clas-sify the otherwise ambiguous entry along with the others as 'Sensory stimulation—cold'. Should the list, however, contain other references, for example, to 'Hot bath', the researcher would probably be inclined to leave the ambiguous reference uncoded or to code it as 'not known' or 'ambiguous'.

Fifthly, the multi-table approach to data classification is useful because it promises to deliver valuable reference material to other researchers. Few scholars will be interested in transported con-victs or the diagnosis and treatment of psychiatric patients at the Gartnavel Royal Hospital. The tables which implement classification schemes for geographic place names, criminal offences and penalties, nineteenth-century occupations, and psy-chiatric treatments, symptoms, and diagnoses, however, may be useful to a much larger audience. These tables and the classification schemes they implement can be incorporated

---

[17] Dates are notoriously difficult where they are given as mere approximations ('c.1765'), inexact ranges ('the late nineteenth century'), or as relative expressions ('a fortnight after Michaelmas in the second year of the reign of James II'). Geographical place names can also be given as mere approximations ('near Birmingham') and as relative expressions ('Foorler's House near the baker's shop'), and currency and commodity measures can also be troublesome. See M. Thaller, 'The Need for Standards: Data Modelling and Exchange', 5, and 'A Draft Proposal for the Coding of Machine Readable Sources', 39, both in D. I. Greenstein (ed.), *Modelling Historical Data: Towards a Standard for Encoding and Exchanging Machine-Readable Texts* (St Katharinen, 1991).

directly into any computerized database provided that comparable data are stored in similarly structured fields. The prospective economies are considerable. In more general terms, historical research produces a significant amount of expertise, for example, about physical and psychological disorders, the geographic location of named places, the meaning and significance of occupational descriptions, the timing of local saints and festival days, and about the value of local currencies. The coding tables of multi-table databases explicitly store this kind of expert knowledge in a way which makes it accessible to other researchers.

*Record linkage with multi-table systems*

Record linkage is an important feature of many computer-aided research projects, as we have already seen in Chapter 1.[18] Generally speaking, it enables the researcher to build up information about a particular object from several different references to it made in one or more sources. In the convicts study, record linkage was straightforward because every piece of information relating to transported convicts was accompanied with the unique identifying tags assigned to the convicts by the colonial administration. Consequently, it was possible to build up convicts' biographical profiles from the *Convict Description Registers* and link these to other information supplied in the *Offence Registers*. The record linkage took place without the aid of a computer while data were being collected and was driven by a simple rule, namely, that all records sharing a unique identifying tag belonged to the same individual.

Obviously, not all historical data are so easily linked. Let us turn to a study of the social origins, university experiences, and career destinations of Oxford University matriculants in the period 1900–70. There, matriculant profiles were built up from two sources including printed lists of matriculants and final honours examination results, respectively. The information from these two sources was entered into the two database tables shown in Figure 3.16.[19] The MATRICS table comprises information on the nearly

---

[18] For a general discussion of record linkage see Ch. 1. For more extensive references see section IID of the bibliography.

[19] These tables are simplified versions of those actually used in the Oxford database. The biographical information shown here has been altered to ensure compliance with the Data Protection Act.

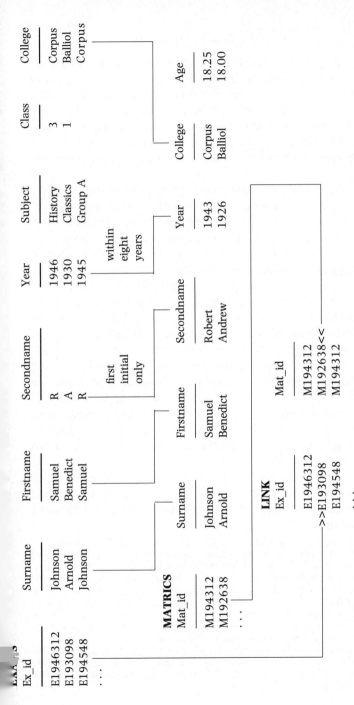

*Note:* Matriculation and examination records are stored in the MATRICS and EXAMS tables, respectively. These nominal records are linked with a multi-table database retrieval whose criteria specify how the values in five fields must match up for any two records from MATRICS and EXAMS before they can be considered as belonging to the same person. The retrievals place the unique identifying tags (*Mat_id* and *Ex_id*) of linked record pairs into a new table called LINK.

Fig. 3.16 Linking nominal records in a multi-table database of Oxford University's twentieth-century members

120,000 people who matriculated in the period including their names, year, and college at time of matriculation. The EXAMS table stores information about the 143,000 finalists from the period and has fields for finalists' names, and the year, subject, and result of their final honours examinations. The values in the tables' respective *Mat_id* and *Ex_id* fields were assigned by the database creator to ensure that the records in both tables are unique.

Unfortunately for the historian, Oxford administrators never assigned matriculants with unique identifying tags to help integrate all of the records produced for university members. Such tags would have helped to join examination results to the matriculants who achieved them. Without them, the researcher is forced to make a judgement based on rather more complicated criteria as to whether any pair of records from the MATRICS and EXAMS tables, respectively, belonged to the same person. Here, examination and matriculation records were said to belong to the same person when the surname, first name, first initial of the second name, and college affiliation in the two records were identical, and when the examination took place within eight years of matriculation. These rules, shown diagrammatically in Figure 3.16, were specified as part of a multi-table database retrieval which placed the *Mat_id* and *Ex_id* values of every joined record pair into a third table called LINK. The LINK table is also shown in Figure 3.16. Using the multi-table database to automate record linkage, it was possible in one afternoon to link 95 per cent of the nearly 263,000 examination and matriculation records, with an estimated rate of accuracy of over 96 per cent. Manual record linkage would have required months of tedious work for the same level of accuracy.[20]

[20] The account is a rather simplified one. Only 75 per cent of the records were actually linked according to the criteria described here. These records were assigned a value of 100 in a third field of the LINK table indicating that they were linked according to the most stringent criteria. Linkage rules were then progressively relaxed in order to link records not matched by the initial criteria. Records linked according to relaxed criteria were assigned values less than 100, indicating the degree of doubt which accompanied their linkage. By keeping track of the probable accuracy of each linked pair of records, it was possible to check ambiguous or surprising statistical results against the subset of data in which there was the utmost confidence. For a comparison of the accuracy of manual and computer-aided record linkage see I. Winchester, 'The Linkage of Historical Records by Man and Computer: Techniques and Problems', *Journal of Interdisciplinary History*, 1 (1970), 107–24.

The multi-table database, then, is preferable to a single-table one where individual fields are likely to contain multiple or recurring values and/or where bulk editing, data classification, or record linkage are required. The Oxford study exploited some of these facilities as did the studies of British convicts and Scottish psychiatry. But a project does not need to be as complex or on the same large scale to benefit from a multi-table system. The Gorbals census data, for example, are very simple. The values in any one field are not recurring. There was never any intention when the database was constructed of linking its nominal records to those collected from other sources (e.g. from probate inventories). Nor is the database big enough (it only had 396 records) to require the kind of editing which was so useful in the study of British convicts. Still, a multi-table database would be beneficial in classifying the Gorbals data for analytical purposes. Independent coding tables would benefit analyses of the geographical origins and occupational profiles of Gorbals residents. With geographical and occupational information coded up for analysis in independent tables, different (perhaps competing) analytical schemes could be used. Even the simplest projects, then, may want to consider a multi-table database, especially as there is nothing to stop the multi-table database user from creating and managing only one table.

## DATABASE SOFTWARE

All database software may be menu- and/or command-driven. With menu-driven systems the user provides instruction to the software by making a selection from a menu of options. Having selected a menu option, another menu of options may appear, selection from which may produce still a further so-called submenu. Making choices at several levels of a menu-driven system effectively builds up the instruction that will be issued to the database. Figure 3.17 shows three menu levels encountered when making a table with a menu-driven database system. With command-driven systems, instructions are built up by typing them onto a so-called command line and issuing the instructions by pressing whatever key is assigned by the software package to mean 'Go' or 'Execute'. Commands must be composed with the

**Menu level 1:** The display shows the available database modules. The user has selected the module which creates tables and is about to execute the selection by using the 'Go' command.

```
         To run a highlighted command, place the cursor over it and
         select the 'Go' menu item.

  ┌─────────────┬───────────────────────────────────────────────────────┐
  │ Commands    │ Description                                            │
  ├─────────────┼───────────────────────────────────────────────────────┤
  │ QUERY       │ RUN simple or saved QUERY                              │
  │ REPORT      │ RUN default or saved REPORT                            │
  │ RUNGRAPH    │ RUN saved GRAPH defined by VIGRAPH                     │
  │             │                                                        │
  │ QBF         │ Use QUERY-BY-FORMS to develop and test query definitions│
  │ RBF         │ Use REPORT-BY-FORMS to design or modify reports        │
  │ VIGRAPH     │ Use VIGRAPH to design, modify or test graphs           │
  │ ABF         │ Use APPLICATIONS-BY-FORMS to design and test applications│
  │             │                                                        │
  │ TABLES      │ CREATE, MANIPULATE or LOOKUP tables in the database    │
  │ VIFRED      │ EDIT forms by using the VISUAL-FORMS-EDITOR            │
  │ QUEL        │ ENTER interactive QUEL statements                     │
  │ SQL         │ ENTER interactive SQL statements                      │
  │ SREPORT     │ SAVE REPORT-WRITER commands in the reports catalog    │
  └─────────────┴───────────────────────────────────────────────────────┘

     Go          Help       Quit
```

**Menu level 2:** The display shows that there are as yet no tables in the database. The user has indicated the desire to create a new table by selecting the 'Create' option from the menu line at the bottom of the display.

```
                         TABLE UTILITY

                      Creating a New Table


                   ┌────────────┬────────────┐
                   │ Table Name │ Owner      │
                   ├────────────┼────────────┤
                   │            │            │
                   │            │            │
                   │            │            │
                   └────────────┴────────────┘

     Create    Destroy    Examine    Find      Help      End
```

**Menu level 3:** At this level, the user is prompted for additional information about the name of the table being created and the name and data types of the table's fields.

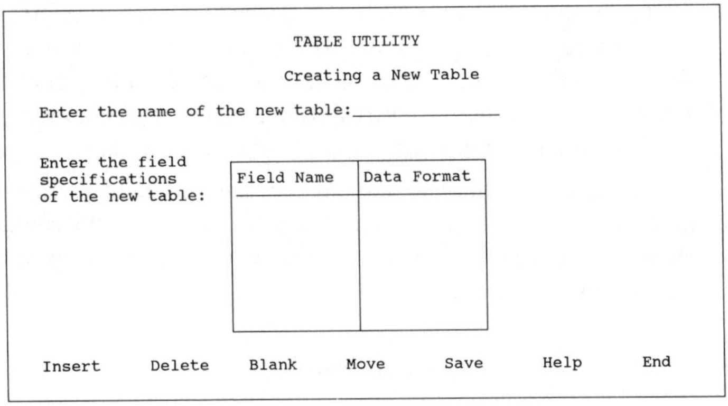

```
                        TABLE UTILITY

                      Creating a New Table

    Enter the name of the new table:_____


    Enter the field
    specifications    Field Name    Data Format
    of the new table:



    Insert      Delete     Blank     Move     Save     Help     End
```

*Note*: The figure shows three levels of menu options that are encountered when creating a table. The selection made at levels one and two are indicated in bold print. It is based on the displays encountered in the *Ingres* database management system.

Fig. 3.17 Using a menu-driven database system

software's own 'command language' and it is important to note that like natural languages, command languages vary considerably—each comprising its own distinctive vocabulary and syntax. When a command contains foreign vocabulary or where its syntax is incorrect, it will fail when the user attempts to execute it. Fortunately for the database user, software companies are beginning to adopt the query language recommended by the International Standards Organization (ISO)—Structured Query Language (SQL).[21] Because SQL is evolving as a *de facto* as well as a *de jure* standard, it has been used in example database commands demonstrated in Figures 3.19, 3.20, 3.23, 3.25.

Whether command- and/or menu-driven, single- and multi-table databases will be available for most computers. Each will boast its own range of utilities but all will offer a bundle of at least four integrated procedures or routines.

1. Table definition procedures allow database tables to be created and their precise field structures defined.

[21] C. J. Date, *A Guide to the SQL Standard*, 2nd edn. (Reading, Mass., 1988); S. Pasleau, *SQL langage et SGBD relationnels* (Paris, 1988).

2. Data entry and data editing procedures enable users to append new records to database tables and to edit and/or delete records already stored in tables.

3. Data retrieval and manipulation procedures allow information stored in the database to be selectively retrieved or transformed according to a number of user-specified criteria.

4. Report generating procedures enable users to retrieve data selectively and output them to a printer or to a file.

Let us look in more detail at database definition, data retrievals and manipulation, and report generating. Data entry and editing is explored in Chapter 6, which focuses generally on project design and implementation.

### Table definition

To create a database table the user assigns the table a name and then names and defines the table's fields. As has already been indicated, considerable thought needs to be given to a database table's definition since field structure determines how information can be selectively retrieved and analysed.[22] Moreover, it is not always convenient to redefine a database table after hundreds of records have been entered into it. The definition of the Gorbals database table is shown above in Figure 3.2. Figures 3.18 and 3.19 show how the table would be a created in menu- and a command-driven system, respectively.

### Data retrieval and manipulation

Data retrieval and manipulation procedures vary from one database package to the next but are fundamentally similar. In general, database retrievals produce tables as a result. Thus, in retrieving from the Gorbals database table the names, addresses, occupations, and ages of Glasgow-born residents of 28 Norfolk St., a five-field table is produced with as many records as there are records in the Gorbals database table which meet the specified criteria. The retrieval itself can be considered as comprising four distinctive parts as shown in Figure 3.20:

- a field selection list indicating which fields of the targeted

---

[22] See pp. 63, 67–8.

```
                      TABLE UTILITY

                  Creating a New Table


Enter the name of the new table: Gorbals
                                 _____


Enter the field
specifications    ┌─────────────┬──────────────┐
of the new table: │ Field Name  │ Data Format  │
                  ├─────────────┼──────────────┤
                  │ HNo         │ integer      │
                  │ PNo         │ integer      │
                  │ Surname     │ c20          │
                  │ Forename    │ c16          │
                  │ Address     │ c20          │
                  │ Relation    │ c12          │
                  │ Sex         │ c1           │
                  │ Age         │ integer      │
                  │ Occupation  │ c20          │
                  │ TBirth      │ c20          │
                  │ Rooms       │ integer      │
                  │ HSize       │ integer      │
                  └─────────────┴──────────────┘


Insert     Delete     Blank     Move     Save     Help     End
```

*Note*: The user has filled in the form indicating the table and field names and the fields' respective data types. All that remains is for the user to select 'Save' from the options shown on the bottom line to create the table. The figure is based on the displays encountered in the *Ingres* database management system.

Fig. 3.18 Creating the Gorbals database table with a menu-driven system

table(s) are to be displayed in the result and the order in which they are to be displayed (in this case, *Surname*, *Forename*, *Address*, *Occupation*, and *Age*);

- a target list which specifies the database table(s) where the desired information is stored (in this case the Gorbals table);[23]
- one or more criteria that must be met by values stored in selected fields of any one record in order for that record to be selected and displayed as part of the result (in this case where *Tbirth* is 'Glasgow' and *Address* is '28 Norfolk St');[24]
- a statement defining the order in which selected records are to be displayed (order by *Surname*, *Forename*).

[23] It may not be necessary to specify the target table in a single-table database system since, by definition, only one table can ever be known to such a system.

[24] Where retrievals involve records from several tables the criteria also need to specify how records in the tables are joined. A retrieval from the ADMISSIONS and TREATMENTS tables of the Scottish psychiatric database, for example, would provide a criterion indicating that the records in the two tables were joined where they shared the same value in their respective *Adid* fields. See Figure 3.25 for examples of how such criteria can be indicated with the command language, SQL.

```
Create table Gorbals                      (
        HNo             integer     ,
        PNo             integer     ,
        Surname         c20         ,
        Forename        c16         ,
        Address         c20         ,
        Relation        c12         ,
        Sex             c1          ,
        Age             integer     ,
        Occupation      c20         ,
        Tbirth          c20         ,
        Rooms           integer     ,
        HSize           integer           )



    Go          Blank           Help            Quit
```

*Note*: The user has typed out the appropriate SQL command and has only to select the 'Go' menu option shown on the bottom line to create the table. The figure is based on a display encountered in the *Ingres* database management system.

Fig. 3.19 Creating the Gorbals database table with a command-driven system using the Structured Query Language (SQL)

Every query at least must indicate a target table and the list of fields to be displayed in the result. With single- and multi-table databases, the results produced by a retrieval can be viewed on the screen, printed onto paper, or saved to a file which can be printed or edited with a word processor, for example. With a multi-table database there are more options. Retrieval result can be inserted into tables with an appropriate field structure or saved as new database tables.

Of these four query components only the criteria require any further discussion since they give automated data retrievals their power and flexibility. Retrieval criteria are made up of so-called operators and functions many of which we have already encountered in example retrievals from the Gorbals database table (Figures 3.3 to 3.8). So-called relational operators are those which indicate that the value in a given field (*Relation, Sex, TBirth*) has to be equal to, greater than, less than, or not equal to a particular expression. We have also encountered 'Boolean' operators, AND and OR, which are used to build up complex retrieval criteria. Figure 3.21 lists relational operators and examples of how they may be used in conjunction with Boolean operators to retrieve selected records from the convicts, Scottish psychiatric,

## a) The original GORBALS table

| HNo | PNo | Surname | Forename | Address | Sex | Age | Occupation | TBirth | Rooms | HSize |
|---|---|---|---|---|---|---|---|---|---|---|
| 1 | 1 | Fletcher | John | 28 Norfolk St | M | 28 | Ironworker | Ayr | 3 | 4 |
| 1 | 2 | Fletcher | Eliza | 28 Norfolk St | F | 28 | Seamstress | Edinburgh | 3 | 4 |
| 1 | 3 | Fletcher | John | 28 Norfolk St | M | 8 | Scholar | Glasgow | 3 | 4 |
| 1 | 4 | Fletcher | James | 28 Norfolk St | M | 6 | Scholar | Glasgow | 3 | 4 |
| 2 | 1 | Hepburn | Robert | 28 Norfolk St | M | 44 | Grocer | Kilmarnock | 5 | 4 |
| 2 | 2 | Hepburn | Janet | 28 Norfolk St | F | 29 | None | Kilmarnock | 5 | 4 |
| 2 | 3 | Hepburn | Mary | 28 Norfolk St | F | 2 | None | Glasgow | 5 | 4 |
| 2 | 4 | Cameron | Margaret | 28 Norfolk St | F | 17 | Domestic | Ayrshire | 5 | 4 |

...

## b) The SQL command with its four principal components identified

| select Surname, Forename, Address, Occupation, Age | } **field selection list** |
|---|---|
| from Gorbals | } **target list** |
| where  TBirth = 'Glasgow' and | } **criterion** |
| Address = '28 Norfolk St' | } **criterion** |
| order by Surname, Forename | } **display order** |

## c) A partial result of the query

| Surname | Forename | Address | Occupation | Age |
|---|---|---|---|---|
| Fletcher | James | 28 Norfolk St | Scholar | 6 |
| Fletcher | John | 28 Norfolk St | Scholar | 8 |
| Hepburn | Mary | 28 Norfolk St | None | 2 |

...

*Note*: The figure shows the original database table, the SQL command, and a partial result. The four principal parts of the retrieval command are identified next to the SQL command in bold.

Fig. 3.20 Retrieving information from the Gorbals database table with SQL

| Operator | Symbol | Example of its use |
|---|---|---|
| Greater than | > | Show the occupations of elderly male convicts who were transported from Britain (*Age* > 64 AND *Sex* = 'M'). |
| Less than | < | Show the age and summary diagnosis of young female paupers admitted to the Gartnavel hospital (*Status* = 'Pauper' AND *Age* < 16 AND *Sex* = 'F'). |
| Equal to | = | Using the coded treatment data in the Scottish psychiatric database retrieve the age, sex, and admission status ('Private' or 'Pauper') of psychiatric patients treated with moral suasion (*TCode* = 'Moral'). |
| Greater than or equal to | => | Occupations of male household heads in Gorbals households with five or more rooms (*Sex* = 'M' AND *Relation* = 'Head' AND *Rooms* => 5). |
| Less than or equal to | =< | Show the names of Oxford matriculants who were Balliol college members, took their Final Honours examinations in History, and got first- or second-class results (*College* = 'Balliol' AND *Class* =< 2 AND *Subject* = 'History'). |
| Not equal to | <> | Occupations of working children in Gorbals less than 16 years of age (*Occupation* <> 'None' AND *Occupation* <> 'Scholar' AND *Age* < 16). |

*Note*: Examples are based on the Gorbals, convicts, Scottish psychiatric, and Oxford databases.

Fig. 3.21 Using relational and Boolean operators to make database retrievals

Gorbals, and Oxford databases. Most databases also will enable users to search for text strings whose exact character sequence is unknown. Notice that two of the records in the Gorbals database table (Figure 3.1) give birthplaces in Ayrshire, only one is far more specific giving the county seat (Ayr) and the other only the county name (Ayrshire). So-called 'wildcard operators' (normally * and ?) enable the user to retrieve all references beginning with the letters 'Ayr'.

So-called arithmetical operators also have been discussed. With these the Gorbals database table was transformed with the addition of a new field giving the average number of persons per room in the households of every enumerated Gorbals resident (Figure 3.8). The arithmetic operators for addition (+), subtraction (−), multiplication (*), division (/), and exponentiation (**) can be used in such transformations. So-called set functions also have been encountered. These enable the user to produce aggregate or summary measures, for example, by counting up the number of records meeting a particular retrieval criterion. A list of these more quantitative functions and examples of how they may be used with the Gorbals, convicts, and Scottish psychiatry databases is provided in Figure 3.22. Other so-called string

| Operator | Example of its use |
|---|---|
| Sum | Show total number of rooms available on Norfolk Street, Gorbals. |
| Count | Count the number of Protestant convicts who gave their occupation simply as 'Labourer' and who had further criminal hearings after arriving in Van Dieman's Land. |
| Average | Show the average age of melancholic women admitted to Gartnavel hospital. |
| Min | Show the age, sex, and summary diagnosis of the youngest person admitted to Gartnavel hospital. |
| Max | Show the age of the oldest gainfully employed person on Norfolk Street, Gorbals. |

*Note*: Examples are based on the Gorbals, convicts, and Scottish psychiatric databases.

Fig. 3.22 Using set functions to make database retrievals

functions can be helpful in managing data in text fields. The
retrieval whose result is shown in Figure 3.23 uses a combination
of string functions to display in upper-case letters and in one field
the surnames and forenames of male Protestant convicts between
the ages of 25 and 45, inclusive. For legibility, the retrieval sup-
plies a comma and a blank space between surnames and forenames as displayed in the result. Finally, as has already been
demonstrated in Figures 3.6 and 3.7, database software allows
users to specify the alphabetical or numerical order in which
retrieved records are displayed.

```
select
    Pid,
    uppercase(Surname) + ', ' +
    uppercase(Forenames) ,
    Age
        from Convicts
            where
                Religion = 'P' and
                Sex = 'M' and
                Age > 24 and
                Age < 46
            order by Pid
```

| Pid | Surname + Forenames | Age |
| --- | --- | --- |
| B3637 | BRYANT, ANTHONY | 26 |
| D1256 | MACDONALD, JOHN | 37 |
| D1348 | DUNCAN, ARCHIBALD | 40 |
| P6166 | MACPHERSON, WILLIAM | 29 |

*Note*: This retrieval from the convicts database table uses the 'uppercase'
function to convert the values in the *Surname* and *Forenames* fields to
upper-case letters and the '+' operator to join the fields together, introducing a comma and a space between them.

Fig. 3.23 Using string functions to make database retrievals

*Report generating*

Most database management systems enable users to format database retrievals for printing. Figure 3.24 shows selected records

Report on Table: Gorbals (style one)

**Address:** 28 Norfolk St

| HNo | PNo | Surname | Forename | Relation | Sex | Age | Occupation | TBirth | Rooms | HSize |
|---|---|---|---|---|---|---|---|---|---|---|
| 1 | 1 | Fletcher | John | Head | M | 28 | Ironworker | Ayr | 3 | 4 |
| 1 | 2 | Fletcher | Eliza | Wife | F | 28 | Seamstress | Edinburgh | 3 | 4 |
| 1 | 3 | Fletcher | John | Son | M | 8 | Scholar | Glasgow | 3 | 4 |
| 1 | 4 | Fletcher | James | Son | M | 6 | Scholar | Glasgow | 3 | 4 |
| 2 | 1 | Hepburn | Robert | Head | M | 44 | Grocer | Kilmarnock | 5 | 4 |
| 2 | 2 | Hepburn | Janet | Wife | F | 29 | None | Kilmarnock | 5 | 4 |
| 2 | 3 | Hepburn | Mary | Daughter | F | 2 | None | Glasgow | 5 | 4 |
| 2 | 4 | Cameron | Margaret | Servant | F | 17 | Domestic | Ayrshire | 5 | 4 |

...

Report on Table: Gorbals (style two)

**HNo:** 1 **PNo:** 1
**Surname:** Fletcher        **Forename:** John
**Relation:** Head          **Occupation:** Ironworker
**Sex:** M   **Age:** 28     **TBirth:** Ayr
**Address:** 28 Norfolk Street
                            **Rooms:** 3
                            **HSize:** 4

**HNo:** 1 **PNo:** 2
**Surname:** Fletcher        **Forename:** Eliza
...

Fig. 3.24 Selected database output formats based on the Gorbals database table

from the Gorbals table printed out in two different formats. So-called report-writing modules incorporate retrieval facilities so users can specify which records and fields to present in the output and how to order them. They also provide some control over page layout (e.g. page and margin sizes), and over the fonts and point-sizes used for printed characters. But here any generalization must cease as the procedures for creating reports vary so much across different database packages.

## COMPUTERIZED DATABASES: SOME LIMITATIONS

Before concluding the chapter it is necessary to review some of the limitations common to all databases which should be given serious consideration before mounting a database project. Three stand out above all others: databases are only suitable for highly structured historical information; the time taken to build a database may be greater than that saved with its automated retrievals and summary measures; databases can make cumbersome analytical tools. Let us look briefly at each of these limitations.

First, computerized databases are only useful where information can be rigorously structured as a collection of records sharing the same well-defined fields. Impressionistic evidence defies this kind of representation. So does rich description of single individuals, events, objects, and ideas that is normally taken down as running prose. Indeed, one could argue that databases are only suitable for information which is actually presented in the original source as a list or table, or information which can be extracted from the source and summarized relatively easily in a list or in tabular form. Censuses, poll books, city directories, and parish registers are primary sources whose information is immediately conducive to database management. Information is already set out as a collection of records each with the same number of pre-defined fields. Poll books, for example, provide a record for each voter, and each record has the same number of fields—surname, forenames, home address, occupation, and vote cast. Manufacturing censuses are lists of firms, where each firm is described by its address, business, and number of employees. Other sources which are not list-like in their appearance but whose information can be abstracted as lists or tables include the hospital's admission and patient records and the convict description and offence records already discussed in this chapter. Collective biographies such as *Who's Who* are another such source. With these it is possible to compile a list of Anglican bishops, for example, in which the same pre-defined range of biographical information (names, father's occupation, date and place of birth, university degrees) can be recorded.

Even where it is possible to represent information as a collection of records sharing the same number of fields, the narrow range of permitted datatypes can act as a constraint. For example, databases insist that numbers be represented in a decimal system, which is wholly inadequate for some of the numeric data of history. Few database fields comprehend a currency measure given in pounds, shillings, and pence, for example. Similarly, database fields defined as dates are not likely to make sense of anything other than fairly recent dates given according to the Gregorian calendar.[25] Lengthy text fields, too, can cause problems as we shall see in Chapter 5. Although some of these problems may be circumvented with innovative table structures, the historian sometimes may feel that data's richness and complexity are sacrificed when they are forced to conform to the rigorous and inflexible requirements of the database software.[26]

A further limitation is that even simple databases are time consuming to construct. Information needs to be collected, entered into the computer, and extensively edited before it can be used in a meaningful way. The larger the database—that is, the more records and/or fields it contains—the longer it will take to compile. Consequently, the first few retrievals are very 'expensive', and the unit cost of retrievals only declines as the number of retrievals made with the computerized system increases. When considering whether to use a computerized database it is worth making three rough calculations: how long it will take to computerize and edit the data; how long it will take to conduct one

[25] Hence, the temporal information recorded in the convicts and Scottish psychiatry databases was separated into fields for days, months, and years, respectively.

[26] Currency values expressed in pounds, shillings, and pence can be stored in three fields instead of one. Fuzzy and non-Gregorian dates can be entered into the field of one table and expressed in standardized fashion in the field of another coding table. Lengthy text fields, however, still cause considerable problems for databases. See pp. 106–7, 175–7.

retrieval manually if the records are managed in a paper-based system; and how many retrievals any one project will require. Where constructing the computerized database requires less time than manually performing the required number of retrievals, the computerized database is worth considering.

A third limitation is that database management systems are systems for managing information, they are not particularly good at analysing it. All databases are helpful for selective data retrieval, transforming information stored in the fields of a database table, and for returning fairly basic summary measures such as counts and averages. Multi-table databases also facilitate bulk editing, data classification, and nominal record linkage, and as we shall see in Chapter 6, accurate data entry. They do not, however, offer much in the way of sophisticated analytical tools. Analyses which rely upon more elaborate measures than the simple summary ones outlined here or on graphical display will require the statistical and spreadsheet software discussed in Chapter 4.[27]

But the constraints on using a database for analysis run deeper than the mere absence of statistical and graphical procedures. As we will see in Chapter 4, meaningful statistical and graphical analysis can only be conducted where the relevant subset of data—that is the selected records and fields which are being analysed—are stored in one table. Where multi-table databases are used, it may prove exceedingly time consuming to merge data stored across several tables into the one required for analysis. To exemplify this point a relatively simple analysis based on the Oxford database is presented in Figure 3.25. The analysis shows the regional origins (place of birth) of a sample of Oxford's British-born male matriculants in four periods 1900–13, 1914–19, 1920–9, and 1930–9. The figures in the table are given in percentage terms. Thus we see, for example, that 25 per cent of British-born men who matriculated in the period 1900–13 were born in the London area.

The analysis was based on three tables, parts of which are also shown in Figure 3.25. The MATRICS table has already been introduced. The ADDRESS table provides information about where

---

[27] Some database software will provide statistical and graphical procedures, but these tend to be primitive when compared to the specialist statistical and graphical software discussed in Ch. 4.

*a*) **The results of the analysis**

| Region | 1900–13 | 1914–19 | 1920–29 | 1930–39 |
|---|---|---|---|---|
| East | 5 | 5 | 4 | 6 |
| Local (to Oxford) | 8 | 7 | 10 | 6 |
| London | 25 | 25 | 21 | 21 |
| Midlands | 5 | 6 | 6 | 5 |
| North | 4 | 3 | 3 | 4 |
| North-east | 7 | 7 | 8 | 7 |
| North-west | 12 | 9 | 10 | 12 |
| South | 5 | 5 | 6 | 4 |
| South-east | 8 | 11 | 9 | 11 |
| South-west | 3 | 2 | 3 | 3 |
| West | 6 | 5 | 7 | 7 |
| Scotland | 6 | 7 | 6 | 7 |
| Wales | 7 | 6 | 7 | 7 |

*b*) **The three tables underlying the analysis**
**MATRICS**

| Mat_id | Surname | Firstname | Secondname | Year | College | Age |
|---|---|---|---|---|---|---|
| M194312 | Johnson | Samuel | Robert | 1943 | Corpus | 18.25 |
| M192638 | Arnold | Benedict | Andrew | 1926 | Balliol | 18.00 |

. . .

**ADDRESS**

| Mat_id | Ptype | Place |
|---|---|---|
| M194312 | fadd | Newport, Mon |
| M194312 | pobt | Salesbury, Lancs |
| >>M192638 | fadd | Slinfold, Sussex |
| M192638 | pobt | Dolgelley, Merioneth |

. . .

**PLACECODE**

| Place | Region |
|---|---|
| Dolgelley, Merioneth | Wales |
| Newport, Mon | West |
| >>Salesbury, Lancs | North-west |
| Slinfold, Sussex | South-east |

*cont. over*/

**c) The SQL commands to produce the above result shown in (*a*) from the three underlying tables shown in (*b*)**

```
create table one
        as select a.mat_id, a.year, c.region
            from matrics a, address b, placecode c
                where       a.mat_id = b.mat_id and
                            b.ptype = 'pobt' and
                            b.place = c.place;


update one set year = 1 where year <1914;
update one set year = 2 where year > 1913 and year < 1920;
update one set year = 3 where year > 1919 and year < 1930;
update one set year = 4 where year > 1929 and year < 1940;


create table two
        as select year, region, numb=sum(mat_id)
                from one group by year, region;


        Create table three (
                region            c16               ,
                1900–13           integer           ,
                1914–19           integer           ,
                1920–29           integer           ,
                1930–39           integer           );


        Insert into three (region, 1900–13)
                select region, numb
                        from two
                                where year = 1;


        Insert into three (region, 1914–19)
                select region, numb
                        from two
                                where year = 2;


        Insert into three (region, 1920–29)
                select region, numb
                        from two
                                where year = 3;


        Insert into three (region, 1930–39)
                select region, numb
                        from two
                                where year = 4;
```

```
Create table next (
        region              c16             ,
        1900–13             integer         ,
        1914–19             integer         ,
        1920–29             integer         ,
        1930–39             integer         );
```

```
Insert into next (region, 1900–13, 1914–19, 1920–29, 1930–39)
        select region,  max(1900–13),
                        max(1914–19),
                        max(1920–29),
                        max(1930–39)
    from three
                    group by region;
```

```
Create table tot
        as select
                        1900–13 = sum(1900–13)      ,
                        1914–19 = sum(1914–19)      ,
                        1920–29 = sum(1920–29)      ,
                        1930–39 = sum(1930–39)
    from next;
```

```
Create table result as select
        region                              ,
        (a.1900–13/b.1900–13) * 100         ,
        (a.1914–19/b.1914–19) * 100         ,
        (a.1920–29/b.1920–29) * 100         ,
        (a.1930–39/b.1930–39) * 100
        from next a, tot b;
```

*Note*: The analysis shows the geographical origins of a sample of Oxford's male matriculants in four periods (1900–13, 1914–19, 1920–9, and 1930–9), a diagram of the tables on which the analysis is based, and the SQL commands necessary to conduct it.

Fig. 3.25 Simple statistical analysis with a multi-table database on Oxford University's twentieth-century members

matriculants were born (records whose *Ptype* field contains the value 'pobt'), and where their fathers lived at time of matriculation (records whose *Ptype* field contains the value 'fadd'). The PLACECODE table codes the place names in the ADDRESS table by region.[28] The records in ADDRESS are joined to those in MATRICS which have the same *Mat_id* and to those in PLACECODE which have the same *Place*. The figure also displays the SQL commands required to produce the analysis from information stored in the three tables.

Although the example has been chosen in part to amuse, it is meant to illustrate the difficulty involved in producing a simple analysis with a multi-table database. In the next chapter we shall see how a similar procedure is conducted much more easily (and, because it involves fewer and less cumbersome commands, more accurately) with a statistical package that is expressly designed for data analysis as opposed to data management.[29] Multi-table databases, then, can be cumbersome analytical tools and as such may inhibit regressive examination of one's data. Imagine having to repeat the analysis shown in Figure 3.25 with only minor variation, for example, to alter the time periods analysed, or to document the geographic origins of men and women or of arts and science students, respectively!

In general then, databases are designed to manage but not to analyse information which can be highly structured without sacrificing its richness and meaning. The information underlying the Gorbals, British convicts, Scottish psychiatric, and Oxford studies was ideally suited to database management. In these studies, the database provided an exceptionally useful tool for editing, storing, and classifying the collected information, and for conducting the simplest retrievals and summary measures by way of analysis. It was inadequate for tabulating, graphing, and analysing the assembled data with more advanced statistical measures. As we shall see in the next chapter, however, the statistical and graphical software which is necessary for these more analytical procedures is readily able to read and thus to use data already stored in the tables of a database. In the four studies discussed in

---

[28] The regions are based on those used by L. Stone, 'The Size and Composition of the Oxford Student Body', in L. Stone (ed.), *The University in Society* (Princeton, NJ, 1975), i. 102.

[29] See pp. 151–2.

this chapter the database was used as a receptacle in which information was compiled, edited, stored, and, where necessary, coded so that it could be analysed later with other software that was less appropriate for data management but more powerful where cross-tabulation, graphical presentation, and statistical measure were concerned.

# 4

## 'Measure for Measure': Numbers, Graphs, and Tables

BASIC numeracy is fundamental for the historian. Numbers crop up regularly in the historical record and as indicated in Chapter 1, measurement is an integral part of historical research.[1] The historian must deal with numbers as well when presenting research results, either by displaying them in tables or representing them graphically, for example, on a line graph or a bar chart. This chapter will look briefly at the quantitative procedures most commonly used in historical research—statistical manipulation, graphical presentation, and tabulation—before going on to examine the computational tools that can help in their conduct.

First, however, a word of caution. To use statistical measures effectively, it is important to know one's statistics. The following discussion is only meant as a brief overview. It will neither provide nor substitute for a basic understanding of statistics. Such a basic knowledge is important, however, especially since the computer enables the fast and accurate production of statistical tests. The computer cannot ensure that the results of these tests are interpreted by the historian with the same degree of precision. Nor can the computer choose the most appropriate statistical test to use when asking a particular question of a given body of data. In other words, with computer applications, quantitative procedures can be conducted by anyone; effective quantitative analysis still requires at least a modicum of statistical knowledge.[2] Given these ominous sounding words, it is perhaps fortunate that most

[1] See Ch. 1.
[2] K. H. Jarausch and K. A. Hardy, *Quantitative Methods for Historians: A Guide to Research, Data, and Statistics* (London, 1991) is a useful guide. Others are listed in the bibliography, section IIв1. More extensive bibliographical treatment can be found in S. R. Grossbart, 'Quantification and Social Science Methods for Historians: An Annotated Bibliography of Selected Books and Articles', *Historical Methods*, 25 (1992), 100–20.

quantitative historical research relies on three relatively simple statistical manipulations: deriving new data by arithmetic manipulation of existing data; summarizing single variables with descriptive statistics (univariate analysis); and cross-tabulating and measuring association between two variables (bivariate analyses).

## SOME COMMON QUANTITATIVE PROCEDURES

### *Deriving new data from old by arithmetic means*

The derivation of new data through arithmetic manipulation is straightforward. A study of municipal finance in the period 1890–1914, for example, required information on the annual cash balance of Philadelphia's city government, but budget statements only provided data on the city's total expenditures and receipts, respectively. Obviously, the required information was easily created from existing data by subtracting annual expenditures from annual receipts. Similarly, an analysis of seventeenth-century European trade needs to equate English currency where there are twelve pence in a shilling and twenty shillings in a pound, with Danish currency where there are sixteen skillings in a merk and six merks in a Danish Reichstaler. Before the two measures can be equated, they need to be expressed in terms of their lowest common denominators—English pence and Danish skillings, respectively—information which once again can be derived by applying simple mathematical formulae to the extant data.

### *Conducting quantitative measures and graphing the results*

Summary or descriptive statistics should be as familiar. These are used to describe the range of values associated with any one variable (field of information) involved in a study. Take as our example the study of the social origins, university experiences, and career destinations of Oxford University's twentieth-century members that was introduced in Chapter 3. In that study, variables included members' place of birth, year and college at matriculation, subject studied, examination result achieved, and subsequent career destinations. The summary measures appropriate for a particular variable depend upon the kind of values it contains. 'Nominal scale' or 'categorical' variables comprise values drawn from a range of mutually exclusive categories. Place of birth, subject studied, and undergraduates' career destinations are examples of categorical variables in the Oxford study. 'Ordinal scale' variables contain values which can be ranked or ordered according to some criterion. In the Oxford study, final examination result is an ordinal variable since its values are ranked into four classes.[3] 'Interval' variables are like ordinal ones in so far as they can be ranked in some order, only here it is possible to specify the distance between individual steps of the ranking scale. Calendar dates are interval variables since the two years separating 1950 and 1952 are equivalent to the two years separating 1956 and 1958. 'Ratio scale' variables have all of the properties of interval variables as well as a meaningfully designated zero point which makes ratio comparison possible. Age is an example drawn from the Oxford study. A person aged 36 is twice as old as another aged 18, thereby implying an age ratio of 2 : 1. Finally, 'continuous' variables represent a special case of interval and ratio variables. With a continuous variable there will be only one observation for every one value. Thus, the variable 'year' would be continuous in a table which showed the total number of university matriculants in each year, 1900–70. It would not be continuous in a table showing matriculation records for Oxford men; there, a particular value of year, for example, 1907, would occur many times, once for every male matriculant in 1907.

## 1. Frequency distributions

Counting up cases or records is a basic statistical procedure which is appropriate for all kinds of variables, and is commonly used to produce so-called frequency distributions. Figure 4.1 shows a frequency distribution for those undergraduates who took final honours examinations in the period 1900–86.[4] The first column shows the four possible values for the variable exam classification. The second column shows the number of times each value for the variable occurred. The third column expresses

---

[3] There were four examination classes until 1964 and three thereafter.

[4] The data exclude undergraduates who failed or achieved an unclassified result in their Final Honours examinations.

| Class Result | Frequency | % | Cumulative Frequency | Cumulative % |
|---|---|---|---|---|
| First | 13,760 | 11.38 | 13,760 | 11.38 |
| Second | 72,888 | 60.28 | 86,648 | 71.66 |
| Third | 29,800 | 24.65 | 116,448 | 96.30 |
| Fourth | 4,469 | 3.70 | 120,917 | 100.00 |

Fig. 4.1 Table showing distribution of Oxford University's finalists' examination results, 1900–1986

the frequencies shown in column two as a percentage of the total number of finalists. Thus, 11.38 per cent of all finalists got first-class results. The fourth column keeps a running total of occurrences. Thus, the cumulative frequency given for second-class results includes the total number of finalists who got first- and second-class results. The final column expresses the cumulative frequency as a percentage of the total number of finalists. The value for thirds tells us that 96.3 per cent of all classified exams were in the third class or above.

Graphically, the frequency distribution shown in the table can be presented as a pie chart or a bar graph as shown in Figures 4.2 and 4.3. With continuous variables, frequency distributions can also be represented with a line graph where the continuous variable is plotted along the X or horizontal axis and the frequency along the Y or vertical axis. Line graphs are especially useful for demonstrating change over time. Figure 4.4 shows the percentage of Oxford finalists who got first-class examination results in every year, 1900–86. There we see that with the exception of the war years, the percentage of first-class finalists was generally steady or in slight decline until 1955 when it began a slow upward drift.[5]

---

[5] Note that where samples are being analysed it may be necessary to use a battery of other measures to determine the extent to which the frequency distribution observed in sample data is representative of that which would be observed in the entire population. For more on sampling see Ch. 6, pp. 203–10. For analyses of variance see Jarausch and Hardy, *Quantitative Methods*, ch. 7, and G. R. Iversen and H. Norpoth, *Analysis of Variance* (Beverley Hills, Calif., 1984).

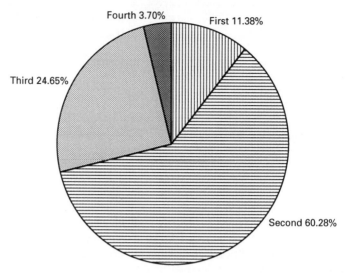

Fig. 4.2 Pie chart showing distribution of Oxford finalists' examination results, 1900–1986

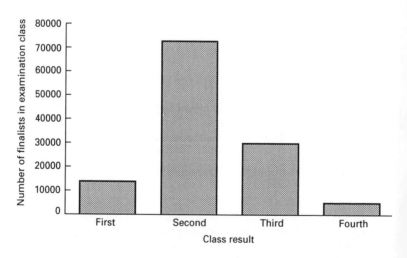

Fig. 4.3 Bar chart showing distribution of Oxford finalists' examination results, 1900–1986

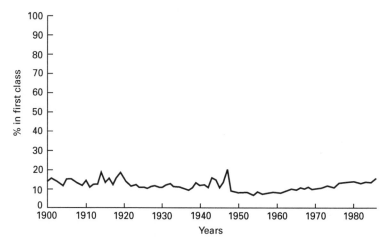

Fig. 4.4 Line graph showing percentage of Oxford finalists obtaining first-class examination results, 1900–1986

## 2. *Measures of central tendency and dispersion*

Measures of central tendency help to describe the distribution of numeric variables (whether measured according to interval or ratio scales). Such measures are shown in Figure 4.5, where they are used to describe the age distribution of a sample of Oxford's female intake in three different periods or cohorts, 1900–9, 1930–9, and 1960–7.[6] Among the measures we see some familiar ones, notably minimum and maximum values which in this case record the youngest and oldest woman entrant in each cohort. The range, shown in the fifth column of Figure 4.5, is

| Cohort | Total Number | Minimum | Maximum | Range | Mean | Median | Mode | Standard Deviation |
|--------|--------------|---------|---------|-------|------|--------|------|--------------------|
| 1900–09 | 55 | 15.3 | 37.7 | 22.4 | 19.8 | 19.7 | 18.2 | 3.5 |
| 1930–39 | 318 | 16.7 | 39.9 | 23.2 | 18.9 | 18.8 | 18.4 | 2.4 |
| 1960–67 | 379 | 16.3 | 30.8 | 14.5 | 18.3 | 18.6 | 18.6 | 1.3 |

Fig. 4.5 Table showing age distribution of a sample of Oxford's female intake, 1900–1909, 1930–1939, and 1960–1967

[6] Women were only eligible to matriculate from 1920. Before that time they were members of one of the five women's societies, but not of the university.

simply the difference between the minimum and maximum values. In this case, it shows the span of years separating the youngest from the oldest matriculant in each cohort. The table also shows another familiar measure of central tendency, the arithmetic mean or average. In this case the number shown expresses the average age for the female intake in each period. Though means are the most frequently used measure of central tendency they do not always provide enough information about the distribution of values in a numeric variable. The means calculated in Figure 4.5, for example, show that over time the average age of the female intake declined. What they do not tell us is whether the trend was caused by a relative decline in the proportion of older women or by a relative increase in the number of younger ones. For this information we need two other measures of central tendency: the median which gives the value above and below which half of all other values reside; and the mode which gives the most commonly occurring value in a set of values. In the case of Oxford's female intake, the median age declines slightly with the average age but the mode actually increases in the last cohort, 1960–7. The pattern suggests that the relative proportion of mature women coming up to Oxford actually declined.

Measures of dispersion further enhance our understanding of how a given set of values is distributed. The standard deviation, for example, summarizes the distance of each value from the arithmetic mean of all values. Where the standard deviation is relatively small, the values are more concentrated around the mean. Where it is relatively large, the values are more dispersed. The last column in Figure 4.5 shows that over the three cohorts, 1900–9 to 1960–7, the standard deviation in the ages of Oxford's female intake declined indicating that more women entrants were near the average age of the entire female intake when they came up to Oxford. That is, female entrants became more like one another in their age and, on the whole, younger. Presumably, with time Oxford was attracting a greater number of its women directly from the schools, and fewer women who had gone on from school to marry or into careers before considering a university place.

Graphically, the central tendency in a set of values can be displayed on a histogram as shown in Figure 4.6 for female under-

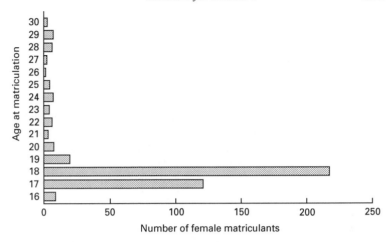

Fig. 4.6 Histogram showing age distribution of a sample of Oxford's female intake, 1960–1967

graduates who matriculated in the period 1960–7. Here, age is plotted along the vertical or Y axis. Out of these values grows a bar whose height is indicative of the frequency with which each value occurs. The graph tells us whether and where the values tend to cluster (in this case around 18 years) or whether they are dispersed. Where the horizontal bars of the histogram are short at either end of the range and grow increasingly in length toward the middle, the distribution of values is 'normal'. Distributions are 'positively skewed' where bars are larger at the lower end of the scale than at the higher, and 'negatively skewed' where the situation is reversed. Here the distribution is positively skewed.[7]

## 3. Cross-tabulation

Cross-tabulations, also called joint-frequency distributions, illuminate the relationship between two variables, one of which is designated as the X or independent variable and the other as the Y or dependent variable. The measure is then calculated to show if and how changes in the values of X are associated with changes in the value of Y. Cross-tabulations are compiled by counting up

[7] Again, it may be necessary to use other measures to determine the extent to which the central tendency or dispersion observed in sample data is representative of those which would be observed in the entire population. See n. 5 above.

the number of times any pair of X and Y values occur together. The cross-tabulation presented in Figure 4.7 was constructed from a sample of Oxford's male finalists, 1900–39, who came up to university directly after leaving a British secondary school. It was constructed to show whether men's educational backgrounds were associated with their performance in Oxford examinations, and was one of a series of tests conducted to see whether and how educational and career trajectories were influenced by social-class background.[8] Here, the independent or X variable, type of school, is used as an indication of social-class background. It has two values: 'Independent schools' indicating private or fee-paying schools, and 'Maintained schools' indicating secondary schools which were funded by central and/or local government authorities and which accepted pupils free of charge. The Y variable is final examination result and has four values, one for each of the four examination classes.

| Frequency Row Pct | E X A M | R E S U L T | | | Row Total |
|---|---|---|---|---|---|
| | First | Second | Third | Fourth | |
| Independent schools | 173 | 553 | 611 | 200 | 1,537 |
| | 11.26 | 35.98 | 39.75 | 13.01 | 72 |
| Maintained schools | 86 | 251 | 190 | 47 | 574 |
| | 14.98 | 43.73 | 33.10 | 8.19 | 28 |
| Column Total | 259 | 804 | 801 | 247 | 2,111 |
| | 12 | 38 | 38 | 12 | 100 |

Fig. 4.7 Cross-tabulation relating the school backgrounds and university examination results of a sample of Oxford's male finalists, 1900–1939

In effect, the table combines four frequency distributions (hence the name joint-frequency distribution). The first shows how first-class results were distributed amongst men from different types of schools, the second how second-class results were distributed, and so on. The values in the cross-tabulation are presented in cells

[8] In Britain, attendance at an independent or fee-paying school is associated by sociologists and historians with social-class position and/or status. See D. Boyd, *Elites and their Education: The Educational and Social Background of Eight Elite Groups* (Windsor, 1973); A. H. Halsey *et al.*, *Origins and Destinations: Family, Class, and Education in Modern Britain* (Oxford, 1980) chs. 2–4, especially pp. 22–31.

each of which describes a particular X : Y pair (e.g. men from independent schools : men who got first-class results). Each cell contains two values, a key to which is provided in the upper-left-most corner of the table. The first (top) value gives the frequency with which the X : Y pair occurs in the data. There, for example we see that 173 men from independent schools got first-class results in their final examinations. The second (bottom) value in the cell gives the frequency as a percentage of the total frequency observed in the particular row of cells. Thus, we see that the 173 first-class men from independent schools represent 11.26 per cent of all men from independent schools. Looking further down the same column of the table headed 'First' we see that this 11.26 per cent does not compare all that favourably with the 14.98 per cent of men from maintained schools who got first-class examination results. At the same time, data in the column headed 'Third' indicates that proportionally more men from independent schools did badly in their final examinations at Oxford than those from maintained schools. The last two rows of values show the number and per cent of men in each examination class. There we see, for example, that 259 men got first-class results making up 12 per cent of the male finalists considered in the sample. The right-most column gives the number and percentage of men from the two types of schools. There we see that 1,537 (72 per cent) of the men in the sample came from independent schools.

Graphically the joint-frequency distribution can be represented on a stacked bar chart as shown in Figure 4.8. The stacked bar chart allows two or more frequencies to be compared visually (there are fewer men from maintained schools in each examination class) and aggregated (there are nearly as many second- and third-class men). A more direct comparison is achieved in Figure 4.9 which uses percentage values and places the bars calculated from the two frequencies side by side rather than on top of one another. Where the independent or X variable is a continuous one line graphs can be used to make such a comparison. Figure 4.10 provides one example. It demonstrates change over time in the distribution of class results for all Oxford finalists, 1900–86.

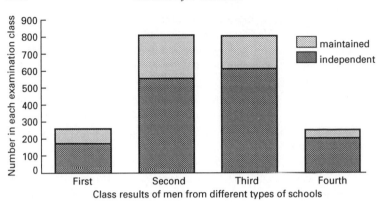

Fig. 4.8 Stacked bar chart relating the school backgrounds and university examination results of a sample of Oxford's male finalists, 1900–1939

### 4. *Measures of association and correlation*

The measures described above are essentially descriptive. That is, they describe the values in a given set of variables. Since such description is all that is ever required in most quantitative historical investigations, these measures will satisfy most historians. There are cases, however, when it is desirable to infer more from the data, for example, about the relationship between two or more variables. Take the cross-tabulation shown in Figure 4.7 as an example. It seems to indicate that men from maintained schools did better in their Oxford examinations than men from independent schools. But how significant are these differences? How can we be sure that the joint-frequency distribution shown there is different from one that would be produced with two variables which had no relation whatever? One test which can help answer this question is known as the Pearson Chi-Square test.[9] It compares the actual or observed joint-frequency distribution with the joint-frequency distribution that would be expected if the two variables had no relation whatever.

Figure 4.11 shows the results of a Pearson Chi-Square test conducted with the data on Oxford men's school backgrounds and

[9] Care needs to be exercised since Pearson's Chi-Square may not be a valid test with interval and ratio variables, cross-tabulations comprising two columns and two rows, or with cross-tabulations in which 25 per cent or more of the cells have observed frequencies of less than five.

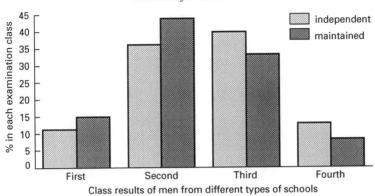

Fig. 4.9 Bar chart relating the school backgrounds and university examination results of a sample of Oxford's male finalists, 1900–1939

examination results in the period 1900–39. The results are displayed in a cross-tabulation. Observed and expected frequencies are the first two (top-most) values presented in each cell. The third value gives the difference between the expected and observed frequencies. First-class examination results were

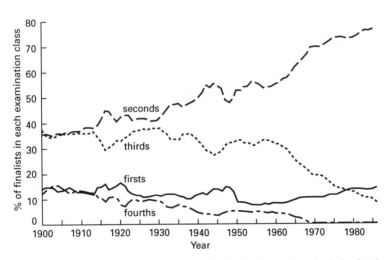

Fig. 4.10 Line graph showing annual distribution of Oxford finalists' examination results, 1900–1986

| Frequency Expected Deviation Cell Chi-Square | EXAM RESULT | | | | |
|---|---|---|---|---|---|
| | First | Second | Third | Fourth | Row Total |
| Independent schools | 173 188.58 −15.58 1.2865 | 553 585.39 −32.39 1.7916 | 611 583.2 27.8 1.3251 | 200 179.84 20.16 2.2603 | 1,537 72 |
| Maintained schools | 86 70.424 15.58 3.4448 | 251 218.61 32.39 4.7975 | 190 217.8 −27.8 3.5482 | 47 67.162 −20.16 6.0524 | 574 28 |
| Column Total | 259 12 | 804 38 | 801 38 | 247 12 | 2,111 100 |

| Statistic | DF | Value | Prob |
|---|---|---|---|
| Chi-Square | 3 | 24.506 | 0.000 |
| Cramer's V | | 0.108 | |

Fig. 4.11 Pearson Chi-Square test based on data relating the school backgrounds and university examination results of a sample of Oxford's male finalists, 1900–1939

obtained by 173 men from independent schools. The expected value was 188.58, and the difference (or deviation) is 173 minus 188.58 or −15.58. The fourth value in each cell expresses the differences between the expected and observed frequencies in a standardized manner and is known as the cell chi-square.

The cell chi-squares are particularly important to the analyst. Those which are relatively large compared to others within the same cross-tabulation may indicate a particularly significant co-occurrence of an X : Y pair. In Figure 4.11, for example, the cell chi-squares indicate the possible significance of the measures which show that in their Oxford examinations men from maintained schools get proportionally more first- and second-class results and proportionally fewer third- and fourth-class results than men from independent schools. The cell chi-squares are important for another reason as well. When added together they produce a chi-square measure for the entire cross-tabulation. That is, a summary measure of the deviation between the observed and expected frequencies in each cell of the cross-tabulation. The chi-square for this table is 24.506. Armed with the chi-square and a measure of the cross-tabulation's overall dimensions known as the degrees of freedom (DF), it is possible to calculate the probability that the deviation between the observed and expected frequencies is that which we would expect from two unrelated variables.[10] In this case the probability that the joint frequency distribution is that of unrelated variables is 0.000. Put another way, we can be close to 100 per cent confident that the observed joint-frequency distribution is not due to chance.[11]

The Pearson Chi-Square test in this case enables us to suggest with some confidence that in the period 1900–39, men from maintained schools did better than those from independent schools in their Oxford examinations. In particular (referring here to the cell chi-squares), men from maintained schools got fewer fourths and more seconds than those from independent schools. The question still remains, however, about the strength of the association between men's school background and their performance in Oxford's final examinations. Here, so-called correlation measures can help. Such measures tend to fall in the range between 0 and 1 where nominal variables are involved with 1 indicating the strongest possible correlation between two variables. We need to be careful, however, as different measures of correlation are sensitive to different kinds of data. Cramer's V which has been calculated for this table as 0.108 indicating a very weak correlation between secondary school background and university examination performance, is normally used where nominal variables are involved.

Other measures of correlation are appropriate where ordinal,

---

[10] Degrees of freedom is a measure of a table's dimensions which is based on the number of its rows and columns. When conducting Pearson Chi-Square tests manually, only the table chi-square and the degrees of freedom need to be calculated. The levels of significance can be ascertained from so-called Chi-Square tables. When conducting Pearson Chi-Square tests with statistical packages, all of the results are calculated automatically.

[11] Be wary of attaching too much significance to a joint-frequency distribution if the confidence level is less than 95 per cent, that is if the probability value is greater than 0.05.

interval, or ratio variables are involved.[12] These may return values ranging from −1, indicating an indirect correlation where an increase in X is associated with a decrease in Y, to 1 indicating a direct correlation where an increase in X is associated with an increase in Y. A value of 0 would indicate no correlation between the variables whatever. Pearson's product moment correlation coefficient, more commonly known as Pearson's r, is perhaps the most familiar measure used to correlate two numeric variables. Its use is demonstrated here with census data compiled for a study of family life in Michigan, 1850–80.[13] Data on the age at marriage of household heads and their spouses show, unsurprisingly, that household heads tended to marry people who were more or less their own age (Pearson's r of 0.8723). Another correlation showed that there was virtually no relationship between the age of a household head and the number of people living in his or her household (Pearson's r was −0.0613).[14]

Graphically, correlations can be displayed as so-called scattergrams. Here the independent variable is plotted along the horizontal (X) axis, the dependent variable along the vertical (Y) axis, and every X : Y pair as a point on the graph. Where there is no correlation between variables as in the case with household size and household head's age, the data points are strewn across the graph with no discernible pattern (Figure 4.12). A direct relationship such as that between the age of household heads and that of their spouses, is indicated by a diagonal pattern running from the bottom-left to the upper-right of the graph (Figure 4.13). When two variables are correlated indirectly, the diagonal pattern is inverted and runs from the top-left to the bottom-right of the graph.

5. *Measures for testing hypotheses*

Regression and other modelling measures about which space permits only the most cursory discussion can help pin-point causal

[12] Since the dependent variable in this case is ordinal (examination result), other measures might have been used to measure correlation, notably Mann-Whitney-U and the Kruskal-Wallis H statistic. See Jarausch and Hardy, *Quantitative Methods*, 117–18, 229.

[13] Data compiled by S. Blomberg *et al.* and obtained from the ESRC Data Archive, study number 90003, *Michigan Family History, 1850–1880*. See S. Blomberg *et al.*, 'A Census Probe into Nineteenth-Century Family History: Southern Michigan, 1850–1880', *Journal of Social History*, 5 (1971), 26–45.

[14] The number of people in a household includes relatives, lodgers, and servants.

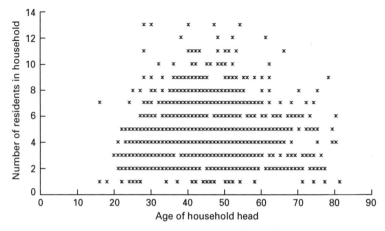

Fig. 4.12 Scattergram correlating age of household head and number of household residents in a sample of Michigan households, 1850–1880

relationships between variables. Various regression procedures have been used, for example, to indicate whether ethnicity or social-class background is more closely associated with people's voting preferences, and whether social-class background or education is a greater influence over individual's social mobility.[15] As their name implies, regression analyses are interactive. The analyst experiments with and progressively refines a mathematical formula in order to derive an equation that explains the maximum number of observations in the data with a minimum of cumulative error. Once derived, the formula is sometimes used as a predictive measure indicating, for example, how people of a particular ethnic group will vote in a given election or how social backgrounds impinge on individuals' chances of experiencing some upward social mobility.

[15] Regression analyses of electoral behaviour have caused some long-standing controversy. See E. T. Jones, 'Ecological Inference and Electoral Analysis', *Journal of Interdisciplinary History*, 2 (1972), 249–62; J. M. Kousser, 'Ecological Regression and the Analysis of Past Politics', *Journal of Interdisciplinary History*, 4 (1973), 237–62; A. J. Lichtman, 'Correlation, Regression, and the Ecological Fallacy', *Journal of Interdisciplinary History*, 4 (1974), 417–33; J. L. Huston, 'Weights, Confidence Intervals, and Ecological Regression', *Journal of Interdisciplinary History*, 21 (1991), 631–54. For the use of modelling measures in social mobility studies, see J. H. Goldthorpe *et al.*, *Social Mobility and Class Structure in Modern Britain* (Oxford, 1980), chs. 3 and 4.

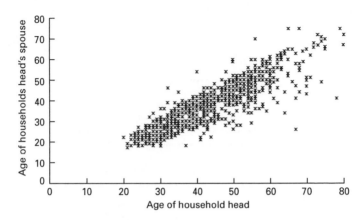

Fig. 4.13 Scattergram correlating ages of household heads and their spouses in a sample of Michigan households, 1850–1880

*Tabulation*

Finally, before looking at the computational tools available to the quantitatively inclined, it is worth considering tabulation. The structure of a table, and its row and column headings, provide essential pointers to the reader as to how the information stored within the table should be interpreted. Tabular presentation requires careful consideration if results are to be displayed with maximum impact. The problem is that there are numerous ways to present even the simplest set of data. Take for example a cross-tabulation showing the geographical origins of Oxford's entire male and female intake in the academic year 1920–1.[16] The same information can be displayed in at least two ways as shown by the tables in Figure 4.14: with men and women comprising the columns and geographical origins comprising the rows or vice versa. The two tables contain the same data but highlight very different trends. The first draws attention to regional variations within gender groups while the second emphasizes variations by sex for each region.

When additional variables are incorporated, the number of permutations in the way they can be represented increases exponen-

[16] The data show where Oxford matriculants' fathers lived at time of matriculation.

Rendition one

| Geographical region | Men (%) | Women (%) |
|---|---|---|
| British | 70 | 94 |
| Commonwealth | 16 | 2 |
| European | 2 | 3 |
| USA | 9 | 1 |
| Other foreign | 3 | 0 |

Rendition two

| Geographical region | British (%) | Common-wealth (%) | European (%) | USA (%) | Other foreign (%) |
|---|---|---|---|---|---|
| Men | 70 | 16 | 2 | 9 | 3 |
| Women | 94 | 2 | 3 | 1 | 0 |

Fig. 4.14 Tables showing geographical origins of Oxford's male and female intake, 1920–1921

tially. There are several ways to compare the geographical origins of the entire male and female intake in two different years, 1920–1 and 1970–1, for example. Two tables can be produced for each year comparing the geographical origins of the male and female intake (Figure 4.15). Here, either gender or geographical region may be used as the row variable. Presenting the data in this way supports static comparisons between men and women or between regions at different times, but tells little about change over time. Alternatively, two tables, one each for men and women, could be used to compare geographical origins by year using year or geographical origins as the row variable (Figure 4.16). This construction shows change over time for men and women, respectively, but makes cross-gender comparisons rather difficult. A further possibility is to construct five tables (Figure 4.17), one for each region, each of which cross-tabulates gender and year using either as the row variable. This construction shows how the gender balance from each region changes over time but obscures cross-regional comparison. Lastly, all of the information could be displayed in a single table (Figure 4.18), but here too there would be nearly as many possible variations depending on how we subdivided the row and/or column variables. Of course there is no 'correct' configuration. Rather, the correct configuration is the one which emphasizes the trends on which the researcher wants to concentrate.

(*a*) Male and female intake, 1920–1

| Geographical region | Men (%) | Women (%) |
| --- | --- | --- |
| British | 70 | 94 |
| Commonwealth | 16 | 2 |
| European | 2 | 3 |
| USA | 9 | 1 |
| Other foreign | 3 | 0 |

(*b*) Male and female intake, 1970–1

| Geographical region | Men (%) | Women (%) |
| --- | --- | --- |
| British | 82 | 90 |
| Commonwealth | 6 | 5 |
| European | 3 | 2 |
| USA | 6 | 2 |
| Other foreign | 3 | 1 |

Fig. 4.15 Tables showing geographical origins of Oxford's male and female intake, 1920–1 and 1970–1: Rendition 1

## COMPUTER SOFTWARE FOR QUANTITATIVE PROCEDURES

### *Spreadsheets*

At last we can turn to the various computer applications that are available to the would-be quantitative historian. Computerized

(*a*) Male intake, 1920–1 and 1970–1

| Geographical region | 1920–1 (%) | 1970–1 (%) |
| --- | --- | --- |
| British | 70 | 82 |
| Commonwealth | 16 | 6 |
| European | 2 | 3 |
| USA | 9 | 6 |
| Other foreign | 3 | 3 |

(*b*) Female intake, 1920–1 and 1970–1

| Geographical region | 1920–1 (%) | 1970–1 (%) |
| --- | --- | --- |
| British | 94 | 90 |
| Commonwealth | 2 | 5 |
| European | 3 | 2 |
| USA | 1 | 2 |
| Other foreign | 0 | 1 |

Fig. 4.16 Tables showing geographical origins of Oxford's male and female intake, 1920–1 and 1970–1: Rendition 2

spreadsheets provide the gentlest introduction.[17] The spreadsheet looks like an empty grid of cells or a checker-board. Horizontal rows of cells are named with numbers in the left-most column, and vertical columns of cells are named by letters in the top-most row. Every cell in the spreadsheet is also named by combining the names of the row and column which intersect at that cell. The sample spreadsheet shown in Figure 4.19 was compiled from the annual accounts of Philadelphia's municipal government for the period 1890–9. The cell containing the value 'Year' has the

---

[17] For a comprehensive overview of computerized spreadsheets see R. Middleton and P. Wardley, 'Annual Review of Information Technology Developments for Economic and Social Historians, 1990', *Economic History Review*, 44 (1991), 349–69. Also see G. Judge, 'Spreadsheets: Flexible Tools for Data Analysis, Model Analysis and Problem Solving', in R. Welford (ed.), *Information Technology for Social Scientists* (Shipley, 1990), 39–74.

(*a*) Britain's contribution to male and female intake 1920–1 and 1970–1

| Sex | 1920–1 (%) | 1970–1 (%) |
| --- | --- | --- |
| Men | 70 | 82 |
| Women | 94 | 90 |

(*b*) Commonwealth's contribution

| Sex | 1920–1 (%) | 1970–1 (%) |
| --- | --- | --- |
| Men | 16 | 6 |
| Women | 2 | 5 |

(*c*) Europe's contribution

| Sex | 1920–1 (%) | 1970–1 (%) |
| --- | --- | --- |
| Men | 2 | 3 |
| Women | 3 | 2 |

(*d*) USA's contribution

| Sex | 1920–1 (%) | 1970–1 (%) |
| --- | --- | --- |
| Men | 9 | 6 |
| Women | 1 | 2 |

(*e*) Other foreign contributions

| Sex | 1920–1 (%) | 1970–1 (%) |
| --- | --- | --- |
| Men | 3 | 3 |
| Women | 0 | 1 |

Fig. 4.17 Tables showing geographical origins of Oxford's male and female intake, 1920–1 and 1970–1: Rendition 3

| Geographical Region | Men (%) | | Women (%) | |
|---|---|---|---|---|
| | 1920–1 | 1970–1 | 1920–1 | 1970–1 |
| British | 70 | 82 | 94 | 90 |
| Commonwealth | 16 | 6 | 2 | 5 |
| European | 2 | 3 | 3 | 2 |
| USA | 9 | 6 | 1 | 2 |
| Other foreign | 3 | 3 | 0 | 1 |

Fig. 4.18 Table showing geographical origins of Oxford's male and female intake, 1920–1921 and 1970–1971: Rendition 4

address A3.[18] The cell immediately to its right, B3, contains the value 'Receipts', and the cell immediately below A3, namely A4, contains the value '1890'. Cell ranges or groups of adjacent cells (which must always be rectangular in shape) also have names. The four cells which give titles to the columns of financial data and include the values 'Year', 'Receipts', 'Expenditures', and 'Surplus/(Deficit)' occupy the cell range A3 : D3. The column of

| | A | B | C | D |
|---|---|---|---|---|
| 1 | Annual cash balance of the City of Philadelphia, 1890-99. | | | |
| 2 | | | | |
| 3 | Year | Receipts | Expenditures | Surplus/(Deficit) |
| 4 | 1890 | $24,443,408 | $22,531,381 | $1,912,027 |
| 5 | 1891 | $23,400,495 | $23,232,671 | $167,824 |
| 6 | 1892 | $24,856,839 | $23,061,526 | $1,795,313 |
| 7 | 1893 | $30,199,515 | $27,977,232 | $2,222,283 |
| 8 | 1894 | $30,689,391 | $32,390,333 | ($1,700,942) |
| 9 | 1895 | $29,838,771 | $31,329,549 | ($1,490,778) |
| 10 | 1896 | $29,425,459 | $29,228,617 | $196,842 |
| 11 | 1897 | $32,683,285 | $29,616,999 | $3,066,286 |
| 12 | 1898 | $26,324,200 | $27,075,013 | ($750,813) |
| 13 | 1899 | $31,948,522 | $27,732,208 | $4,216,314 |
| 14 | | | | |
| 15 | | | | |
| 16 | Average balance | | | $963,436 |

Fig. 4.19 Sample spreadsheet of municipal finance data for the city of Philadelphia, 1890–1899

[18] Data from D. I. Greenstein, 'Politics and the Urban Process: Two Case Studies of Philadelphia, 1800–1854 and 1890–1914' (Oxford University D.Phil. thesis, 1987), ch. 4.

|    | A               | B            | C            | D                  |
|----|-----------------|--------------|--------------|--------------------|
| 1  |                 |              |              |                    |
| 2  |                 |              |              |                    |
| 3  | Year            | Receipts     | Expenditures | Surplus/(Deficit)  |
| 4  | 1890            | 24443408     | 22531381     | = B4-C4            |
| 5  | 1891            | 23400495     | 23232671     | = B5-C5            |
| 6  | 1892            | 24856839     | 23061526     | = B6-C6            |
| 7  | 1893            | 30199515     | 27977232     | = B7-C7            |
| 8  | 1894            | 30689391     | 32390333     | = B8-C8            |
| 9  | 1895            | 29838771     | 31329549     | = B9-C9            |
| 10 | 1896            | 29425459     | 29228617     | = B10-C10          |
| 11 | 1897            | 32683285     | 29616999     | = B11-C11          |
| 12 | 1898            | 26324200     | 27075013     | = B12-C12          |
| 13 | 1899            | 31948522     | 27732208     | = B13-C13          |
| 14 |                 |              |              |                    |
| 15 |                 |              |              |                    |
| 16 | Average balance |              |              | = AVERAGE(D4:D13)  |

Fig. 4.20 Sample spreadsheet of municipal finance data showing underlying formulae

municipal receipts data occupies the range B4 : B13. The cell range containing both receipts and expenditures is referred to as B4 : C13.

Various data types are permitted in spreadsheet cells.[19] Cells can accommodate numeric data, for example, and these can take on several different formats. The numbers in A4 : A13 are formatted as whole or counting numbers, those in B4 : D13 as US dollars with negative numbers surrounded by parentheses. Other formats available for numeric data include calendar dates, real numbers with a fixed number of places to the right of the decimal point, and scientific notation. Text values are also permitted as shown in cells A1, A16, and A3 : D3. They may be formatted by centring or right or left justifying them within a cell and by determining their font and point size.

Formulae also may be placed in spreadsheet cells, and it is this type of cell entry that gives the spreadsheet its power. In Figure 4.19 cells D4 : D13 contain numbers formatted as positive or negative currency measures. Figure 4.20 shows that formulae which subtract annual receipts from annual expenditures actually underlie these numbers. Note that the formulae comprise cell addresses instead of numbers. Thus, the formula in cell D4 subtracts the number stored in cell C4 (expenditures for 1890) from that stored in cell B4 (receipts for 1890) to yield the annual cash

---

[19] For more on data types see Ch. 3, pp. 66–8.

balance. When a formula is entered into a cell the resultant value is displayed (as in Figure 4.19) rather than the formula. Figure 4.20 shows that cell D16 has another kind of formula. It uses one of the spreadsheet's many functions, in this case to take an average of the values in the cell range D4 : D13, producing an average cash balance for the years 1890–9. Spreadsheets offer a range of functions too numerous to describe here in any greater detail. They include mathematical functions (e.g. absolute value, square root, logarithmic value), statistical functions (e.g. standard deviation, variance, sum, average), and financial functions (net present value, loan payment, and future and present value estimates). By combining functions and formulae, the most complex calculations are possible with a spreadsheet.

One of the spreadsheet's greatest assets is that it automatically recalculates formula values whenever the data in the cells they address are altered. When the number indicating 1890 receipts (cell B4) is edited to read $22,943,408, for example, the 1890 balance (cell D4) is automatically recalculated as $412,027 and the 1890–9 average balance (cell D16) as $813,787. This automatic recalculation facility ensures the spreadsheet's success in a business setting. Companies trying to predict how a particular financial decision will affect annual profits, for example, no longer have to recalculate the entire annual account when a few new pieces of information are introduced. The result is available instantly.

The spreadsheet's use is straightforward. Commands are selected from a hierarchically arranged menu which normally appears at the top of the screen.[20] Entering and editing data entails moving the cursor through the spreadsheet with a mouse and/or directional and page-up and page-down keys and, where necessary, by scrolling the spreadsheet vertically and/or horizontally. With a cursor positioned over a cell, the cell's data may be entered or existing data edited from the keyboard. Other basic editing procedures include moving and copying information between individual cells or cell ranges. For example, the range of cells indicating annual expenditures (C3 : C13) might be moved to the range F3 : F13 as shown in Figure 4.21. Notice that the data from C3 : C13 appear unaltered in their new position, F3 : F13,

[20] For more on hierarchical menus see Ch. 3, p. 95.

|   | A | B | C | D | E | F |
|---|---|---|---|---|---|---|
| 1 | Annual cash balance of the City of Philadelphia, 1890-99 | | | | | |
| 2 | | | | | | |
| 3 | Year | Receipts | | Surplus/(Deficit) | | Expenditures |
| 4 | 1890 | $24,443,408 | | $1,912,027 | | $22,531,381 |
| 5 | 1891 | $23,400,495 | | $167,824 | | $23,232,671 |
| 6 | 1892 | $24,856,839 | | $1,795,313 | | $23,061,526 |
| 7 | 1893 | $30,199,515 | | $2,222,283 | | $27,977,232 |
| 8 | 1894 | $30,689,391 | | ($1,700,942) | | $32,390,333 |
| 9 | 1895 | $29,838,771 | | ($1,490,778) | | $31,329,549 |
| 10 | 1896 | $29,425,459 | | $196,842 | | $29,228,617 |
| 11 | 1897 | $32,683,285 | | $3,066,286 | | $29,616,999 |
| 12 | 1898 | $26,324,200 | | ($750,813) | | $27,075,013 |
| 13 | 1899 | $31,948,522 | | $4,216,314 | | $27,732,208 |
| 14 | | | | | | |
| 15 | | | | | | |
| 16 | Average balance | | | $963,436 | | |

Fig. 4.21 Sample spreadsheet of municipal finance data demonstrating effects of moving cells with formulae

and cells C3 : C13 are empty. But notice, too, that the values in range D4 : D13 still show the same value for the city's cash balance; the formulae used in the range D4 : D13 have been rewritten automatically to reflect the new position of the expenditure data now in F4 : F13.[21]

Data can be copied as well. A cell entry can be copied into any other single cell. The entry in cell A4, 1890, could be copied into cell Z18. Alternatively, the entry in a single cell can be copied to a range of cells. Thus, the entry, 1890, in cell A4, can be copied into cells Z18 : Z24, each of which would then contain the value 1890. If a formula is copied, the cell names addressed in the formula are updated so that both the copied formula and the source formula address cells in the same 'relative' position. For example, by copying the formula in cell D16 to cell C16 the formulae in cell C16 would read '= AVERAGE(C4 : C13)'. The value in cell D16 would still show the average cash balance, 1890–99, while the new value in cell C16 would show the average expenditure over the same period. The original formula in cell D16 addresses the ten cells in the column which begins twelve cells above it. So does the formula now in cell C16. This level of semi-intelligence can speed up spreadsheet composition. The formula that was used to calculate the city's annual cash balance had to be entered only

[21] Had the expenditure data been left in place in the range C4 : C13 and the formulae in D4 : D13 moved to F4 : F13, the formulae would remain the same leaving cells F4 : F13 to display the same values for annual cash balance.

once into cell D4. Thereafter, the formula in cell D4 was copied to the range D5 : D13.

Some of the data manipulations which are normally associated with database management systems are also available with spreadsheets. The cells in a specified range may be sorted according to the ascending or descending value of the data in any one or more columns. Thus, the municipal finance data displayed in Figure 4.19 could be sorted in descending order of the data on annual cash balance contained in column D as shown in Figure 4.22. Procedures for selective data retrieval are also available with spreadsheets. In general, however, the sorting and retrieval facilities available with a spreadsheet are primitive when compared with those available in database management systems and so their consideration need not detain us here.

| | A | B | C | D |
|---|---|---|---|---|
| 1 | Annual cash balance of the City of Philadelphia, 1890-99 | | | |
| 2 | | | | |
| 3 | Year | Receipts | Expenditures | Surplus/(Deficit) |
| 4 | 1894 | $30,689,391 | $32,390,333 | ($1,700,942) |
| 5 | 1895 | $29,838,771 | $31,329,549 | ($1,490,778) |
| 6 | 1898 | $26,324,200 | $27,075,013 | ($750,813) |
| 7 | 1891 | $23,400,495 | $23,232,671 | $167,824 |
| 8 | 1896 | $29,425,459 | $29,228,617 | $196,842 |
| 9 | 1892 | $24,856,839 | $23,061,526 | $1,795,313 |
| 10 | 1890 | $24,443,408 | $22,531,381 | $1,912,027 |
| 11 | 1893 | $30,199,515 | $27,977,232 | $2,222,283 |
| 12 | 1897 | $32,683,285 | $29,616,999 | $3,066,286 |
| 13 | 1899 | $31,948,522 | $27,732,208 | $4,216,314 |
| 14 | | | | |
| 15 | | | | |
| 16 | Average balance | | | $963,436 |

Fig. 4.22 Sample spreadsheet of municipal finance data demonstrating sorting facilities

Spreadsheets can be enormously helpful in handling the numeric data of history wherever they crop up, for example, in accounts and ledgers or in population and manufacturing censuses. Rarely are these data usable without at least some manipulation. Categories of information not kept up in the original source but which are useful for analysis have to be calculated, just as Philadelphia's annual cash balance had to be calculated from data giving the city's total annual expenditures and receipts for the period 1890–9. Here, the spreadsheet's editing and automatic recalculating facilities can save time as has already been explained.

High-quality graphics including pie charts, bar graphs, stacked bar graphs, histograms, scattergrams, and line graphs can also be produced with most spreadsheets. The relevant graph type (e.g. pie, bar, line) is selected from the appropriate menu option and the underlying data from the spreadsheet's cells. A line graph (Figure 4.23) showing the annual receipts and expenditures of Philadelphia's city government, 1890–9, is based on one prepared from the spreadsheet displayed in Figure 4.19. The values in cells A4 : A13 were selected for the graph's X axis, and two series of values in cell ranges B4 : B13 and C4 : C13, respectively, were selected for presentation along the graph's Y axis. Graph formatting facilities were then used to supply the graph with titles, legends, data-point symbols, and so on. Some idea of what can be achieved is indicated in the graphs presented in this chapter. They are based on ones prepared with spreadsheet software.

Spreadsheets have some limitations which are worth mentioning. Where complex statistical formulae or functions are used repeatedly with different data sets, the spreadsheet may prove cumbersome. The function required to calculate Pearson's r, for example, may be entered into a spreadsheet cell in order to correlate values stored in two cell ranges.[22] Should the function be required for use with other data ranges either in the same or another spreadsheet, it would have to be comprehensively edited. As we shall see below, statistical packages are more simply command driven. The different measures are called by name as in a spreadsheet, but variables are not identified by their values' relative location in a matrix. Instead they are defined, as in a database, by a field name. Thus, where a correlation requires cumbersome editing in a spreadsheet, a command such as 'correlate field_1 with field_2' is sufficient in a statistical package. Consequently, where data-processing requirements involve the repetitive use of standard statistical measures, it might be best to consider statistical software from the outset.

Another limitation with spreadsheet software is that relatively large data sets can be awkward to manage. When information is spread over hundreds, even thousands of cells, the user is all too easily lost in a sea of numbers.[23] Spreadsheets are also inappro-

---

[22] Most spreadsheet packages will provide functions for commonly used statistical measures.

[23] The size of a data set need not be constrained by the spreadsheet software.

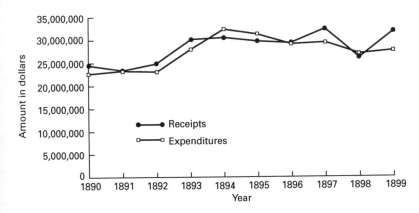

Fig. 4.23 Line graph drawn with municipal finance data, showing annual receipts and expenditures of Philadelphia's city government, 1890–1899

priate where analyses depend as much on reorganizing data as they do on calculation. Imagine analysing the spreadsheet shown in Figure 4.24 which comprises decennial Scottish employment statistics by region, gender, and occupational category, 1841–1971.[24] Aggregating the regional information shows change over time in the distribution of Scottish men's and women's respective employment patterns (Figure 4.25), and requires comprehensive formula writing and spreadsheet editing. More formula writing and editing is required to produce another simple serial analysis shown in Figure 4.26, this time of the occupational distribution of Strathclyde's gainfully employed population. Similar problems are encountered where analyses require data reclassification, for example with the employment data to determine changes in the number of men employed in all heavy industries. Had the employment data been entered up into a

My current spreadsheet software has 16,384 rows and 256 columns, making a total of 4,194,304 cells. The effective limit on the size of any one spreadsheet is the amount of RAM available to the machine. Yet as the memory available in desktop computers expands in leaps and bounds, constraints on spreadsheets' maximum size are rapidly relaxed. For more on computer memory specifications see Ch. 6, p. 211.

[24] I am grateful to M. Black and J. Wakeling for making these data available to me in machine-readable form, based on data presented in C. Lee, *British Regional Employment Statistics, 1841–1971* (Cambridge, 1979).

142 'Measure for Measure'

|  | A | B | C | D | E | F | G | H | I |
|---|---|---|---|---|---|---|---|---|---|
| 1 | Decennial Scottish employment statistics, 1841-1971. | | | | | | | | |
| 2 | Gender | Year | Region | | | Occupational Categories | | | |
| 3 | | | | 1 | 2 | 3 | 4 | 5 | 6 |
| 4 | males | 1841 | Strathclyde | 46911 | 16139 | 8882 | 945 | 9281 | 1699 |
| 5 | males | 1841 | Dumfries and Galloway | 18069 | 553 | 1179 | 49 | 991 | 103 |
| 6 | males | 1841 | Borders | 13259 | 122 | 873 | 35 | 714 | 227 |
| 7 | males | 1841 | Lothian | 15111 | 2564 | 5127 | 438 | 3408 | 409 |
| 8 | males | 1841 | Central and Fife | 17282 | 4330 | 2583 | 199 | 2256 | 384 |
| 9 | males | 1841 | Tayside | 26349 | 757 | 3071 | 129 | 2406 | 804 |
| 10 | males | 1841 | Grampian | 43138 | 422 | 2444 | 177 | 2390 | 377 |
| 11 | males | 1841 | Highland | 41464 | 148 | 1068 | 45 | 1032 | 77 |
| 12 | females | 1841 | Strathclyde | 3032 | 323 | 1416 | 117 | 52 | 143 |
| 13 | females | 1841 | Dumfries and Galloway | 3632 | 33 | 285 | 2 | 3 | 0 |
| 14 | females | 1841 | Borders | 2395 | 28 | 177 | 3 | 1 | 0 |
| 15 | females | 1841 | Lothian | 2092 | 335 | 961 | 47 | 12 | 3 |
| 16 | females | 1841 | Central and Fife | 1078 | 389 | 401 | 16 | 5 | 6 |
| 17 | females | 1841 | Tayside | 1939 | 4 | 705 | 3 | 6 | 3 |
| 18 | females | 1841 | Grampian | 3465 | 0 | 608 | 1 | 6 | 1 |
| 19 | females | 1841 | Highland | 4995 | 0 | 137 | 15 | 1 | 2 |
| 20 | males | 1851 | Strathclyde | 51864 | 34185 | 16766 | 2303 | 18539 | 5985 |
| 21 | males | 1851 | Dumfries and Galloway | 22224 | 1258 | 1784 | 84 | 1171 | 156 |
| 22 | males | 1851 | Borders | 14693 | 295 | 1479 | 54 | 848 | 221 |
| 23 | males | 1851 | Lothian | 15939 | 6044 | 8151 | 753 | 4629 | 1205 |
| 24 | males | 1851 | Central and Fife | 17009 | 8348 | 3724 | 366 | 3912 | 739 |
| 25 | males | 1851 | Tayside | 27612 | 1343 | 4841 | 206 | 2960 | 1089 |
| 26 | males | 1851 | Grampian | 51106 | 1055 | 4304 | 277 | 2733 | 540 |
| 27 | males | 1851 | Highland | 55167 | 618 | 2051 | 99 | 1315 | 141 |
| 28 | females | 1851 | Strathclyde | 11434 | 176 | 3243 | 503 | 69 | 11 |
| 29 | females | 1851 | Dumfries and Galloway | 4451 | 3 | 615 | 9 | 1 | 0 |
| 30 | females | 1851 | Borders | 4738 | 3 | 336 | 1 | 4 | 0 |
| 31 | females | 1851 | Lothian | 5282 | 76 | 1520 | 95 | 11 | 2 |
| 32 | females | 1851 | Central and Fife | 4223 | 190 | 795 | 21 | 4 | 2 |
| 33 | females | 1851 | Tayside | 6666 | 13 | 1083 | 12 | 6 | 0 |
| 34 | females | 1851 | Grampian | 10403 | 10 | 1135 | 187 | 5 | 0 |
| 35 | females | 1851 | Highland | 13446 | 14 | 379 | 2 | 3 | 0 |
| 36 | ... | | | | | | | | |
| 37 | KEY TO OCCUPATIONAL CATEGORIES | | | | | | | | |
| 38 | | 1 | Agriculture, forestry, and fishing | | | | | | |
| 39 | | 2 | Mining and quarrying | | | | | | |
| 40 | | 3 | Food, drink, and tobacco | | | | | | |
| 41 | | 4 | Chemicals and allied products | | | | | | |
| 42 | | 5 | Metal manufacture | | | | | | |
| 43 | | 6 | Mechanical engineering | | | | | | |
| 44 | | | ... | | | | | | |
| 45 | KEY TO REGIONAL DEFINITIONS | | | | | | | | |
| 46 | Strathclyde | | | Argyll, Ayr, Bute, Dumbarton, Lanark | | | | | |
| 47 | Dumfries | and Galloway | | Dumfries, Kirkcudbright, Wigtown | | | | | |
| 48 | Borders | | | Berwick, Peebles, Roxburgh, Selkirk | | | | | |
| 49 | Lothian | | | East Lothian, Midlothian, West Lothian | | | | | |
| 50 | Central and Fife | | | Clackmanan, Fife, Stirling | | | | | |
| 51 | Tayside | | | Angus, Kinross, Perth | | | | | |
| 52 | Grampian | | | Aberdeen, Banff, Kincardine, Moray | | | | | |
| 53 | Highland | | | Caithness, Inverness, Nairn, Orkney and | | | | | |
| 54 | | | | Shetland, Ross and Cromarty, Sutherland | | | | | |

Fig. 4.24 Sample spreadsheet of Scottish employment statistics, 1841–1971

|   | A | B | C | D | E | F | G | H |
|---|---|---|---|---|---|---|---|---|
| 1 | Decennial Scottish employment statistics, 1841-1971. | | | | | | | |
| 2 | | | | | | | | |
| 3 | Occupational distribution of employed men and women in Scotland. | | | | | | | |
| 4 | | | | | | | | |
| 5 | Gender | Year | | | Occupational Categories | | | |
| 6 | | | 1 | 2 | 3 | 4 | 5 | 6 |
| 7 | female | 1841 | 22628 | 1112 | 4690 | 204 | 86 | 158 |
| 8 | female | 1851 | 60643 | 485 | 9106 | 830 | 103 | 15 |
| 9 | female | 1861 | 48924 | 526 | 11739 | 672 | 93 | 26 |
| 10 | female | 1871 | 51022 | 509 | 12121 | 612 | 157 | 260 |
| 11 | ... | | | | | | | |
| 12 | | | | | | | | |
| 13 | male | 1841 | 221583 | 25035 | 25227 | 2017 | 22478 | 4080 |
| 14 | male | 1851 | 255614 | 53146 | 43100 | 4142 | 36107 | 10076 |
| 15 | male | 1861 | 248462 | 62013 | 48566 | 4606 | 44342 | 15353 |
| 16 | male | 1871 | 273960 | 76461 | 50087 | 6994 | 58635 | 23938 |
| 17 | ... | | | | | | | |
| 18 | | | | | | | | |
| 19 | | | | | | | | |
| 20 | Key to occupational categories | | | | | | | |
| 21 | | | | | | | | |
| 22 | | 1 | Agriculture, forestry, and fishing | | | | | |
| 23 | | 2 | Mining and quarrying | | | | | |
| 24 | | 3 | Food, drink, and tobacco | | | | | |
| 25 | | 4 | Chemicals and allied products | | | | | |
| 26 | | 5 | Metal manufacture | | | | | |
| 27 | | 6 | Mechanical engineering | | | | | |
| 28 | ... | | | | | | | |

Fig. 4.25 Scottish employment statistics aggregated to show men's and women's employment, 1841–1971

database instead of a spreadsheet, any one of these results would have been achieved simply and far more quickly with a few basic selective retrievals.

Finally, the prospects for table presentation are at best mixed. A variety of custom editing options determine how text is formatted (fonts, point sizes, and pitch), and how cells and cell ranges are displayed (surrounded by borders, underlined, and/or shaded for emphasis). Some of these facilities were used to prepare the tables on which Figures 4.1, 4.5, and 4.14–4.18 are based. Again, however, the spreadsheet should be abandoned in favour of a database or a statistical package wherever tabular presentation requires persistent data recoding and/or reorganization. The problem is that constructing a table with a spreadsheet involves physically entering the table's values into the relevant spreadsheet cells. Changing the table's structure can be enormously time consuming as values have to be shifted to new locations often by editing them manually. In a database or statistical package,

*'Measure for Measure'*

| | A | B | C | D | E | F | G | H |
|---|---|---|---|---|---|---|---|---|
| 1 | Decennial Scottish employment statistics, 1841-1971. | | | | | | | |
| 2 | | | | | | | | |
| 3 | | | | | | | | |
| 4 | Occupational distribution of employed people in the Strathclyde region. | | | | | | | |
| 5 | | | | | | | | |
| 6 | Year | | | Occupational Categories | | | | |
| 7 | | 1 | 2 | 3 | 4 | 5 | 6 |... |
| 8 | 1841 | 49943 | 16462 | 10298 | 1062 | 9333 | 1842 | |
| 9 | 1851 | 63298 | 34361 | 20009 | 2806 | 18608 | 5996 | |
| 10 | 1861 | 57780 | 40461 | 26043 | 2845 | 25553 | 9741 | |
| 11 | 1871 | 56634 | 49255 | 26215 | 3970 | 37719 | 16672 | |
| 12 | 1881 | 46037 | 54185 | 33467 | 4758 | 45650 | 23422 | |
| 13 | | | | | | | | |
| 14 | | | | | | | | |
| 15 | Key to occupational categories | | | | | | | |
| 16 | | | | | | | | |
| 17 | 1 | Agriculture, forestry, and fishing | | | | | | |
| 18 | 2 | Mining and quarrying | | | | | | |
| 19 | 3 | Food, drink, and tobacco | | | | | | |
| 20 | 4 | Chemicals and allied products | | | | | | |
| 21 | 5 | Metal manufacture | | | | | | |
| 22 | 6 | Mechanical engineering | | | | | | |
| 23 | ... | | | | | | | |

Fig. 4.26 Scottish employment statistics aggregated to show employment in the Strathclyde region, 1841–1971

comprehensive manipulations of this sort are generally possible with simple database commands.

## *Statistical Packages*

The recurrent problem with spreadsheets, then, is that they do not offer the same range of data-manipulation facilities that are available in database management systems. At the same time, database management systems which are good at data reclassification, selective retrieval, and data restructuring, do not offer a very wide range of recalculating, statistical, or graphical facilities. Occupying something of a middle ground is so-called statistical software, which combines some of the database's data-handling facilities with analytical and graphic functions that are more powerful than those found in a spreadsheet. Like databases, statistical packages bundle together four routines in a menu-and/or command-driven environment: data definition, data entry and editing, data retrieval and manipulation, and report generat-ing. In addition, statistical packages offer analytical and graphical modules which are not available or very primitive in database packages. The principal modules are examined here in turn with the exception of data entry which is discussed in Chapter 6. Examples are based on *SAS*, a statistical package which can be menu or command driven. The examples here are command driven. As such, they use *SAS*'s command language whose nuances and idiosyncrasies do not need to detain us any longer than it takes to recognize that with a statistical package a handful of terse statements have a powerful manipulative effect on data stored in tabular form.

### 1. *Table definition*

Data definition, data entry, and data-manipulation facilities are the *raison d'être* of a database package. With a statistical package, they play a supporting role for the analytical and graphical procedures. Before these can be applied to any data set, the data set must be prepared in a tabular format comprising that subset of records and fields on which any one analysis relies.[25] As with database tables, statistical tables are created by assigning them a name and by defining their fields by giving them names and data types. The difference is that statistical packages permit an even narrower range of data types than databases, normally consisting only of text and real numbers (numbers which may have decimal points).[26] Another difference is that most statistical packages are even more uncomfortable with text fields than databases, preferring highly abbreviated text fields where they are used at all.

The *SAS* command shown below demonstrates how a table called STATGORB is created in a statistics package. In this case, the command also populates the new database table with records read into the table from an external file named 'gorbals.dat' which contains the records of the Gorbals database table discussed in Chapter 3.[27]

---

[25] Statistical software refers to observations and variables where database software refers to records and fields. This chapter continues with the database terminology already introduced in Ch. 3, notably records and fields.

[26] Statistical packages vary. Some will only accept numeric fields, others may accept abbreviated text fields as well. Very few will recognize date or currency data types.

[27] For more on the Gorbals database table see Ch. 3, pp. 64–8, and Figures 3.1, 3.2, 3.18, and 3.19. For more on data exchange between software applications see Ch. 6, pp. 225–9.

```
data Statgorb;
infile 'gorbals.dat';
input HNo 1–3 PNo 4–6 $ Surname 7–26 $ Forename 27–42
    $ Address 43–62 $ Relation 63–74 $ Sex 75–75 Age 76–78
    $ Occupation 79–98 $ Tbirth 99–118 Rooms 119–121 HSize 122–124;
run;
```

The command identifies the external file 'gorbals.dat' where the data are located and defines the new table by assigning it a name and by naming its fields (e.g. *HNo*, *PNo*). It also indicates fields' datatypes. Those fields whose names are preceded with a dollar sign (*Surname*, *Forename*) are text fields, those without a dollar sign are numeric. Finally, the command indicates that every line in the external file corresponds to a record in the STATGORB table and that both comprise 124 characters, the first three of which go into the *HNo* field, the next three into *PNo*, and so on. With statistical packages as with databases, new tables also can be created from the results of selective data retrievals. The *SAS* command:

```
data New (keep = HNo PNo Occupation Age);
set Statgorb;
if Age > 21 and Sex = "M" then output;
run;
```

creates a four-field table from the records in STATGORB pertaining to men over 21 years of age.

## 2. *Data retrieval and manipulation*

Data retrieval and manipulation facilities are normally used to prepare from one or several tables that subset of data required for a particular statistical or graphical analysis. To exemplify the point and some of the data-manipulation facilities normally found in statistical packages, let us refer to an extended example based on the Oxford data which were introduced in Chapter 3. The example draws on three familiar tables from the study of Oxford University members, 1900–70—MATRICS, ADDRESS, and PLACECODE.[28] The tables, shown in Figure 4.27, were read into the statistical package from external files in a manner similar to that demonstrated above with the Gorbals census data. Data manipulations in the statistical package follow directly on from analytical aims which focus on a sample of male and female matriculants in the periods 1900–9 and 1960–7. The aims are as follows:

[28] See Ch. 3, pp. 92–4, 108–12, and Figure 3.25.

- to measure change over time in the geographical origins of Oxford's matriculants;
- to cross-tabulate the geographical origins of Oxford's men and women matriculants, respectively, in particular periods;
- to see whether regional patterns of recruitment differ significantly when different measures of matriculants' geographical origins are used (i.e. place of birth and father's address at time of matriculation);
- to enquire into the average age of men and women matriculants and whether this changed over time.

Before the analyses can be conducted, a subset of the data in the three tables has to be retrieved, recoded, and recombined in one table as shown in Figure 4.28. The table has six fields: *Mat_id* and *Age* come from the MATRICS table. *Cohort* and *Sex* are calculated from the MATRICS table's *Year* and *College* fields, respectively (all Oxford colleges were single sex until 1974). *Fadd* and *Pobt* are two measures of matriculants' geographical origins: fathers' address at matriculation and place of birth, respectively. Both fields will contain the coded regional place-name values stored in the PLACECODE table. Let us briefly review the five data manipulations which created this table from the records stored in MATRICS, ADDRESS, and PLACECODE.

The first step demonstrates a selective data retrieval. It selects only those records from MATRICS which refer to Oxford matriculants in the periods 1900–9 and 1960–7 and saves them in a new table called MATRICS1. At the same time, it renames the *Year* and *College* fields to *Cohort* and *Sex*, respectively.

```
data matrics1 (rename = (cohort = year sex = college));
set matrics;
if cohort > 1899 and cohort < 1910 then output;
if cohort > 1959 and cohort < 1968 then output;
run;
```

MATRICS1

| Mat_id | Surname | Firstname | Secondname | Cohort | Sex | Age |
|--------|---------|-----------|------------|--------|-----|-----|
| M19001000 | Daniels | Andrew | Robert | 1900 | Corpus | 18.25 |
| M1900101 | Williams | Benjamin | Daniel | 1900 | Balliol | 19.00 |
| M1965104 | Hampshire | Anna | Marie | 1965 | St Hugh's | 18.75 |
| M1960106 | Johnston | Fiona | | 1960 | Somerville | 19.25 |

...

**MATRICS**

| Mat_id | Surname | Firstname | Secondname | Year | College | Age |
|--------|---------|-----------|------------|------|---------|-----|
| M19001000 | Daniels | Andrew | Robert | 1900 | Corpus | 18.25 |
| M1900101 | Williams | Benjamin | Daniel | 1900 | Balliol | 19.00 |
| M1920123 | Willis | Sebastian | Louis | 1920 | New | 18.50 |
| M1965104 | Hampshire | Anna | Marie | 1965 | St Hugh's | 18.75 |
| M1960106 | Johnston | Fiona | | 1960 | Somerville | 19.25 |

...

**ADDRESS**

| Mat_id | Ptype | Place |
|--------|-------|-------|
| M19001000 | fadd | Newport, Mon |
| M19001000 | pobt | Salesbury, Lancs |
| M19001001 | fadd | Slinfold, Sussex |
| —>M19001001 | pobt | Dolgelley, Merioneth |
| M1920123 | fadd | Ayr |
| M1920123 | pobt | Glasgow |
| M1965104 | fadd | Long Buckby |
| M1965104 | pobt | Long Buckby, Northampton |
| M1960106 | fadd | Stoke on Trent |
| M1960106 | pobt | Stoke on Trent |

...

**PLACECODE**

| Place | Region |
| --- | --- |
| Ayr | Scotland |
| Glasgow | Scotland |
| Dolgelley, Merioneth | Wales |
| >>Long Buckby | Midlands |
| Long Buckby, Northampton | Midlands |
| Newport, Mon | West |
| Salesbury, Lancs | North-west |
| Slinfold, Sussex | South-east |
| Stoke on Trent | Midlands |

*Note:* The arrows indicate how the records in the three tables are related.

Fig. 4.27 Tables from the Oxford database underlying a statistical analysis of university members' geographical origins in two periods, 1900–9 and 1960–7

| Mat_id | Cohort | Sex | Age | Fadd | Pobt |
|--------|--------|-----|-----|------|------|
| M19001000 | 1 | m | 18.25 | West | North-west |
| M1900101 | 1 | m | 19.00 | South-east | Wales |
| M1965104 | 2 | f | 18.75 | Midlands | Midlands |
| M1960106 | 2 | f | 19.25 | Midlands | Midlands |
| . . . | | | | | |

Fig. 4.28 Oxford data recombined for statistical analysis of members' geographical origins

The second step demonstrates selective data retrieval and one other data manipulation which is essential to many analytical inquiries, notably data recoding. In this case, the redundant name fields are eliminated and the values in the new *Cohort* field are updated so that those between 1900 and 1909 are changed to 1 and those between 1960 and 1967 are changed to 2. The values in the new *Sex* field are also updated so that Lady Margaret Hall, Somerville, St Anne's, St Hilda's, and St Hugh's—the names of Oxford's five women's societies (later colleges)—are changed to 'f' for female, and all other values are changed to 'm' for male.

```
data matrics1 (keep = Mat_id Cohort Sex Age);
set matrics1;
if cohort < 1910 then cohort = 1;
if cohort > 1959 then cohort = 2;
if sex = "LMH" or sex = "Somerville" or sex = "St Anne's"
   or sex = "St Hilda's" or sex = "St Hugh's" then sex = "f";
if sex > "f" or sex < "f" then sex = "m";
run;
```

MATRICS1

| Mat_id | Cohort | Sex | Age |
|--------|--------|-----|-----|
| M19001000 | 1 | m | 18.25 |
| M1900101 | 1 | m | 19.00 |
| M1965104 | 2 | f | 18.75 |
| M1960106 | 2 | f | 19.25 |
| . . . | | | |

The third step demonstrates a selective data retrieval from records stored in two tables, ADDRESS and PLACECODE. The result is

entered into a new table, NEWADDS where the specific geographical
place names from the address table are replaced by their regional
equivalents found in PLACECODE.

```
data newadds (drop = place);
merge address (in = w) placecode;
by place;
if w;
run;
```

NEWADDS

| Mat_id | Ptype | Region |
|--------|-------|--------|
| M19001000 | fadd | West |
| M19001000 | pobt | Northwest |
| M1900101 | fadd | Southeast |
| M1900101 | pobt | Wales |
| M1965104 | fadd | Midlands |
| M1965104 | pobt | Midlands |
| M1960106 | fadd | Midlands |
| M1960106 | pobt | Midlands |

. . .

Step four transforms the data in the NEWADDS table so that the
field values 'fadd' and 'pobt' become field or column headings of
variables which give the regional location of matriculants'
father's address and place of birth, respectively. This data manipulation which creates column headings from row values is the
same one which proved particularly cumbersome when it was
tried with a database management system, requiring numerous
SQL statements as shown in Figure 3.25. Notice how simply the
same manipulation is achieved here with a statistical package.

```
data newadds(keep = Mat_id fadd pobt);
   array comb{2} fadd pobt;
   do Mat_id = 1 to 2;
      set newadds;
      by Mat_id;
      comb{Mat_id} = Mat_id;
      if last.Mat_id then return;
end;
```

NEWADDS

| Mat_id | Fadd | Pobt |
|--------|------|------|
| M19001000 | West | Northwest |
| M1900101 | Southeast | Wales |
| M1965104 | Midlands | Midlands |
| M1960106 | Midlands | Midlands |
| ... | | |

Step five is another database retrieval which draws related records from two tables to produce a new table. Here records from MATRICS1 and NEWADDS are merged to create the RESULT table required for analyses as already shown in Figure 4.28.

```
data result;
merge newadds (in = w) matrics1;
by Mat_id;
if w;
run;
```

Having at last retrieved and recoded the appropriate subset of data, analyses can begin. With a statistical package analytical commands normally indicate the measure or graphical procedure which the user wants to perform, the fields on which the procedure is to operate, and the records which should be considered. With our RESULT table we might begin by analysing individual variables, for example by constructing a frequency distribution showing the number and percentage of matriculants born in each region. The relevant *SAS* command and a partial result appear in Figure 4.29.

An analysis better suited to demonstrating change over time and to comparing men and women is shown in Figure 4.30. It cross-tabulates the place of birth (*Pobt*) and cohort (*Cohort*) variables, and represents only a minor variation on the frequency procedure shown above. A variation on the same theme would include a number of statistics with the cross-tabulation—Chi-Square and Cramer's V, for example—to indicate whether there were significant differences in British men's and women's regional origins. Measures of central tendency and of dispersion can also be calculated for numeric variables. Figure 4.31 shows such mea-

```
proc freq;
tables pobt;
run;
```

| Place of birth | Frequency | % | Cumulative Frequency | Cumulative Per cent |
|---|---|---|---|---|
| East | 195 | 6.2 | 195 | 6.2 |
| Local (to Oxford) | 315 | 10.0 | 510 | 16.2 |
| London | 695 | 22.0 | 1205 | 38.2 |
| Midlands | 163 | 5.2 | 1368 | 43.3 |
| North | 116 | 3.7 | 1484 | 47.0 |
| North-east | 250 | 7.9 | 1734 | 54.9 |
| North-west | 364 | 11.5 | 2098 | 66.5 |
| Scotland | 135 | 4.3 | 2233 | 70.8 |
| South | 173 | 5.5 | 2406 | 76.2 |
| South-east | 296 | 9.4 | 2702 | 85.6 |
| South-west | 79 | 2.5 | 2781 | 88.1 |
| Wales | 177 | 5.6 | 2958 | 93.7 |
| West | 198 | 6.3 | 3156 | 100.0 |

Fig. 4.29 Command-driven analysis of the Oxford data using a statistical package: a simple frequency distribution showing region of birth for a sample of British-born Oxford members 1900–9 and 1960–7

sures calculated for the age of men and women matriculants in the sample.

High-quality graphical output can be produced with other procedures. Here commands need to indicate the required graph type, the fields whose data values are to be graphed, and the subset of records to be considered. With statistical packages graphs can be customized to a far greater extent than with spreadsheets enabling the user to specify, for example, the thickness, colour, and scale of graph axes, how graphs are positioned on the printed page, the placement, font, colour, and point size used with graph titles, legends, and footnotes, and so on. The price of this flexibility, however, is the number of commands needed to tailor graphical output. Figure 4.23 was drawn by a spreadsheet with only a few simple menu selections. Assuming that the data were also available in *SAS*, the same graph, without a legend, would be drawn with the following command sequence:

Goptions
    title1  J = C  H = 1  F = simplex  c = BLACK  A = 90
        'Philadelphia's Annual Receipts and Expenditures, 1890–9'
        H = 3 F = Simplex A = 90 ' '
        H = 3 F = Simplex A = –90 ' ';
    symbol1  W = 1  C = black  I = join  V = square
    symbol2  W = 1  C = black  I = join  V = triangle;
Proc gplot data results;
    Plot (exenditures receipts) * year /overlay
                    haxis = 1890 to 1899
                    vaxis = 0 to 5000000 by 35000000;
run;

Finally, statistical packages offer procedures which can be used to create a wide range of differently formatted tables from one or more variables stored in a data set. Here the user determines the table's configuration, that is, which variables are represented as rows and columns and/or as subdivisions of rows and columns (as in Figure 4.18 where the cohort columns are subdivisions of the gender columns). Tables can be customized as well. For example, to print column- and row-boundary lines in bold, to shade columns and/or rows, and to attach and format text as table titles and column and row headings. Once again, however, flexibility is achieved at a price—having to specify in some considerable detail how each one of a table's many features is to be formatted.

## SELECTING THE RIGHT SOFTWARE FOR NUMERIC DATA AND QUANTITATIVE PROCEDURES

In conclusion, it is worth specifying some criteria to help the user choose between spreadsheet, statistical, and database software, all of which is capable of managing tabular data. Firstly, consider the required output. Where extensive recalculation of numeric data, graphical, or statistical analyses is required, then spreadsheet and statistical software is preferred to database management systems. In choosing between a spreadsheet and a statistical pack-

---

Fig. 4.30 Command-driven analysis of the Oxford data using a statistical package: a cross-tabulation showing region of birth for a sample of British-born male and female Oxford members, 1900–9 and 1960–7

```
proc freq;
tables cohort * pobt * sex;
run;
```

TABLE 1 OF POBT BY SEX: COHORT 1 (1900–9)

POBT                          SEX

Frequency

| Col Pct | men | women | Total |
|---|---|---|---|
| East | 74 | 8 | 82 |
| | 4.6 | 6.6 | |
| Local (to | 134 | 12 | 146 |
| Oxford) | 8.3 | 9.7 | |
| London | 410 | 32 | 442 |
| | 25.3 | 25.8 | |
| Midlands | 74 | 3 | 77 |
| | 4.6 | 2.4 | |
| North | 64 | 8 | 72 |
| | 4.0 | 6.5 | |
| North- | 107 | 12 | 119 |
| east | 6.6 | 9.7 | |

. . .

TABLE 2 OF POBT BY SEX: COHORT 2 (1960–7)

POBT                          SEX

Frequency

| Col Pct | men | women | Total |
|---|---|---|---|
| East | 78 | 35 | 113 |
| | 7.6 | 8.9 | |
| Local (to | 118 | 51 | 169 |
| Oxford) | 11.6 | 12.9 | |
| London | 184 | 69 | 253 |
| | 18.0 | 17.5 | |
| Midlands | 66 | 20 | 86 |
| | 6.5 | 5.1 | |
| North | 29 | 15 | 44 |
| | 2.8 | 3.8 | |
| North- | 91 | 40 | 131 |
| east | 8.9 | 10.2 | |

. . .

```
proc univariate;
var age;
by sex;
run;
```

*SEX = male Variable = AGE*

Univariate Procedure

Moments

| | | | |
|---|---|---|---|
| N | 3264 | Sum Wgts | 3264 |
| Mean | 19.40891 | Sum | 63350.67 |
| Std Dev | 3.627498 | Variance | 13.15874 |
| Skewness | 5.586581 | Kurtosis | 47.91793 |
| USS | 1272504 | CSS | 42936.97 |
| CV | 18.68986 | Std Mean | 0.063494 |
| T:Mean = 0 | 305.6814 | Prob>|T| | 0.0001 |
| Num ^ = 0 | 3264 | Num > 0 | 3264 |
| M(Sign) | 1632 | Prob>|M| | 0.0001 |
| Sgn Rank | 2664240 | Prob>|S| | 0.0001 |

Quantiles(Def = 5)

| | | | | |
|---|---|---|---|---|
| 100% | Max | 79.083 | 99% | 37.417 |
| 75% | Q3 | 19.167 | 95% | 24.75 |
| 50% | Med | 18.417 | 90% | 22.083 |
| 25% | Q1 | 17.917 | 10% | 17.583 |
| 0% | Min | 15.25 | 5% | 17.333 |
| | | | 1% | 16.833 |

*SEX = FEMALE Variable = AGE*

Univariate Procedure

Moments

| | | | |
|---|---|---|---|
| N | 581 | Sum Wgts | 581 |
| Mean | 19.04445 | Sum | 11064.82 |
| Std Dev | 3.067479 | Variance | 9.409429 |
| Skewness | 5.706413 | Kurtosis | 43.3398 |
| USS | 216180.9 | CSS | 5457.469 |
| CV | 16.10695 | Std Mean | 0.12726 |
| T:Mean = 0 | 149.6493 | Prob>|T| | 0.0001 |
| Num ^ = 0 | 581 | Num > 0 | 581 |
| M(Sign) | 290.5 | Prob>|M| | 0.0001 |
| Sgn Rank | 894535.5 | Prob>|S| | 0.0001 |

Quantiles(Def = 5)

| | | | | |
|---|---|---|---|---|
| 100% | Max | 49.167 | 99% | 30.75 |
| 75% | Q3 | 18.833 | 95% | 23.417 |
| 50% | Med | 18.333 | 90% | 21.083 |
| 25% | Q1 | 17.917 | 10% | 17.5 |
| 0% | Min | 14 | 5% | 17.167 |
| | | | 1% | 16.5 |

age, the data's structure should be determinant. If analyses are likely to rest on a small handful of formulae—as in the study of municipal finance data described above—or on the production of high-quality graphics from data which require little in the way of reclassification and restructuring, then the spreadsheet may be the most useful tool. If, on the other hand, statistical analyses are likely to require repetitive use of sophisticated measures or if graphical and statistical analyses require constant data reorganization and recoding, then a statistical package is preferred to a spreadsheet. The statistical package has a wider range of 'canned' or preprogrammed analytical procedures than a spreadsheet and its data management facilities are more powerful.

Statistical packages' data management facilities are so powerful that the reader might rightly ask why they do not simply supplant the database management system, especially as data stored in databases often require statistical packages anyway for their analysis. The question is taken up in Chapter 6, where we shall see that statistical packages offer rudimentary data entry and editing facilities which are not as user-friendly and flexible as those offered by database management systems. Where a project involves relatively lengthy character fields or data whose structure is highly complex and is best represented in hierarchies of associated tables, data entry and editing with a statistical package may be nothing short of nightmarish and error prone. One consequence is that at present, there remains a rather strict division of labour between database management and statistical software which forces projects that are involved in analysing large and complexly structured data sets to rely on both. Fortunately, the mechanisms for exchanging data between databases and software packages are reasonably straightforward, as we have already seen to a limited extent in this chapter and as will be demonstrated in Chapter 6.

Fig. 4.31 Command-driven analysis of the Oxford data using a statistical package: measures of central tendency based on a sample of British-born male and female Oxford members, 1900–9 and 1960–7

# 5

# Text and Text Processing

HISTORIANS who use computers currently concentrate most of their attention on database management systems, statistics software, and spreadsheet packages. Wedded to the idea that computers are only useful where information comes highly structured in records and fields, they ignore packages which manage and analyse running prose. That is, of course, with the exception of word processors. This narrowness is remarkable for three reasons. First, because the vast bulk of historical information is only available as running prose. Secondly, because computerized text-processing software replicates with greater speed and precision many of the operations historians currently conduct with textual information. And thirdly, because movement into this new area does not require pioneering innovation; only more and better cross-fertilization with linguistic and literary scholars who have fruitfully exploited the computer's text-editing, managing, and analysing facilities for several decades.

## TEXT EDITING: WORD PROCESSORS, TEXT EDITORS, AND TEXT-FORMATTING SOFTWARE

### *Word processors*

An obvious starting-point is word processing—a computing application whose appeal has grown so widely with the microcomputer revolution as to need little introduction here. The word processor is another example of software which bundles together several computational routines. The routine which the user sees most often is the editor with which text is created and edited on screen. The formatter works 'behind the scenes'. It takes care of how the text appears on the screen and when it is printed, for example, by controlling line length, right and left justification, spacing between lines, and the use of different fonts and type-faces. A third module is the user interface which governs how editing and formatting facilities are seen by the user and provides more or less helpful instructions about how to use the software. Word processors have changed fundamentally the nature of document preparation. Visual- or screen-editing facilities provide instant access to the entire contents of a document. Consequently, the user can go directly and immediately to those parts of a document which require editing. 'Global editing' is also available, for example, to turn in one instant a single-spaced document into a double-spaced one, or all occurrences of 'dog' into 'cat'. Word processors also enable documents to be reformatted automatically as they are edited. Word- and page-wrap facilities ensure that when three words are deleted from the centre of a paragraph, for example, a large white space is not left in their place. Instead, the surrounding text is joined together and the paragraph which once contained the deleted words and the document's pagination are both reformatted accordingly. Automatic and interactive reformatting also ensure that when the 35th footnote is deleted from a text originally containing 100 footnotes, footnotes 36 to 100 are renumbered from 35 to 99. Finally, word processors dis-play text on the computer screen as it will appear when printed. This facility is known as WYSIWYG, or 'What You See Is What You Get'. But in providing this facility, wordprocessors are forced to rely upon another: WYSINWT, or, 'What You See Is Not What's There'.[1] And what there is in a word-processed document is a plethora of horrible-looking characters which govern the docu-ment's appearance on screen and when printed, and which are hidden from view by the software's user interface. Take for exam-ple the first two sentences of this paragraph. What the computer sees in those sentences when they are saved as a file by the word-processing package, *Word5*, is shown in Figure 5.1. The same sentences saved by *Wordstar* are shown in Figure 5.2.

These figures tell us that different word processors use different formatting characters and consequently create files which are mutually incomprehensible. Some of these formatting characters

---

[1] For other relevant acronyms including GOKWYG ('God Only Knows What You Get') see S. Rahtz, 'The Processing of Words', in S. Rahtz (ed.), *Information Technology in the Humanities: Tools, Techniques and Applications* (Chichester, 1987), 75.

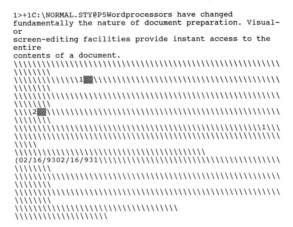

```
1>+1C:\NORMAL.STY@P5Wordprocessors have changed
fundamentally the nature of document preparation. Visual-
or
screen-editing facilities provide instant access to the
entire
contents of a document.
\\\\\\\\\\\\\\\\\\\\\\\\\\\\\\\\\\\\\\\\\\\\\\\\\\\\\\\\\
\\\\\\\\
\\\\\\\\\\\\\\1█\\\\\\\\\\\\\\\\\\\\\\\\\\\\\\\\\\\\\\\\\
\\\\\\\\
\\\\\\\\\\\\\\\\\\\\\\\\\\\\\\\\\\\\\\\\\\\\\\\\\\\\\\\\\\
\\\\\\\\
\\\\2█\\\\\\\\\\\\\\\\\\\\\\\\\\\\\\\\\\\\\\\\\\\\\\\\\\\\
\\\\\\\\
\\\\\\\\\\\\\\\\\\\\\\\\\\\\\\\\\\\\\\\\\\\\\\\\\\\\1\\\\
\\\\\\\\\\\\\\\\\\\\\\\\\\\\\\\\\\\\\\\\\\\\\\\\\\\\\\\\\\
\\\\\
\\\\\\\\\\\\\\\\\\\\\\\\\\\\\\\\\\\\\\\\\
(02/16/9302/16/931\\\\\\\\\\\\\\\\\\\\\\\\\\\\\\\\\\\\\\\\\\
\\\\\\\\
\\\\\\\\\\\\\\\\\\\\\\\\\\\\\\\\\\\\\\\\\\\\\\\\\\\\\\\\\\
\\\\\\\\
\\\\\\\\\\\\\\\\\\\\\\\\\\\\\\\\\\\\\\\\\\\\\\\\\\\\\\\\\\
\\\\\\\\
\\\\\\\\\\\\\\\\\\\\\\\\\\\\\\\\\\\\\\\\\\
\\\\\\\\\\\\\\\\\\\\\\\\\
```

Fig. 5.1 A sentence shown in its internal *Word5* format

```
Wordprocessorμ havî changeô fundamentall· thî naturî oμ documen¶ î
preparation« Visual- o· screen-editinô facilitieμ providî instan¶ î
access to the entire contents of a
document.
```

Fig. 5.2 The same sentence shown in its internal *Wordstar* format

may be unrecognizable to communications software making the electronic transfer of word-processed documents prone to corruption.[2] Most word processors can strip formatting characters from their documents and save the rest (letters, numbers, and punctuation) in ASCII form; that is, as characters whose machine-readable representation conforms to the American National Standard Code for Information Interchange. And since most text-handling and communications software recognizes characters represented in this standard form, documents which contain only ASCII characters are more easily and accurately transferred. The problem is that word-processed documents saved as ASCII files lose the formatting features for which the word processor was initially used. Word- and page-wrap facilities are lost. So are the features which indicate what characters are to be printed in bold, underlined, or as super-scripts. Admittedly some word processors are capable of reading formatted documents created by other packages and of creating

---

[2] See Ch. 2, p. 54.

formatted documents that can be read by other packages.[3] But a truly free market in the transfer of word-processed documents is still some way off.

Word processors have other limitations. With their bundled routines operating together and consuming the computer's processing power, editing gets slower as documents get longer. Should the chapters of this book be combined into one word-processing document, even the simplest edit would take a long time. And if the combined chapters of this book proved cumbersome, the complete works of Shakespeare or thousands of records retrieved from an on-line database would be positively unwieldy.[4] Global editing, too, can be limited in word processors, especially where semi-intelligent editing is required. For example, word-searching facilities are universally available. But few word processors can determine a word's position in a line (find 'dog' where the word begins at the fifteenth character position on the line; or find the line which begins with the letter 'T'). Thus, while word processors are useful for document preparation, they have limitations where machine-readable documents are created for widespread use and exchange, are particularly lengthy, or require semi-intelligent editing.

## *Text editors*

So-called 'text editors' take over where word processors leave off.[5] These are ASCII editors or document-preparation software which read and create only ASCII files. Ten or even five years ago, text editors were distinctly different from word processors (which, in fact, they antedate by several computing generations). They were on the whole line editors as opposed to screen editors. A screen full of text might be displayed but the cursor could not be moved freely around it. Instead, editing took place by typing out explicit

---

[3] Microsoft's word processor, *Word for Windows* version 3.1, for example, reads and writes files in the formats used by its competitors.

[4] See Ch. 2, pp. 55–8.

[5] D. Andrews and M. Greenhalgh, *Computing for Non-Scientific Applications* (Leicester, 1987), 210. For an outrageous account of the development of word processors and text editors see T. H. Nelson, *Literary Machines: The Report on, and of, Project Xanadu Concerning Word Processing, Electronic Publishing, Hypertext, Thinkertoys, Tomorrow's Intellectual Revolution, and Certain Other Topics Including Knowledge, Education and Freedom*, edn. 87.1 (San Antonio, 1987), 1/22–1/38.

instructions on a so-called command line normally displayed separately from the text at the bottom of the screen as shown in
Figure 5.3. Commands might be relatively simple: 'delete three
lines of this document' (k3 in the command language known to
the line editor, *ECCE*). They might also be chained together and
made extremely complex, even semi-intelligent as shown in
Figure 5.4.

```
>p18
(00001)Historians who use computers currently concentrate most
(00002)of their attention on database management systems,
(00003)statistics software, and spreadsheet packages. Wedded to
(00004)the idea that computers are only useful where information
(00005)comes highly structured in records and fields, they
(00006)ignore packages which manage and analyse running prose.
(00007)That is, of course, with the exception of wordprocessors.
(00008)This narrowness is remarkable for three reasons. Firstly,
(00009)because the vast bulk of historical information is only
(00010)available as running prose. Secondly because computerized
(00011)text-processing software replicates with greater speed
(00012)and precision many of the operations historians currently
(00013)conduct with textual information. And thirdly, because
(00014)movement into this new area does not require pioneering
(00015)innovation; only more and better cross-fertilization with
(00016)linguistic and literary scholars who have fruitfully
(00017)exploited the computer's text editing, managing, and
(00018)analyzing facilities for several decades.
>
```

*Note*: The command line begins with an angle bracket (>). The first command, p18 (print 18 lines), has been issued and the result displayed on
the screen with numbered lines. The command line at the bottom of the
figure is empty, awaiting the user's next command.

Fig. 5.3 A paragraph as seen in the ASCII line editor, *ECCE*

During the 1980s the gulf between word processors and text
editors narrowed. Today, many text editors support full-screen as
well as line editing. Similarly some word processors mimic text
editors' semi-intelligent editing with so-called macros or recorded
keystroke sequences which are played back when a designated
key is struck.[6] But distinctions still exist. Text editors do not offer
WYSIWYG-style formatting and as a result they do not embed
into a document the hidden formatting characters which impede
the interchange of word-processed files. Secondly, text editors are
still more powerful than word processors. They operate more

---

[6] With a macro, the Alt-F10 key combination, for example, can be pro-
grammed to play back the keystrokes necessary to type out a frequently used
postal address or to replace in a document every occurrence of the word 'pro-
gramme' with 'program'.

```
>(v/t/\r0i/$/m,r6i/&/m)*m-*p18
(00001)Historians who use computers currently concentrate most$
(00002)of their attention on database management systems,$
(00003)statistics software, and spreadsheet packages. Wedded to$
(00004)the i&dea that computers are only useful where information
(00005)comes highly structured in records and fields, they$
(00006)ignore packages which manage and analyse running prose.$
(00007)That is, of course, with the exception of wordprocessors.$
(00008)This narrowness is remarkable for three reasons. Firstly,$
(00009)because the vast bulk of historical information is only$
(00010)available as running prose. Secondly because computerized$
(00011)text-&processing software replicates with greater speed
(00012)and precision many of the operations historians currently$
(00013)conduct with textual information. And thirdly, because$
(00014)movement into this new area does not require pioneering$
(00015)innovation; only more and better cross-fertilization with$
(00016)linguistic and literary scholars who have fruitfully$
(00017)exploited the computer's text editing, managing, and$
(00018)analyzing facilities for several decades.$
>
```

*Note*: The command enters an ampersand in the sixth column of any line beginning with the letter 't', and a dollar sign at the right-most column of lines not beginning with the letter 't'. After searching the entire text, the editor is instructed to return to the beginning (m-*) and print out the first eighteen lines (p18), which are displayed here.

Fig. 5.4 A semi-intelligent line-editing command in *ECCE*, and a partial result

quickly and efficiently especially with large files, and they provide more powerful semi-intelligent editing.

Given these particular strengths, text editors might typically be used with large ASCII files such as those produced for or retrieved from on-line data or text bases.[7] For example, a text editor was used with the machine-readable version of the *Federalist Papers* from which examples of computer-aided text retrieval and analysis were compiled for this chapter. The machine-readable text was obtained over the network from a US computer installation managed by the Gutenberg Project.[8] The text weighed in at 1.2 megabytes—equivalent to nearly four 100,000-word (250-page) monographs. Helpfully, the machine-readable text's creator had inserted before the text of each paper the number (e.g. 'Federalist No. 10') by which individual papers are known. Wherever these lines occur, they begin with the phrase 'Federalist No.' and are followed with the appropriate numeral (from 1 to 85). The text's creator also inserted under the number lines of each paper the surname of the paper's author (e.g. 'Hamilton', 'Jay', and

[7] See Ch. 2, pp. 55–8.

[8] Project Gutenberg 1.1 release of *The Federalist Papers*, made available over ftp by M. S. Hart, Director, Project Gutenberg, 1 Sept. 1991.

'Madison').[9] In effect, the author and number lines indicated the beginning of each paper and thus the end of the paper preceding it. But this structure needed to be made explicit to the text-analysis and retrieval software which could not otherwise identify lines beginning with 'Federalist No.' or with 'Hamilton', 'Jay', or 'Madison' as number and author lines respectively. The number and author lines had, in other words, to be explicitly identified for the software, and this was done by inserting at their start the characters '<number>' and '<author>', respectively.

Though possible with a word processor, the task would have been time consuming because it would require scrolling through nearly 19,000 lines of text. It would have been slowed as well because word processors take a long time when saving changes made to such lengthy documents. Moreover, the editing task was a programmable one—it could be governed by a very simple set of rules—and thus ideal for a semi-intelligent text editor. All occurrences of 'Federalist No.' had to be found and replaced with '<number>'. Lines beginning with 'Hamilton', 'Jay', or 'Madison' had to be identified and preceded with '<author>'. In a text editor, a few simple commands made the amendments and saved the revised file within minutes.

### Text-formatting software and mark-up languages

Of course, there are many instances where it is desirable to format and print documents stored as ASCII files and/or to incorporate into ASCII files a wider range of formatting and printing enhancements than even word processors afford. How, in such cases, are text formatting features to be incorporated? The answer is with text-formatting software. Text-formatting software interprets characters which are embedded in a document to instruct a printer, for example, to use a specific typeface or point size, to use or stop using bold or underlined characters, or to justify lines of text to the left and right. Although this sounds very similar to word processing, which also relies upon embedded characters for its formatting instructions, there are two significant differences. First, the characters used by text formatters are standard ASCII

---

[9] Alexander Hamilton, John Jay, and James Madison. The papers were initially signed with the pseudonym 'Publius'.

characters. They appear when a document is viewed on the screen. They also appear when a document is printed without the intervention of formatting software which interprets the formatting characters as printing instructions. Secondly, with text formatters, formatting characters are explicitly entered by the user into a document, normally after the document has been completely and finally edited. With word processors, documents are formatted dynamically as they are being created. Moreover, with a word processor the user is unaware that formatting characters are being inserted into the document by the software; the characters themselves are invisible to the user.

The range of characters comprehensible to any one text formatter is referred to as its mark-up language, and character combinations which indicate a particular instruction are called tags. Tags are inserted in a document preceding or surrounding the text elements to which they immediately refer. Thus, in a document where Latin words are to be printed in italic the phrase 'per se' might be marked up as follows: {\it per se}. Although mark-up languages differ considerably from one text formatter to another, two generic types may be identified: procedural and descriptive.[10] Procedural mark-up languages consist of tags which provide explicit instruction about how each tagged element in a text should be printed. Section headings might be tagged with printing instructions which, for example, translate into 'indent one-half inch, type line in bold capital letters, then insert two blank lines'. Documents tagged with procedural mark-up will normally have an initial section called a header (sometimes stored in a separate file). The header defines the tags permitted in a document and the characters which distinguish tags from text (often curly braces, back slashes, or angle brackets). Headers also might contain user-defined shorthands with which complex tag sequences are abbreviated.[11] Documents tagged with procedural mark-up will normally be comprehensible to one specific formatting program only. The examples here refer to *TeX*, text-formatting software

[10] L. D. Burnard, 'Tools and Techniques for Computer-Assisted Text Processing', in C. S. Butler (ed.), *Computers and Written Texts* (Oxford, 1992), 1–28.

[11] With the text-formatting software known as *TeX*, an instruction to use a magnified bold font normally given as 'cmbx10 scaled' might be shortened to 'mbf'.

which is widely used in the scientific and publishing communities.[12]

Take as an example the first page of a chapter in a Ph.D. thesis shown in Figure 5.5.[13] When printed, the chapter heading and title appear in a bold font and centred at the top of an 8.5″ by 11″ page. In addition, the title includes within it a footnote number in superscript. The text of the footnote is set out on the bottom of the same page. It uses a smaller font than that which is used in the title, and is not printed in bold. Figure 5.6 shows some of the tagged (synonyms include 'marked up' and 'encoded') machine-readable text which produced the printed version. The chapter heading, 'Chapter 3', is to be centred and printed in a bold font according to the tags '\centerline{\bf Chapter 3}'. So are the two lines of the chapter title; and the first line of the chapter title is separated from the chapter number by two blank lines '\bigskip\noindent'. The title which occurs in the footnote, on the other hand, 'De Anima Brutorum', is printed in italic '{\it De Anima Brutorum . . .}', and the footnote number '1' is in superscript as indicated by the dollar signs which surround and the up-arrow which precedes it. Immediately after the title is the text of footnote 1; it is introduced by the '\note' tag, enclosed in curly braces, and formatted with the tags that read '\openup2\jot'. Some of these tags are immediately comprehensible to the *TeX* text-formatting software (e.g. \bigskip, \centerline, \noindent). Others, including the tags for characters in superscript and footnote formats, are user-defined shorthand conventions which are specified in the header. The part of the header which defines the footnote format used in this particular example is shown in Figure 5.7. If procedural mark-up seems somewhat involved when formatting the first page of a dissertation chapter, that used to format a simple table or list is very complex indeed.

---

[12] *TeX* was developed as a 'publishing system' by Donald E. Knuth and is currently in the public domain, that is, distributed either without charge or at cost. For information contact the *TeX* Users' Group via BITNET at TUG@MATN.AMS.COM or by subscribing to the Group's discussion list TEX-L at the same BITNET address (see Ch. 2 for a description of discussion lists and how to subscribe to them). Also see D. E. Knuth, *The TeXbook* (Reading, Mass., 1984).

[13] I am grateful to Dr J. Andrews, Wellcome Unit for the History of Medicine, Glasgow University, for advising me on the use of procedural mark-up and for providing these examples from his Ph.D. thesis, 'Bedlam Revisited: A History of Bethlem Hospital *c*.1634–1770' (University of London, 1991), 134, 189.

Chapter 3

'The Discipline of the House':[1]
Environment, Management & Architecture

## Introduction

The 'squalor' of Bethlehem, depicted in Swift's (and other contemporaneous) portraits of naked, starved, 'slovenly' and abused patients, dabbling in their own excreta; languishing in dark cells, or picking out the straws of their beds; and of a filthy, stench ridden hospital; taken for granted as fact by some historians, or by literary critics, like Max Byrd; has been considerably exaggerated[2]. On any literal reading of Augustan literature, one would indeed gain the impression that all, or most, of Bethlem's patients were shut away in 'darken'd room[s]'; were incontinent, unwashed, unclothed and slept on straw; were subjected to 'daily' lashings, and were constantly in chains. Yet modern commentators have made little attempt to test this image of the environment of Bethlem by reference to the hospital's own records, or to the more matter of fact accounts of other contemporary visitors, nor has provision for the insane at Bethlem been thoroughly placed in the context of other contemporary alternatives. The hospital's environment has generally been portrayed as a static time-capsule of sustained squalor. Taken to its worst extremes, this image led one historian as recently as 1982, to declaim:-

> Bedlam (or Bethlem) was [in the eighteenth century]...a wretched place...The records
> show that patients were beaten, starved and manacled, and for months at a time they
> were placed in filthy dungeons, with no light or clothing; they were given only excre-
> ment-sodden straw on which to lie. Amputations of the toes and fingers of patients,
> due to frostbite, were not uncommon"...[3].

1 For quote, see e.g. Willis, *De Anima Brutorum...* (1672), trans Pordage as *Two Discourses Concerning the Soul of Brutes...* (London, 1683), 208; the "inveterate and habitual' insane, 'seldom admit to any Medical Cure; but...being placed in Bedlam, or an Hospital for Mad people, by the ordinary discipline of the place, either at length return to themselves, or else they are kept from doing hurt'; & testimony of John Haslam before the Madhouses Committee, 1st Report, 1815, 105, re. discharge from Bethlem of the 'sick and weak' and those 'not...able to undergo the discipline of the house'.

2 See Swift, *The Legion Club*, 1s 52, 154, 234–5; *Gulliver's Travels*, 'Voyage to Laputa', pt. 3. chaps v & vi, esp. 178–82; *Tale of a Tub*, 111–13; & Byrd, *Visits to Bedlam*, chap. 3, esp 85 & note to plate 6. Byrd refers to 'the...squalor of Bedlam', and to Yahoos dabbling in their dung 'like the inmates of Bedlam'.

3 Beatrice Saunders, *Our Ancestors of the Eighteenth Century* (sSussex, The Book Guild, 1982). See, also, Roderick E. McGrew, *Encyclopedia of Medical History* (London, Macmillan, 1985), who speaks more generally about the 'unspeakable' 'conditions under which' the insane 'existed', but only less sensationally:- 'The mad cells were usually dark, dank, cold, and rat-infested. Sanitation was virtually nonexistent, clothing was minimal in the coldest weather, and it was not uncommon for both men and women to be seen lying entirely naked on beds of rotten straw...The only consideration was to make escape impossible. Health or comfort meant nothing'. Similarly, reliant on little more than the 1815/16 Madhouses Committee Reports, Singer & Underwood

Fig. 5.5 Printed version of a dissertation chapter's opening page, formatted using *TeX*

```
\centerline{\bf Chapter 3}
\bigskip\noindent
\centerline{\bf `The Discipline of the House':{$^1$}}
\centerline{\bf Environment, Management \& Architecture}
\note{\openup2\jot{For quote, see e.g. Willis, {\it De
Anima Brutorum...} (1672)...
\bigskip\noindent
\openup2\jot
```

```
The rest of the chapter goes here...
```

Fig. 5.6 Text of the same page encoded with *TeX*'s procedural mark-up language

```
%footnote
\newcount\notenumber
\def\clearnotenumber{\notenumber=0}
\def\note#1{\global\advance\notenumber by 1
        \global\footnote{$^{\the\notenumber}$}
        {\footnotefont\begingroup\openup-
2\jot\def\it{\footnoteital}#1\vskip 0pt\endgroup}}
\clearnotenumber
\def\prosevskip{\bigskip}
\long\def\versequote{\prosevskip\begingroup\narrower\obey
lines\textfont\raggedright\baselineskip=8pt}
\def\endvq{\prosevskip\endgroup}
\def\prosequote{\baselineskip=8pt\begingroup\narrower\pro
sevskip}
\def\endpq{\prosevskip\endgroup}
```

Fig. 5.7 Portion of the *TeX* header defining the mark-up which formats the dissertation's footnotes

The printed and marked-up versions of a table taken from the same dissertation are shown in Figures 5.8 and 5.9, respectively.

The principal difference between descriptive and procedural mark-up languages is that the former are process independent. That is, they identify the structural elements or features of a document rather than a procedure to be adopted at different points within it.[14] Thus, new section headings might be tagged simply to indicate 'new section heading begins here', and Latin words which are normally italicized in print might be tagged as 'foreign word'. To produce formatted output from a document tagged with descriptive mark-up, it is necessary to instruct the formatting software in the procedures to adopt when encountering each generically described text feature. Documents encoded with descriptive mark-up, like those encoded with procedural mark-up, will have a

[14] Rahtz, 'The Processing of Words'; B. Boguraev and M. Neff, 'Text Representation, Dictionary Structure, and Lexical Knowledge', in D. Ross and D. Brink (eds.), *ACH/ALLC '91. 'Making Connections': Conference Handbook* (Tempe, Ariz., 17–21 Mar. 1991), 17–22.

BRIDEWELL DIET (1647)

SUNDAYS-TUESDAYS & THURSDAYS: Meat Days

Dinner:

⅓lb of boiled, boned beef

¼ of pottage

½ of a 1½d loaf

¼ pint of 4/- beer

Supper:

⅓ lb of boiled, boned beef

¼ of a 1½d loaf

1 pint of 4/- beer

WEDNESDAYS, FRIDAYS & SATURDAYS: Dairy Days

Dinner:

⅙ lb of butter or ¼lb of cheese

¼ of milk pottage

½ of a 1½d loaf

¼ pint of 4/- beer

Supper:

¼ of a 1½d loaf

1 pint of 4/- beer

Fig. 5.8 Printed version of a table in the dissertation

header. In both cases the header will define permitted tags and the characters used to distinguish the tags from the text. But there are differences. The header used with procedural mark-up comprises a list of tags each of which is instantly associated with some printing instruction. Where descriptive mark-up is used, an independent set of instructions has to be provided to make the tags comprehensible to text-formatting software and thus the printer, for example, by instructing the formatter to indent and use bold capital letters where section headings are encountered, or to print foreign words in italic. Rather than specifying procedural conventions, the header used with descriptive mark-up explicitly describes the elements which make-up a document by indicating how they are tagged and by defining their relationship to one another. Take the Ph.D. chapter again as an example.

```
\centerline{{\bf BRIDEWELL DIET (1647)}}
\smallskip\noindent
\centerline{{\bf SUNDAYS-TUESDAYS \& THURSDAYS: Meat Days}}
\vskip 0.2in
\+{\bf Dinner:}\cr
\vskip 0.1in
\+&{$1\over3$lb of boiled, boned beef}\cr
\vskip 0.08cm
\+&{$1\over4$ of pottage}\cr
\vskip 0.08cm
\+&{$1\over2$ of a 1$1\over2$d loaf}\cr
\vskip 0.08cm
\+&{$1\over4$ pint of 4/ beer}\cr
\vskip 0.1in
\+{\bf Supper:}\cr
\vskip 0.1in
\+&{$1\over3$lb of boiled, boned beef}\cr
\vskip 0.08cm
\+&{$1\over4$ of a 1$1\over2$d loaf}\cr
\vskip 0.08cm
\+&{1 pint of 4/ beer}\cr
\vskip 0.3in
\centerline{\bf WEDNESDAYS, FRIDAYS \& SATURDAYS: Dairy Days}
\vskip 0.2in
\+{\bf Dinner:}\cr
\vskip 0.1in
\+&{$1\over6$lb of butter or $1\over4$lb of cheese}\cr
\vskip 0.08cm
\+&{$1\over4$ of milk pottage}\cr
\vskip 0.08cm
\+&{$1\over2$ of a 1$1\over2$d loaf}\cr
\vskip 0.08cm
\+&{$1\over4$pint of 4/ beer}\cr
\vskip 0.1in
\+{\bf Supper:}\cr
\vskip 0.1in
\+&{$1\over4$ of a 1$1\over2$d loaf}\cr
\vskip 0.08cm
\+&{1 pint of 4/ beer}\cr
\vskip 0.3in}
\par
```

Fig. 5.9 Text of the same table encoded with *TeX*'s procedural mark-up
language

Where a procedural mark-up language is used to format the text,
the header will contain a simple list of the procedural tags that
will be encountered in the document, including tags for indents,
line breaks, and italic fonts. Where a descriptive mark-up language is used, the header will list the generic elements that are
likely to be found—chapter, heading, title, paragraph, footnote—
and indicate, for example, that chapters are allowed to contain
headings, titles, and paragraphs, that any of these features are
allowed to contain footnotes, and, by implication, that footnotes
are not allowed to contain chapters.

The same first page of the dissertation chapter marked up in
Figure 5.6 for use with *TeX* might be encoded with the descriptive
mark-up language known as SGML (Standard Generic Mark-up
Language), as shown in Figure 5.10. The tags are more compre-

```
<chapter>
    <head>Chapter 3
    </head>
    <ctitle>The Discipline of the House':
        <note>For quote, see e.g.
            <citation>
                <author>Willis
                </author>,
                <title>De Anima Brutorum...
                </title>
                <date>(1672)
                </date>...
            </citation
        </note>
        Environment, Management & Architecture
    </ctitle>

    <p> The text of the first paragraph goes here...
    </p>

    ... More paragraphs in chapter go here...

</chapter>
```

Fig. 5.10 Dissertation chapter's opening page encoded with the descriptive mark-up language, SGML

hensible than those of procedural mark-up languages and there is more information, for example in the footnote where bibliographic citations and their authors and titles are explicitly indicated. The document's header, a portion of which is shown in Figure 5.11, defines the tagged elements and how they are related to one another. In effect, it defines the dissertation's structure. The first element defined in the header is called dissertation, and refers to the document in its entirety. It comprises three elements—front, body, and back. Only the second of these, body, is defined in Figure 5.11 in any further detail, though we might assume that the front contains at least the elements title-page and table of contents while the back contains elements bibliography and appendix. Elements which occur in the body of the dissertation include an element called chapter, which in turn includes elements called head, ctitle (for chapter title), and paragraph. These elements are themselves comprised of text (indicated by #PCDATA or parsable character data). The note element may occur anywhere in the document; that is, within any of the elements described so far. It comprises citations which in turn comprise authors, titles, and dates which themselves comprise text.[15] The

---

[15] Document preparation with SGML is a rapid growth area. See L. D. Burnard, 'What is SGML and How Does it Help?', in D. I. Greenstein, *Modelling Historical Data* (St Katharinen, 1991), 65–80 and his gentle introduction to SGML in C. M. Sperberg-McQueen and L. D. Burnard (eds.), *Guidelines for the Encoding and Interchange of Machine-Readable Texts*, edn. P1 (Oxford, 1990), Ch. 2.

```
< ! ELEMENT dissertation      – – (front, body, back)        >
< ! ELEMENT front. . . elements in the front defined here. . .   >
< ! ELEMENT body              – – (chapter)                   >
< ! ELEMENT chapter           – – (head, ctitle, p*)          >
< ! ELEMENT head              – – (#PCDATA)                   >
< ! ELEMENT ctitle            – – (#PCDATA)                   >
< ! ELEMENT p                 – – (#PCDATA)                   >
< ! ELEMENT back. . . elements in the back defined here. . .   >
< ! — These elements may appear anywhere in the text        —>
< ! ELEMENT note              – – (citation)                  >
< ! ELEMENT citation          – – (author, title, date)       >
< ! ELEMENT author            – – (#PCDATA)                   >
< ! ELEMENT title             – – (#PCDATA)                   >
< ! ELEMENT date              – – (#PCDATA)                   >
```

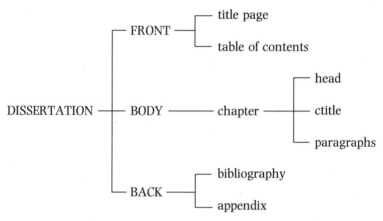

Fig. 5.11 Portion of the SGML header which defines the mark-up and the dissertation's structure: a schematic diagram shows the dissertation's structure as defined in the header

structure of the dissertation defined in the header is represented schematically in Figure 5.11.

Using descriptive mark-up to define a document's structure independently of any processing considerations (e.g. how to print particular elements) offers four advantages. First, the mark-up is generic. As such it can be made comprehensible to different text formatters. Secondly, the same tags can be interpreted differently by different users or at different times. For example, the dissertation element <head> might govern the creation of centred, enumerated, and emboldened chapter headings in one printed version of the dissertation and left-aligned, italicized, lower-case chapter headings in another. With descriptive mark-up, then, the user is not committed to a particular printing format or style which is rigidly fixed when a text is encoded with procedural mark-up.

Thirdly, since texts encoded with descriptive mark-up can be printed according to any number of very different formats, the user can design so-called style sheets which associate particular printing instructions with elements as appropriate for the type of document being printed. For example, a style sheet designed for business letters might position any text encoded as a 'sender's address' at the top left-hand side of the document, not indent the first line of new paragraphs, and italicize and enclose in parentheses text encoded as 'references'. A style sheet designed for journal articles, on the other hand, might place text encoded as 'sender's address' at the bottom left-hand side of the document, indent the first line of new paragraphs by a half inch, and sequentially enumerate text elements encoded as references, placing them together at the end of the document and printing them with smaller characters than those used in the text of the document itself. Once defined, style sheets can be used time and again with any document so long as the document uses mark-up that the style sheet understands.[16] Fourthly, as we shall see below, effective use of text-retrieval and analysis systems depends upon the use of descriptive mark-up to define the structure of machine-readable texts. Only once a text's various elements are defined and demarcated with tags can their contents be isolated, retrieved, and/or analysed.

Whether procedural or descriptive mark-up is used for text formatting, the preparation of printed materials is far more involved with text-formatting software than with word processors. Why, then, would the word-processing cognoscenti give up the luxuriant WYSIWYG environment for one with unsightly angle brackets, curly braces, and seemingly incomprehensible tags? There are at least four reasons. First, text editors antedate word processors and some diehard partisans simply refuse to abandon their old friends. Secondly and more seriously, it is sometimes necessary to

---

[16] Some word processors enable users to create style sheets which can be used to format new documents when they are first created or to reformat existing documents.

format documents whose length makes word processors impracticable. Thirdly, text-formatting programs offer features not found in most word processors. Some of these features, like the preparation of tables of contents and indexes, require a degree of semi-intelligence not always available in word processors. For example, a text formatter can be instructed more easily than a word processor to compile a table of contents and an index from the text of a document encoded with 'chapter title' and 'index term' tags, respectively. Other features only available with text-formatting software include some of the eccentric character sets necessary, for example, for scientific notation. Finally, since the documents encoded for use with text-formatting packages are created as ASCII files, they are more easily exchanged between different computers and, especially where descriptive mark-up is used, between different formatting software.

Text formatters also have limitations and these are worth mentioning if only in brief. First, they do not all provide for the same range of specialist needs. Scientists interested in printing complex mathematical formulae or intricate tables from machine-readable files, for example, will be catered for with *TeX*, but poorly served by other formatters. Thus it is important to ensure that the formatting package you choose provides the print enhancements you require. A second problem is that mark-up languages differ widely. Consequently, to print a machine-readable text that has been tagged with a particular mark-up language, it is essential to have a formatter which recognizes that mark-up language. Using any other formatter may require that the text be comprehensively edited to replace foreign tags with ones that are known to the available system. The problem is compounded wherever there isn't a one-to-one mapping between tags used by different mark-up languages. Fortunately there are signs that the computing industry may be gravitating toward SGML as its standard descriptive mark-up language.[17] What remains is for more text-formatting (and word-processing) software to become capable of reading and writing documents marked up in SGML.

---

[17] SGML is now recognized by the International Standards Organization (ISO), see *ISO: 8879: Information Processing: Text and Office Systems: Standard General Markup Language (SGML)* (Geneva, 1986).

## TEXT MANAGEMENT AND TEXT RETRIEVAL

Word processors, line editors, and text formatters are also woefully inadequate at managing and analysing collections of machine-readable texts. For these facilities, the user needs to migrate to so-called full-text retrieval and text analysis software, respectively.[18] Text retrieval software provides ready access to selected elements of a machine-readable text or collection of texts. For example, it might be used to retrieve from the machine-readable edition of the *Federalist Papers* those papers written by Alexander Hamilton, or all paragraphs (irrespective of author and paper number) containing the words 'party' or 'faction'. In effect, the text retrieval system acts very much like a database, and the reader might well ask why not use a database for such purposes. Surely the database table shown in Figure 5.12 would accommodate the *Federalist Papers* very nicely. Each row of the table represents one paper, each column a characteristic of that paper including number, author, and the text of the paper itself. The problem is that databases cannot yet handle lengthy character fields efficiently because of the indivisible nature of the values entered into them.[19] Thus, it would be quite impossible to search the *Pap_text* field shown in Figure 5.12 for lines containing the

| ID | Author | Number | Pap_text |
| --- | --- | --- | --- |
| F9 | Hamilton | 9 | A FIRM Union will be of the utmost moment to the peace and liberty of the States. . . |

Fig. 5.12 A database table designed to accommodate the text of the *Federalist Papers*

[18] J. H. Ashford and P. Willett, *Text Retrieval and Document Databases* (London, 1988); J. J. Hughes, 'Text Retrieval Programs – A Brief Introduction', *Bits & Bytes Review* (July and Aug. 1987); M. Bland *et al.*, *Free Text Retrieval Systems: A Review and Evaluation* (London, 1989); I. Lancashire (ed.), *The Humanities Computing Yearbook, 1989/90: A Comprehensive Guide to Software and Other Resources* (Oxford, 1991), 508–17; D. A. Spaeth, *A Guide to Software for Historians* (Glasgow, 1991), 73–82.

[19] There are indications that some of the more sophisticated database products are incorporating better text-handling facilities.

word 'liberty'. The database software has no way of distinguishing lines or paragraphs in the value entered into a character field. The entire text of any record containing the word 'liberty' could be retrieved but this may not be the desired result. Nor would the retrieval be efficient or quick. To locate 'liberty' in the *Pap_text* field, the database looks for the required string by reading the characters in the field sequentially. Where character fields are particularly lengthy and where tables have several hundreds of records, the search can be quite time consuming.

Some of these problems are overcome if, for example, each word is treated as a unique record in a database table which includes fields describing the word's exact position within the text as shown in Figure 5.13.

| ID | Para | Line | Word | Author | Number | Pap_text |
|----|------|------|------|--------|--------|----------|
| F9 | 1 | 1 | 1 | Hamilton | 9 | A |
| F9 | 1 | 1 | 2 | Hamilton | 9 | FIRM |
| F9 | 1 | 1 | 3 | Hamilton | 9 | Union |
| F9 | 1 | 1 | 4 | Hamilton | 9 | will |
| F9 | 1 | 1 | 5 | Hamilton | 9 | be |
| F9 | 1 | 1 | 6 | Hamilton | 9 | of |
| F9 | 1 | 1 | 7 | Hamilton | 9 | the |
| F9 | 1 | 1 | 8 | Hamilton | 9 | utmost |
| F9 | 1 | 1 | 9 | Hamilton | 9 | moment |
| F9 | 1 | 1 | 10 | Hamilton | 9 | to |
| F9 | 1 | 1 | 11 | Hamilton | 9 | the |
| F9 | 1 | 1 | 12 | Hamilton | 9 | peace |
| F9 | 1 | 1 | 13 | Hamilton | 9 | and |
| F9 | 1 | 1 | 14 | Hamilton | 9 | liberty |
| F9 | 1 | 1 | 15 | Hamilton | 9 | of |
| F9 | 1 | 1 | 16 | Hamilton | 9 | the |
| F9 | 1 | 1 | 17 | Hamilton | 9 | States |

Fig. 5.13 An alternative database table designed to accommodate the text of the *Federalist Papers*

Searching this table for lines of text containing the word 'liberty' is possible if somewhat convoluted. But having solved one problem the table structure presented in Figure 5.13 introduces an altogether different one. That is, it becomes difficult to reconstruct the linear structure of the original text. The first line of

*Federalist* 9 as retrieved from the database table shown in Figure 5.13 would be displayed as follows:

Pap_text

---

A
FIRM
Union
will
be
of
the
utmost
moment
to
the
peace
and
liberty
of
the
States

The desired result, however, is likely to look somewhat different, notably:

A FIRM Union will be of the utmost moment to the peace and liberty of the States

The linear output is retrievable but not without the enormous effort required to turn row values into column headings as demonstrated in Chapter 3 with a profusion of SQL commands.[20]

Full-text retrieval systems succeed where databases fail in managing running prose. Though they differ considerably, a generic description is possible. Like databases, full-text retrieval systems consist of a collection of records, often referred to as documents. Just as the structure of a database record is described in terms of a collection of explicitly defined fields, the structure of a text retrieval document is described in terms of a collection of explicitly defined elements. There are three important differences, however. First, in the database, the maximum length of any one field is for all practical purposes restricted. In the full-text retrieval

---

[20] See Ch. 3, pp. 109–11.

system an element's length is virtually unrestricted and might contain the entire text of a treatise, pamphlet, or book. Secondly, the full-text retrieval system can distinguish between lines, words, and, depending on the software, paragraphs which occur within each element. The database cannot distinguish between words, lines, and paragraphs which occur within fields. Thirdly, data are rarely entered interactively into full-text retrieval systems as they are into databases. Instead, data are normally loaded in bulk from external ASCII files which use a descriptive mark-up language to tag where documents and their elements begin and end.[21]

Of course what elements are defined, named, and tagged for the documents stored in a text retrieval system depends entirely on the kinds of retrievals the user wants to conduct. The *Federalist Papers* might be simply structured as a collection of 85 documents, one for each paper. And each document would comprise tags indicating its number, author, date of initial publication, title, and then the beginning and end of its text body as shown in Figure 5.14. The structure supports selective retrievals based on the contents of any of the defined elements, and on the words, lines, and paragraphs within the text body of each of the *Federalist Papers*.[22] In another implementation, it might be desirable to extend the range of elements, for example, to include the opening and closing sections of each paper so they can be examined for particularly inflammatory rhetoric. This rather more sophisticated rendition is shown in Figure 5.15. In yet a third implementation shown in Figure 5.16, individual papers are not distinguished from one another. Instead the corpus is structured as a sequence of individual pages of text. Should an analyst wish to identify both pages, on the one hand, and individual papers on the other, the corpus would have to be encoded according to two independent but 'concurrent' mark-up schemes as the two could not be expected to coincide. The beginning and end of individual papers might not, for example, coincide with page breaks as shown in Figure 5.16.[23]

[21] See Ch. 6, pp. 225–9.

[22] Most full-text retrieval systems will recognize the elements word, line, and paragraph without the user having to mark up where they start and end. The elements are implicitly marked up anyway by spaces in the case of words and by line breaks and indentation in the case of lines and paragraphs, respectively.

[23] Very few software packages can manage concurrent mark-up schemes, hence they receive only passing mention here.

```
<paper>

    ...the marked up text of Papers 1-8 goes here...

</paper>

<paper>

    <number>Federalist 9
    </number>
    <author>Hamilton
    </author>
    <date>21 November 1787
    </date>
    <title>The Union as a Safeguard Against Domestic
        Faction and Insurrection. To the People of the
        State of New York:
    </title>
    <text>A FIRM Union will be of the utmost moment to
        the peace and liberty of the States...

    ...more text of Federalist 9 goes here...

    </text>
</paper>

<paper>

    ...the marked up text of Papers 10-85 goes here...

</paper>
```

*Note*: This Rendition creates a series of sequential documents called <paper> (one for each of the *Federalist Papers*). The <paper> elements in turn comprise the elements <number>, <author>, <date>, <title>, and <text>.

Fig. 5.14 Structuring the *Federalist Papers* with the descriptive mark-up language, SGML: Rendition 1

With the structure of the machine-readable text explicitly marked up, the user can call on a range of retrieval facilities which are far more powerful and more appropriate to full texts than those which are available in databases. The full-text retrieval system will permit many of the operators and functions available in a database system and which are fully documented in Chapter 3. Briefly, these include the 'Boolean' operators AND and OR and the 'relational' operators including greater than (>), less than (<), equal to (=), and not equal to (<>). Some statistical operators may also be available, notably those which count occurrences of specified keywords within a selected text element. The text retrieval system also permits a range of operators and functions not found in the database. Especially important are the spatial operators (so-called proximity, positional, and field operators) which specify the relative position between two or more keywords. Proximity operators would be used to determine whether the words 'faction' and 'evil' occurred within five words of one

```
<paper>

    ...the marked up text of Papers 1-8 goes here...

</paper>

<paper>
    <number>Federalist 9
    </number>
    <author>Hamilton
    </author>
    <date>21 November 1787
    </date>

    <title>The Union as a Safeguard Against Domestic
        Faction and Insurrection. To the People of the
        State of New York:
    </title>

    <text>

        <preamble>A FIRM Union will be of the utmost
            moment to the peace and liberty of the
            States...

            ...rest of the preamble goes here...
        </preamble>

        <body>
            ...body goes here
        </body>

        <conclusion>In the Lycian confederacy, which
            consisted of twenty three CITIES or
            republics...
        </conclusion>

    </text>
</paper>


<paper>

    ...the marked up text of Papers 10-85 goes here...

</paper>
```

*Note*: This Rendition is like Rendition 1, only the <text> element is subdivided into <preamble>, <body>, and <conclusion> elements.

Fig. 5.15 Structuring the *Federalist Papers* with the descriptive mark-up language, SGML: Rendition 2

another anywhere within the *Federalist Papers*. With positional operators the same search could be refined by specifying a particular sequence for the word pair (e.g. where 'pernicious' occurs within up to four words after 'faction'). And field operators could specify that a word pair had to occur within the same 'implied' field, for example, within the same line or paragraph.[24]

More sophisticated text retrieval systems provide thesauri to make searches for particular words more comprehensive. For example, a thesaurus might enhance the search for proximate

---

[24] Hughes, 'Text Retrieval Programs'.

```
<page>
    ...text of of the first page of Federalist 1 goes
here...
</page>

<page>
    ...more pages of text go here...

</page>

<page>
    ...text of Federalist 8 ends here...

    Federalist 9
    Hamilton
    21 November 1787
    The Union as a Safeguard Against Domestic Faction
    and Insurrection. To the People of the State of New
    York: A FIRM Union will be of the utmost moment to
    the peace
</page>

<page>
    and liberty of the States...
</page>

<page>

...other pages of text go here...

</page>
```

*Note*: This Rendition creates a series of sequential documents called <page>. Notice that the text of *Federalist 9* does not begin on a new page.

Fig. 5.16 Structuring the *Federalist Papers* with the descriptive mark-up language, SGML: Rendition 3

occurrences of 'faction' and 'evil' by looking as well for proximate occurrences of any relevant pair of synonyms e.g. 'faction' and 'iniquity', or 'party' and 'infamy'. Many systems will even permit users to construct their own thesauri or edit supplied ones, thereby tailoring their entries to the text concerned. Soundex dictionaries may also be included. These facilitate searches for words which sound like the keyword and are particularly important with corpora where inconsistent spellings are common. Still other systems might use standard lexicons which lemmatize keywords—reduce them to their root form—and search for words sharing the same root. The accuracy of automated lexicons, however, is limited by the ambiguities inherent in any language. Homographs, words which are spelled the same but mean different things (e.g. 'lead' and 'lead'), present particular problems.

Text retrieval systems are also far more flexible than databases in allowing users to determine how retrieval results should be displayed. They need to be. The Gorbals database table discussed in Chapter 3 might be queried to supply the names of people born in Glasgow. Records which meet the query condition are displayed as part of the result; those which do not meet the query condition are not displayed. In the full-text retrieval system, a document can meet a query condition several times over. For example, searching the *Federalist Papers* for the word 'party' we discover that there are several occurrences of the keyword 'party' in *Federalist 10*. The multiple occurrence of a single keyword within a given document or element is very common. And text retrieval software, unlike database software, is able to distinguish and display as individual 'hits' the several occurrences of a given keyword within any document or element. It is also possible with text retrieval software to determine the context in which individual keyword occurrences are displayed. The context is normally specified in terms of the number of words, lines, and paragraphs that surround each keyword occurrence. In Figure 5.17 occurrences of the keyword 'party' and 'faction' in the *Federalist Papers* are displayed by author and paper number in a context defined as one line of text on either side of the line containing the keyword.

(Hamilton,8)
The army under such circumstances may usefully aid the magistrate to suppress a small **faction**, or an occasional mob, or insurrection; but it will be unable to enforce encroachments against the united

---

(Hamilton,8)
It deserves the most serious and mature consideration of every prudent and honest man of whatever **party**. If such men will make a firm and solemn pause, and meditate dispassionately on the

---

(Hamilton,9)
A FIRM Union will be of the utmost moment to the peace and liberty of the States, as a barrier against domestic **faction** and insurrection. It is impossible to read the history of the petty

---

. . .

*Note*: The keywords 'party' and 'faction' are displayed by author and paper number.

Fig. 5.17 Keyword searches based on the *Federalist Papers*

Text retrieval systems are ideal for managing text corpora (the *Federalist Papers*, the collected works of Thomas Jefferson) and annotated bibliographies. Consequently, they are the stock and trade of commercial on-line database manufacturers whether they are providing on-line access to the British Library's catalogue or to recent editions of the *New York Times*. For the historian, they offer a means of organizing large quantities of machine-readable information, whether it consists of personal bibliographies, research notes, and lectures as described in Chapter 2, or the electronic texts used for analytical purposes, as described below.

## TEXT ANALYSIS

The line separating text retrieval systems and text analysis software is obscured in many places. Both require machine-readable texts whose structure is explicitly tagged with some descriptive mark-up language. Moreover, many text retrieval systems have some analytical facilities while text analysis software may support basic text management and retrieval. The principal difference is similar to that which distinguishes database management and statistical software. The latter provides a suite of analytical procedures while the former provides for data management. Because text analysis software differs so widely the analyses rather than their conduct in any particular package will form the focus here.[25]

### Content analysis

Content analysis is an obvious starting-point.[26] It is widely used by librarians automatically to classify texts based on the words they contain. Word frequencies, which show how many times selected words occur in a text or some part thereof, are central. Frequently occurring words are looked up in a computerized thesaurus, where they are associated with standard subject headings.

[25] For software-specific discussion and reviews see Lancashire, *Humanities Computing Yearbook, 1989/90*, 477–507; Spaeth, *A Guide to Software*, 73–82.

[26] Content analysis in literary and linguistic computing was already becoming well developed in the late 1950s. See I. de Sola Pool (ed.), *Trends in Content Analysis* (Urbana, Ill., 1959); O. Holsti, *Content Analysis for Social Science and Humanities Research* (Reading, Mass., 1969). For more up-to-date information see R. Weber, *Basic Content Analysis* (Newbury Park, Calif., 1990), the bibliography, section IIc; and Lancashire, *Humanities Computing Yearbook, 1989/90*, 489–97.

Content analysis is useful outside the library as well.[27] An analysis of the *Federalist Papers*, for example, shows that together 'party' and 'faction' occur 109 times in 41 of the 85 papers—results which might indicate to the uninitiated that the terms reflect a theme of some interest to Hamilton, Jay, and Madison. The distribution of these terms is also indicative. Figure 5.18 shows that uses of 'party' and 'faction' are particularly concentrated in *Federalist 10* (25 occurrences) and *Federalist 76* (10 occurrences), and to a lesser extent in *Federalist 9* and *Federalist 49* (5 occurrences in each). Without any prior knowledge about the *Federalist Papers* or an index to their contents, the reader interested in the subject of party and faction knows precisely where to turn. Arguably, the same conclusion and much more beside would result from a thorough reading of the *Federalist Papers*. But a thorough reading is not always practicable. Historians of public-health policy or of diplomacy in the late twentieth century, for example, already face a vast and growing quantity of poorly indexed (even unindexed) government and other documents which are only stored in machine-readable form. If the selective use of these documents has to depend upon browsing through them, research in several areas of contemporary history will grind to a halt.[28]

[27] For historical applications see T. F. Carney, 'Content Analysis: A Review Essay', *Historical Methods Newsletter*, 4 (1971), 52–61; R. L. Merritt, 'The Emergence of American Nationalism: A Quantitative Approach', *American Quarterly* (1965), 319–35; P. Dautrey, 'Les Déclarations des droits de l'homme: une approche quantitative', Centre National de la Recherche Scientifique, *L'Ordinateur et le métier d'historien. IVe Congrès 'History and Computing': volume des actes* (Bordeaux, 1990), 65–73; P. Tavernier, 'L'Héritage de 1789 et de 1848 dans la Déclaration universelle de 1948', in *Les Droits de l'homme et la conquête des libertés* (Grenoble, 1988); M. Olsen and L.-G. Harvey, 'Computers in Intellectual History: Lexical Statistics and the Analysis of Political Discourse', *Journal of Interdisciplinary History*, 18 (1988); M. Olsen, 'The Language of Enlightened Politics: The Société de 1789 in the French Revolution', *Computers and the Humanities*, 23 (1989), 357–64.

[28] See J. M. Clubb, 'Computer Technology and the Source Materials of Social History', *Social Science History*, 10 (1986), 97–114; D. I. Greenstein, 'Historians as Producers or Consumers of Standard-Conformant, Full-Text Datasets? Some Sources of Modern History as a Test Case', in Greenstein, *Modelling Historical Data*, 179–94; R. W. Zweig, 'Virtual Records and Real History', *History and Computing*, 4 (1992), 174–82.

---

Fig. 5.18 Distribution of the keywords 'party' and 'faction' in the *Federalist Papers*

| Federalist Paper Number | Occurrences of 'party' and 'faction' | Graph of distribution |
|---|---|---|
| 1 | 1 | X |
| 3 | 3 | XXX |
| 8 | 2 | XX |
| 9 | 5 | XXXXX |
| 10 | 25 | XXXXXXXXXXXXXXXXXXXXXXXXX |
| 14 | 1 | X |
| 15 | 1 | X |
| 16 | 2 | XX |
| 18 | 4 | XXXX |
| 19 | 2 | XX |
| 21 | 2 | XX |
| 22 | 2 | XX |
| 26 | 2 | XX |
| 27 | 2 | XX |
| 29 | 1 | X |
| 37 | 1 | X |
| 42 | 1 | X |
| 43 | 2 | XX |
| 46 | 1 | X |
| 49 | 5 | XXXXX |
| 50 | 3 | XXX |
| 51 | 3 | XXX |
| 55 | 1 | X |
| 59 | 1 | X |
| 61 | 2 | XX |
| 63 | 1 | X |
| 64 | 1 | X |
| 65 | 3 | XXX |
| 67 | 1 | X |
| 70 | 2 | XX |
| 71 | 1 | X |
| 73 | 2 | XX |
| 74 | 1 | X |
| 76 | 10 | XXXXXXXXXX |
| 78 | 1 | X |
| 79 | 1 | X |
| 80 | 3 | XXX |
| 81 | 4 | XXXX |
| 83 | 1 | X |
| 84 | 1 | X |
| 85 | 1 | X |

Total: 109

| a | 4059 | abridged | 5 |
|---|---|---|---|
| abandon | 5 | abridgements | 1 |
| abandoned | 3 | abridging | 1 |
| abandoning | 1 | abridgment | 5 |
| abate | 1 | abroad | 8 |
| abatements | 1 | abrogate | 1 |
| abetted | 2 | abrogating | 1 |
| abhorrence | 1 | absence | 1 |
| abilities | 8 | abservation | 1 |
| ability | 7 | absolute | 45 |
| abject | 1 | absolutely | 21 |
| able | 75 | absolves | 1 |
| ablest | 2 | absorb | 3 |
| abolish | 13 | absorbed | 2 |
| abolished | 11 | abstain | 3 |
| abolishing | 1 | abstained | 1 |
| abolition | 8 | abstract | 6 |
| abortive | 2 | abstracted | 2 |
| abounding | 1 | abstraction | 1 |
| abounds | 2 | abstruse | 1 |
| about | 26 | absurd | 10 |
| above | 14 | absurdities | 1 |
| abraham | 1 | absurdity | 8 |
| abridge | 6 | absurdly | 1 |

Fig. 5.19 Part of a global word-frequency list based on the *Federalist Papers*

With most text analysis and some text retrieval software word frequencies can be compiled for user-selected keywords like 'party' and/or 'faction'. Alternatively, global lists can be compiled showing the number of times each distinct word occurs in a text. Figure 5.19 shows the first several entries of a global word-frequency list prepared from the *Federalist Papers*. With global word frequencies, some software will permit the specification of so-called stop words, that is words which are excluded from the frequency list. High-frequency words such as 'a', 'and', and 'the' are often designated as stop words since they indicate little about the themes addressed in a particular text. Some text analysis software will come equipped with ready-made 'stop-word' lists which can be edited to suit particular analytical needs. More sophisticated packages compile word lists from words which sound alike or which share the same lemma. Thus the words 'abridge', 'abridged', 'abridgements', 'abridging', and 'abridgment', which are considered separately in Figure 5.19, could be treated as instances of the same lemma whose frequency would be given in a lemmatized list as 18.

## Concordances

Concordances are also used to examine a text's contents, but focus more explicitly on defining what particular words and phrases mean.[29] A concordance is not a statistical measure. Instead it is a means of reorganizing textual information to illuminate the contexts in which particular words are used.[30] Take the *Federalist Papers* again as an example. How and when parties met with at least grudging acceptance amongst leading political figures in the USA is still an issue which provokes some debate. Central to it is an understanding of the Founding Fathers' views on the subject. The concordance in Figure 5.20 shows the first few occurrences of the term 'faction' in Hamilton's contributions to the *Federalist Papers* and leaves us in little doubt as to his disdain for, indeed fear of, political combinations. Another concordance compiled from the *Federalist Papers* for the word 'American'

```
(8)            to suppress a small >faction, or an occasional mob,
(9)  a Safeguard Against Domestic >Faction and Insurrection | For
(9)    a barrier against domestic >faction and | insurrection. It
(9)          as well to suppress >faction and to guard the
(9)    Union to repress domestic >faction and insurrection. | A
...
```

*Note*: This Rendition shows the keyword 'faction' in *Papers* written by Hamilton. The keyword is displayed in context and by paper number.

Fig. 5.20 Concordance based on the *Federalist Papers*: Rendition 1

[29] Concordances antedate the computer age, having been compiled and used extensively by religious devotees determined to establish more precisely the exact meaning of sacred words attributed to God and his prophets. Thus, it should come as no surprise that the first computer-assisted research in a humanities discipline was that conducted by Father Busa who compiled concordances for the works of Thomas Aquinas. See S. Hockey, 'An Historical Perspective', in Rahtz, *Information Technology in the Humanities*, 22.
[30] S. Hockey, *A Guide to Computer Applications in the Humanities* (London, 1980), 41–9; Lancashire, *The Humanities Computing Yearbook, 1989/90*, 485.

is shown in Figure 5.21. It helps to assess whether leading proponents of the US Constitution felt or helped promote a distinctly American national identity. The result may suggest that Hamilton—amongst the most nationalistic of the Founding Fathers, according to some historians—only considered an American way of doing business. James Madison, on the other hand, may have had a very powerful sense of an American identity.

```
(Hamilton,11)       that may threaten their >American dominions
(Hamilton,11)           in favor of the >American trade,
(Hamilton,11)          the genius of the >American merchants
(Hamilton,11)          in the system of >American affairs.
(Hamilton,11)      in erecting one great >American system,
(Madison,14)           in the veins of >American citizens,
(Madison,14) innovations displayed on the >American theatre,
(Madison,18)      | Confederation of the >American States.
...
```

*Note*: This Rendition shows the keyword 'American' in *Papers* written by Hamilton and Madison. The keyword is displayed in context, in order of appearance in the text, and indicated by author and paper number.

Fig. 5.21 Concordance based on the *Federalist Papers*: Rendition 2

Procedures for compiling concordances differ from one text analysis package to another but may be described in general terms. A keyword or a list of keywords is selected as is the range of text for which the concordance is to be compiled. In the first of the two preceding examples 'faction' was chosen as the keyword and the *Federalist Papers* written by Hamilton as the range of text. In the second example, the selected keyword was changed to 'American' and the range of text extended to include papers written by Madison as well as Hamilton. Wherever it is possible to create a global concordance—that is, a concordance for all of the words occurring in a text—it also should be possible to create or tailor a stop-word list. Thesauri, lemmatization, and Soundex facilities may also be available.

Concordance procedures also should provide some control over the context in which the keyword is displayed. In Figures 5.20 and 5.22 the context is identical. The keyword, 'faction' is surrounded by four words on either side with a pipe (|) representing a line break and considered as the equivalent of one word. In Figure 5.21, the keyword 'American' is preceded by four words (or line breaks) and followed by one. The order in which occur-

rences are displayed also may be determined. Figures 5.20 and
5.21 show occurrences in the order that they appear in the text
of the *Federalist Papers*. This arrangement helps to indicate where
and how words tend to cluster. In Figure 5.22 occurrences are
ordered alphabetically by the context on the left of the keyword—
a method which may be more suited to the identification of
themes or grammatical elements (adjectives, nouns) which pre-
cede or follow the keyword. Finally, the user may specify the format in which each occurrence is displayed. Normally there are at
least two formats to choose between. 'Keyword in context'
(KWIC) shows the keyword surrounded by contextual information
as in Figures 5.20 to 5.22. 'Keyword out of context' (KWOC)
presents the keyword to the left or right of the contextual information.

```
(9)    a barrier against domestic >faction and | insurrection. It
(9) a Safeguard Against Domestic >Faction and Insurrection | For
(9)         as well to suppress >faction and to guard the
(8)         to suppress a small >faction, or an occasional mob,
(9)     Union to repress domestic >faction and insurrection. | A
...
```

*Note*: This Rendition shows the keyword 'faction' in *Papers* written by
Hamilton. The keyword is displayed in context, ordered alphabetically by
left-hand context, and indicated by paper number.

Fig. 5.22 Concordance based on the *Federalist Papers*: Rendition 3

### Collocate analysis

Collocate analysis, the analysis of word combinations, provides a
rather more quantitative measure of word usage. Here the aim is
to determine which of the words or collocates used in conjunction
with selected keywords are used principally or only in conjunction with those keywords. Figure 5.23 displays a partial result
of an analysis of the collocates used with 'party' and 'faction' in
the *Federalist Papers*. It reveals that 'pestilential' occurred only
twice in the entire text of the *Federalist Papers* (type frequency
equals 2), both times within five words of the keywords 'party'
or 'faction' (collocate frequency also equals 2). Intuitively, the
result does not seem a random or coincidental one: 'pestilential' is
clearly part of the authors' vocabulary, but one which is reserved
for use in combination with words indicating political combina-

| Collocates | Collocate Frequency | Type Frequency | Z-Score |
|---|---|---|---|
| minor | 4 | 6 | 21.900 |
| assaults | 2 | 2 | 19.018 |
| dislikes | 2 | 2 | 19.018 |
| likings | 2 | 2 | 19.018 |
| pestilential | 2 | 2 | 19.018 |
| suppress | 2 | 2 | 19.018 |
| governing | 3 | 6 | 16.380 |
| predominant | 3 | 6 | 16.380 |
| sedition | 3 | 6 | 16.380 |
| controlling | 2 | 3 | 15.486 |
| partialities | 2 | 3 | 15.486 |
| insurrection | 4 | 15 | 13.680 |
| antidote | 1 | 1 | 13.448 |
| associate | 1 | 1 | 13.448 |
| coloring | 1 | 1 | 13.448 |
| curing | 1 | 1 | 13.448 |
| demon | 1 | 1 | 13.448 |
| fountains | 1 | 1 | 13.448 |
| invented | 1 | 1 | 13.448 |
| outnumber | 1 | 1 | 13.448 |
| precipitancy | 1 | 1 | 13.448 |
| rays | 1 | 1 | 13.448 |
| rightful | 1 | 1 | 13.448 |
| sown | 1 | 1 | 13.448 |
| stimulate | 1 | 1 | 13.448 |
| waves | 1 | 1 | 13.448 |
| victories | 2 | 4 | 13.374 |
| victory | 2 | 4 | 13.374 |
| domestic | 5 | 30 | 11.940 |
| disease | 2 | 5 | 11.929 |
| major | 2 | 5 | 11.929 |
| removing | 2 | 5 | 11.929 |
| diseases | 2 | 6 | 10.860 |
| rage | 2 | 6 | 10.860 |
| uniting | 2 | 6 | 10.860 |

Fig. 5.23 Collocate analysis of the keywords 'party' and 'faction' in the *Federalist Papers*

tion. But how significant is this result? How can we compare the authors' use of pestilential with their use of 'insurrection', which occurs fifteen times in the *Federalist Papers* (type frequency) but only four times within five words of 'party' or 'faction' (collocate frequency). The so-called Z-score goes some way in providing an objective measure of the significance of any particular word combination. The measure is based upon three values: the number of times a collocate appears in a text, the number of times it appears in proximity to the keyword, and the span of words within which collocates are sought (in this case, within five words on either side of the keyword).[31] The higher the Z-score the less likely the collocate's appearance in proximity to the keyword is a random or coincidental one.

Procedures for conducting collocate analyses vary so much as to prohibit any but the most general description. Keywords and the span of words surrounding them within which the collocates will be sought, are selected by the user. Stop-word lists may be available to exclude selected words from consideration and it may be possible to determine the order in which collocates are displayed (i.e. in ascending or descending alphabetical, collocate frequency, type frequency, or Z-score order).

*Stylistic analysis*

Stylistic analyses also may prove useful in historical research. According to one scholar, they

normally aim at a statistical description of quantities, lengths, and types of affixes, inflections, words, parts-of-speech, phrases, clauses and sentences in a writer's work so as to discover either his or her 'fingerprint' or the subset of characteristics distinguishing it from that of other writers.[32]

Using a battery of so-called stylometric tests on different texts and comparing the results, literary scholars have attempted to identify the authorship of unattributed texts and to determine the

[31] See G. L. M. Berry-Rogghe, 'Computation of Collocations and their Relevance in Lexical Studies', in A. J. Aitken *et al.* (eds.), *The Computer and Literary Studies* (Edinburgh, 1972) and the very useful explanation in Olsen and Harvey, 'Computers in Intellectual History', 456–8.
[32] B. Brainerd *et al.*, 'Text Analysis', in Lancashire, *Humanities Computing Yearbook, 1989/90*, 500.

influence that different authors had on one another. The measures range from relatively simple calculations of average sentence and word length to more sophisticated measures of vocabulary size and richness. A selection of stylometric analyses of Hamilton's and Madison's vocabularies in their respective contributions to the *Federalist Papers* are shown in Figure 5.24. Briefly, the results suggest that Madison's vocabulary is slightly richer and larger than that of Hamilton's. The 'type/token ratio' which divides the vocabulary (number of distinct words or types) by the total number of words in the text (tokens) is slightly larger for Madison than for Hamilton.[33] Moreover, words or types which occur only once in Madison's papers contribute more towards his vocabulary (41.57 per cent) and towards the total number of words in his texts (3.4 per cent) than is the case for Hamilton, where the figures are 38.72 per cent and 2.39 per cent respectively. Another measure of the same phenomenon is given in the table's second column which calculates words' relative frequencies. There we see that each word which occurs only once contributes 0.144 per cent (given as 0.001444) to the total number of words in Madison's texts and only 0.085 per cent (given as 0.00085) to Hamilton's texts.[34]

Using these and other stylometric analyses literary scholars have developed descriptive measures for works from different genres (e.g. plays in prose, plays in verse, novels), different authors (e.g. Giraudoux, Hugo, Proust, and Chateaubriand), and from the same author but written at different periods (e.g. the collected works of Giraudoux). The measures are not purely descriptive. At least it is possible to build up for any one text a stylistic profile which allows that text to be compared with others, for example, to determine its authorship or trace its intellectual or literary heritage.[35] One needs to be careful, however. Many measures are extremely sensitive to a text's length (measured in number of

[33] Type/token ratios travel in the range between 0 and 1. The larger the ratio, the richer the vocabulary; that is, the more distinctive types occur within it.

[34] The statistic is calculated by dividing the frequency count (in this case 1 for words which occur once) by the total number of words considered in the text (in Madison's case 69,207 words). A percentage is then calculated by multiplying the result by 100.

[35] See J. Haynes, *Introducing Stylistics* (London, 1989); E. Brunet, 'What Do Statistics Tell Us?', in S. Hockey *et al.* (eds.), *Research in Humanities Computing 1* (Oxford, 1991), 70–92 and other works listed in the bibliography, section IIв2.

words) and to its subject content.[36] Longer texts and specialist texts prepared for expert audiences, for example, may have larger vocabularies than shorter texts and those written for general audiences. Genre, too, has an impact. A collection of newspaper articles and an autobiographical account all by the same author may differ considerably in their measurable style. Clearly, then, stylistic analyses are fallible and cannot provide positive identification of a text's authorship or literary heritage. They can contribute another kind of evidence which deserves consideration. Thus far, however, stylometric analyses have only benefited historical studies indirectly through work conducted in other disciplines. The disputed authorship of *Federalist 62* and *Federalist 63*, for example, was resolved through stylistic analyses conducted by statisticians.[37] Historians have also benefited from stylistic analyses conducted by those philosophers, theologians, and literary critics who have focused on works of historical interest.[38]

### Pitfalls and prospects of text analysis

With any of the techniques outlined above there are pitfalls which can and should be avoided. First, two software-related problems. The market for text analysis software is a queer and tricky one which reflects the very *ad hoc* way in which text analysis techniques have been developed and implemented as home-grown solutions to very local or particular problems. Consequently, the market is filled with *ad hominem* software much of which has been tailored to specific texts or analytical problems, and thus may be limited in its general applicability.[39] Text analysis packages have not yet, anyway, emulated statistical software

[36] For example, the type/token ratio calculated for Alexander Hamilton's total contribution to the *Federalist Papers* (117,036 words in all) was 0.07, but 0.38 when calculated on the basis of the 1,624 words in his *Federalist 1*.

[37] F. Mosteller and D. Wallace, *Inference and Disputed Authorship: The Federalist* (New York, 1964); and *Applied Bayesian and Classical Inference: The Case for 'The Federalist Papers'* (New York, 1984).

[38] Examples include A. J. P. Kenny, *The Aristotelian Ethics* (Oxford, 1974) and his *A Stylometric Study of the New Testament* (Oxford, 1987). For a comprehensive guide see J. J. Hughes, *Bits, Bytes & Biblical Studies: A Resource Guide for the Use of Computers in Biblical and Classical Studies* (Grand Rapids, Mich., 1987) and the sections on biblical studies, philosophy, and literary studies in Lancashire, *Humanities Computing Yearbook, 1989/90*, 18–31 and 194–380.

[39] For an example see H. Ehrlich and G. Vallasi, 'The James Joyce Text Machine', in Ross and Brink (eds.), *ACH/ALLC '91. 'Making Connections'*, 137–40.

## HAMILTON

| Freq. | Relative Frequency | Number Such | Words in Freq. | Vocab. Total | Word Total | % of Vocab. | % of Words | % of Words in Freq. |
|---|---|---|---|---|---|---|---|---|
| 1 | 0.00085 | 2794 | 2794 | 2794 | 2794 | 38.72 | 2.39 | 2.39 |
| 2 | 0.00171 | 1082 | 2164 | 3876 | 4958 | 53.71 | 4.23 | 1.85 |
| 3 | 0.00256 | 650 | 1950 | 4526 | 6908 | 62.72 | 5.90 | 1.67 |
| 4 | 0.00342 | 447 | 1788 | 4973 | 8696 | 68.92 | 7.43 | 1.53 |
| 5 | 0.00427 | 308 | 1540 | 5281 | 10236 | 73.18 | 8.74 | 1.32 |
| 6 | 0.00512 | 208 | 1248 | 5489 | 11484 | 76.07 | 9.81 | 1.07 |
| 7 | 0.00598 | 196 | 1372 | 5685 | 12856 | 78.78 | 10.98 | 1.17 |
| 8 | 0.00683 | 127 | 1016 | 5812 | 13872 | 80.54 | 11.85 | 0.87 |
| 9 | 0.00769 | 138 | 1242 | 5950 | 15114 | 82.46 | 12.91 | 1.06 |
| ⋮ | | | | | | | | |

## MADISON

| Freq. | Relative Frequency | Number Such | Words in Freq. | Vocab. Total | Word Total | % of Vocab. | % of Words | % of Words in Freq. |
|---|---|---|---|---|---|---|---|---|
| 1 | 0.00144 | 2356 | 2356 | 2356 | 2356 | 41.57 | 3.40 | 3.40 |
| 2 | 0.00289 | 956 | 1912 | 3312 | 4268 | 58.43 | 6.17 | 2.76 |

| | | | | | | | | |
|---|---|---|---|---|---|---|---|---|
| 3 | 0.00433 | 505 | 1515 | 3817 | 5783 | 67.34 | 8.36 | 2.19 |
| 4 | 0.00578 | 344 | 1376 | 4161 | 7159 | 73.41 | 10.34 | 1.99 |
| 5 | 0.00722 | 252 | 1260 | 4413 | 8419 | 77.86 | 12.16 | 1.82 |
| 6 | 0.00867 | 158 | 948 | 4571 | 9367 | 80.65 | 13.53 | 1.37 |
| 7 | 0.01011 | 118 | 826 | 4689 | 10193 | 82.73 | 14.73 | 1.19 |
| 8 | 0.01156 | 100 | 800 | 4789 | 10993 | 84.49 | 15.88 | 1.16 |
| 9 | 0.01300 | 86 | 774 | 4875 | 11767 | 86.01 | 17.00 | 1.12 |
| . . . | | | | | | | | |

| | HAMILTON | MADISON |
|---|---|---|
| TOTAL WORDS SELECTED (or 'tokens') | 117075 | 69207 |
| TOTAL VOCABULARY (distinct words or 'types') | 7216 | 5668 |
| TYPE/TOKEN RATIO | 0.06164 | 0.08190 |

*Note*: The tables show statistics for words which occur fewer than ten times.

Fig. 5.24 Stylistic analysis based on the *Federalist Papers*, comparing Madison's and Hamilton's respective contributions

by bundling together in one product a comprehensive range of measures and analytical procedures.[40] Anyone interested in textual analysis therefore will be well advised to select their software carefully ensuring that it caters to envisaged needs. Having selected the appropriate package, one must be careful not to be lulled into a false sense of security by the ease with which results can be produced. It is never enough simply to understand how to generate a particular result. One must also understand how the result has been derived and what it means with respect to the data upon which it is based.[41]

Marking up a machine-readable text is another possible stumbling block. As with text retrieval systems, text analysis software recognizes words and lines by default. Some will recognize paragraphs. Other text elements on which analyses might depend need to be tagged explicitly just as the machine-readable text of the *Federalist Papers* was tagged to distinguish papers from one another. Untagged elements cannot be analysed. Thus, a machine-readable version of a book tagged to distinguish page breaks in the original printed edition can be used to compile a word-frequency list for pages 16–20. It cannot be used to compile a word-frequency list for chapter 3. Similarly, analyses of where and how Hamilton, Jay, and Madison used classical and literary references cannot be conducted until the relevant literary references are explicitly tagged. The lesson is a simple one: before marking up a machine-readable text, consider what elements are likely to form the basis of analysis and/or retrieval. The exercise is similar to the design and definition of database fields. In both cases, recovering from mistakes made at an early stage can be costly, especially where lengthy machine-readable texts or large databases are concerned.

Ambiguities inherent in written language also pose problems. For a start, computers cannot yet, anyway, understand the meaning of words. They can only recognize distinctive character combinations which occur between spaces and/or punctuation. The problem, of course, is that in so many applications it is preferable to distinguish words by what they mean in context rather than

[40] See Ch. 4.

[41] Hockey, *A Guide to Computer Applications*, and A. J. P. Kenny, *The Computation of Style: An Introduction to Statistics for Students of Literature and Humanities* (Oxford, 1982) are very approachable guides. Others are listed in section IIB2 of the bibliography.

by their graphical representation. For instance, had the examples in this chapter been based on the autobiography of a prominent twentieth-century political figure and socialite rather than on the *Federalist Papers*, content analyses based on the word 'party' might have turned out somewhat differently. Though so-called disambiguation routines exist, none will distinguish between the different meanings of any one word with 100 per cent accuracy. Consequently, where analyses depend upon disambiguating homographs, they may require comprehensive text editing, for example, to change occurrences of 'party' to 'partya' and 'partyb' to indicate occurrences referring to social engagements and political combinations, respectively. The manual solution, too, has its problems especially with lengthy machine-readable texts or with texts where words are frequently used in a manner which is no clearer to the researcher than it is to the computer.[42] Ambiguity crops up as well where textual features have to be classified for analytical purposes, for example, where noun clauses and reductive idioms are tagged for stylistic analyses.[43] Identifying such features is at best a subjective exercise which can never be entirely above dispute and it is incumbent upon the researcher to provide comprehensive documentation explaining how classification schemes were derived and applied.

Despite these potential stumbling blocks, text analyses promise to open out onto new analytical horizons. Content and collocate analyses can bring new evidence to bear on questions currently answered with a battery of selected quotations. Did the evangelists of the Great Awakening introduce or borrow radical precepts about individuals' obligations to God and the community, respectively? Surely, important evidence might be produced by analysing the words and phrases used by the Awakeners to describe these obligations, the contexts in which such words and phrases occurred, and the stylistic characteristics of Awakeners and sixteenth-century dissenters. Similarly, systematic analyses of how the Founding Fathers in the USA used words such as 'people', 'leaders', and 'government' might provide a whole new dimension to a debate once actively engaged by Charles Beard

---

[42] N. M. Ide and J. Veronis, 'Caught in the Web of Words: Using Networks Generated from Dictionaries for Content Analysis', in Ross and Brink (eds.), *ACH/ALLC '91. 'Making Connections'*, 231–6.
[43] Hockey, *A Guide to Computer Applications*, 130–3.

about their political motivations.[44] The extent of Locke's influence over Jefferson or, more generally, traces of the Scottish enlightenment in American revolutionary thought might be investigated through stylistic analyses. Similarly, the genealogy of eighteenth-century American radicalism and its influence on American political discourse could be charted with stylistic and content analyses comparing revolutionary pamphlets with the tracts produced by nineteenth- and twentieth-century political parties and interest groups.[45]

Historians should also borrow from linguists who draw on word distributions, concordances, and collocate analyses to assess how the same language is used by different social and regional groups, and how different languages impinge on one another through the use of borrowed words.[46] In history these techniques can illuminate the relationship between immigration and the transmission of culture and values.[47] They can add as well to recent debate which concentrates on political discourse to determine the extent to which nineteenth-century working-class culture and politics were developed autonomously of bourgeois influence.[48] Admittedly there will be problems. Modern linguists collect data about word usage through surveys and interviews; methods not, on the whole, available to the historian. None the less, it is possible to compile machine-readable linguistic corpora

[44] C. Beard, *An Economic Interpretation of the Constitution of the United States* (New York, 1913).

[45] See for example the discussion in S. Srinivasan, 'Style in Syntax: A Computer Aided Quantitative Study', in S. Lusignan and J. S. North (eds.), *Computing in the Humanities: Proceedings of the Third International Conference on Computing in the Humanities* (Waterloo, Ont., 1977), 85–97. Also see Olsen and Harvey, 'Computers in Intellectual History'.

[46] Hockey, *A Guide to Computer Applications*, 79–84; J. Kirk, 'Word Maps of East Central Scots: A Computerised Package', in A. Fenton (ed.), *Third International Conference on the Languages of Scotland, Edinburgh. 25–27 July 1991* (forthcoming); J. Kirk and G. Munroe, 'A Method for Dialectometry', *Journal of English Linguistics*, 22 (1989), 97–110; J. Kirk, G. Munroe, and M. D. J. O'Kane, 'Electronic Word Maps', in S. Hockey and N. Ide, (eds.), *Research in Humanities Computing 2* (forthcoming).

[47] There may be especial need for such work in immigration history, particularly now as the debate about immigration and cultural transmission has been reopened with respect to the peopling of British North America. See D. H. Fischer, *Albion's Seed: Four British Folkways in America* (Oxford, 1989).

[48] O. Smith, *The Politics of Language, 1791–1819* (Oxford, 1989), and G. Stedman Jones, 'Rethinking Chartism', in G. Stedman Jones (ed.), *The Languages of Class: Studies in English Working-Class History, 1832–1982* (Cambridge, 1983), 90–178.

comprising samples from hundreds or even thousands of extant texts likely to indicate common word usage (personal papers, autobiographies, popular fiction, newspapers, and plays taken from different regions of any country where a national language predominates). Here, folklorists who transcribe orally transmitted songs, stories, and plays might point a way forward.[49]

In sum, as far as applying computer-aided text analysis to historical research is concerned, virtually everything remains to be borrowed and tried. But there is at least one reason more compelling than intellectual curiosity which will in time force a migration amongst some historians, anyway, towards text retrieval and analysis software. That is, the increasing volume of historical information which is only available and accessible in machine-readable form. This will be central to the history of the late twentieth century—a history which will remain beyond the grasp of anyone unwilling to branch out and try new methods of handling traditional historical material—that is, texts.

---

[49] M. J. Preston, 'Solutions to Classic Problems in the Study of Oral Literature', in Lusignan and North, *Computing in the Humanities*, 117–32.

# 6

## Putting It All Together

CAREFUL preparation and design is the key to successful computer-aided projects, especially where the projects are expected to
be costly, time consuming, and labour intensive. Care needs to be
taken with simpler tasks as well. Nothing is more soul-destroying
than discovering that machine-readable data lovingly prepared
over several hours (or worse, months) will not support the desired
analyses or printed presentation owing to a project-design flaw. In
an effort to direct researchers away from potential pitfalls, this
chapter offers an eight-step guide to the design of computer-aided
work.

### CONDUCT A COST–BENEFIT ANALYSIS

Surely the first consideration is whether the results promised by a
computer-aided project justify the cost involved in mounting it.
The cost is not just the financial one incurred acquiring hardware, software, and in some instances research and clerical assistance. It also involves the time spent crawling up new learning
curves as each stage of a project is begun. Software packages
have to be mastered, sampling techniques considered even if not
applied, statistical measures investigated, and innumerable procedures from record linkage to data classification learned. So when
do the ends justify the computational means? There is no
definitive answer to this question; only two further questions
which should be considered before even looking at a computer
keyboard.

First, is the desired result likely to be found somewhere in the
extant archival record? Weeks and even months can be wasted
computerizing census-like data to estimate the population of an
eighteenth-century town, for example, when a perfectly reliable
estimate is available in some primary or secondary source.

Secondly, does the computer offer the most efficient means of obtaining the desired result? The answer to this question will depend on the amount of information involved and the number of manipulations envisaged for it. A researcher interested in a very basic social profile of Glasgow's nearly 600 nineteenth-century city councilmen, for example, might achieve results more quickly by storing biographical data on note cards and manually compiling the required frequency distributions and cross-tabulations by reshuffling and recounting the cards for each quantitative result. Similarly, a bibliography which is being prepared for publication but not for future selective retrievals is probably not worth entering into a full-text retrieval or bibliographic package. There is no fixed rule of thumb that can be applied to determine when a project is worth computerizing. Still, it is possible to estimate the value of a computerized project in terms of its intellectual contribution, its financial cost, and the time it will take to conduct. Once made, these calculations can be weighed up against the costs incurred by acquiring the same result manually or not at all. Irrespective of the outcome, it will always be worth spending the time necessary to make these calculations as carefully and as precisely as possible.

### CRITICIZE THE SOURCE

Source criticism is particularly important for computer-aided research. Do the intended sources give an accurate account of the phenomena under investigation? The most detailed and comprehensive eighteenth-century port book, for example, may be irreparably corrupted by merchants' attempts to avoid an excise. This does not mean that inaccurate sources must be rejected. Robert Fogel has argued convincingly that sensitivity to one's data and a competence in statistical method can correct for biases found in some of the most distorted sources.[1] None the less, 'Garbage In, Garbage Out' is a well-worn phrase which is worth remembering at the early stages of a computer-aided investigation.[2]

[1] R. W. Fogel, 'The New History: Its Findings and Methods', in D. K. Rowney and J. Q. Graham, Jr. (eds.), *Quantitative History* (Homewood, Ill., 1969), 320–5.
[2] See L. Stone, 'History and the Social Sciences', in L. Stone, *The Past and the Present* (Boston, 1981), 33.

Even where a source's data are reliable they may be too ambiguous to measure confidently. In a reliable manufacturing census, for example, the number of employees given for a firm might be '5 to 8'. The value may be beyond dispute but it is not easily represented in a database, spreadsheet, or statistical package. Nor is it easy to analyse. Marginalia and glosses are another source of ambiguity. How does one interpret entries on the manufacturing census manuscript which appear to be scored out in a hand other than that of the enumerator, or a marginal comment which reads 'figures are low due to hard winter'? Where a large proportion of the data are ambiguous, their computerized manipulation and analysis may produce worthless results.

Consistency in a serial source is another problem where trend data are required. The information sought by census takers in the UK and in the USA, for example, changed over time making some trend data impossible to reconstruct. In the UK the occupational data gathered by census takers changed dramatically during the nineteenth century while in the USA census takers continually refined and changed the categories used to take account of the foreign-born population. It is also essential to evaluate every source in light of the historical questions on which it will be brought to bear. Too often, it is tempting to computerize data which are readily available but only tangentially related to the central aims of research. In the Oxford study, for example, a rich and accurate record of matriculants' preliminary examinations (as opposed to their final honours examinations) was ignored. It promised to illuminate various routes to an Oxford degree which were intrinsically interesting but not particularly helpful in a study of matriculants' social origins and career destinations.


PLUNDER DATA ARCHIVES

Clearly, the best possible source is one which is relevant, accurate, unambiguous, and already available in machine-readable form. Admittedly the prospects of discovering machine-readable information relevant to a study of Byzantine town planning or of the Scottish Enlightenment and its impact on revolutionary thought in the American colonies may seem quite remote. Still, it is worth remembering that computer-aided historical, literary, and linguistic investigations have been conducted now for almost thirty years, and the machine-readable results of many of these projects will be on deposit in data and text archives. Though a union catalogue of machine-readable holdings does not yet exist, a thorough review of the available data is both possible and worthwhile. At best it can eliminate the need for time-consuming and costly data entry. A study of US party development during the era of Reconstruction (1865–76), for example, might rely entirely on election returns data held by the Inter-University Consortium for Political and Social Research.[3] A more likely result will be the discovery of a machine-readable subset of the information that is ultimately required in a particular research project, or information that will prove useful for comparative purposes.

The search for machine-readable material will be guided in part by the kind of data that are required. Machine-readable texts, the *Federalist Papers* or the collected works of Milton, for example, will be found in text archives. Highly structured data, the like of which emanate from databases and/or statistical projects, are stored in social-science data archives. The names and addresses of some of the major data and text archives are given in the bibliography.[4]

SAMPLE WHERE NECESSARY

*General considerations*

Whether or not the relevant data are already available in machine-readable form, the researcher will want to consider the extent to which they are representative of the phenomena under investigation. So-called sampling is almost always a consideration in computer-aided historical research, even where there is a scarcity of information about the phenomena being investigated.[5]

[3] See bibliography, section IIIʙ1.     [4] See bibliography, section IIIʙ.
[5] For much of the discussion I am indebted to Hamish Maxwell-Stewart's fine unpublished paper, 'Sampling Design and Data Interpretation' delivered to Glasgow University's History and Computing Seminar Series, February 1992. Useful introductions include R. S. Schofield's 'Sampling in Historical Research', in E. A. Wrigley (ed.), *Nineteenth-Century Society: Essays in the Use of Quantitative Methods for the Study of Social Data* (Cambridge, 1972), 146–90; K. H. Jarausch

Take, for example, a study of criminal justice in eighteenth-century England based on scarce court records.[6] Are the court proceedings for which records exist representative of all such proceedings including those for which records have not survived? Here a sample has effectively been chosen for the researcher by the ravages of time. Sampling also may be forced on a project which uses sample data from a text or data archive.

More frequently, sampling is forced onto the historian because the extant record is too voluminous to computerize in its entirety. Economy is not the sole justification for sampling, however. Accurate measures of a given phenomenon do not require that every instance of that phenomenon or case be investigated, just as it is unnecessary to drink an entire bottle of wine in order to appreciate its taste, colour, and aroma. According to one textbook for would-be quantitative historians: 'statistical accuracy changes little after a certain sample size has been reached . . . Additional cases yield minimal error reduction, while the effort required to improve results further will increase exponentially'.[7] The question then is twofold: how to draw a sample without bias, and what is the optimum sample size for any given project which will yield the most accurate (that is representative) results for the minimum expenditure? The first question involves technique, the second, statistical expertise mixed with a touch of witchcraft.

Before either can be evaluated in any detail, a few definitions are required. First, the statistician talks about the 'sampling universe', that is, the total number of cases that could be examined. In the Oxford study, the universe included every matriculant in the period 1900–70. In a study of eighteenth-century English criminal justice, the universe includes every court proceeding in the relevant period. Defining the sampling universe is important at two levels. First, it forces an investigation to define its aims and the phenomena undergoing investigation. A collective biography

and K. A. Hardy, *Quantitative Methods for Historians* (London, 1991), Ch. 4. More comprehensive texts include W. E. Deming, *Some Theory of Sampling* (New York, 1950); R. Parsons, *Statistical Analysis: A Decision-Making Approach* (New York, 1974); W. G. Cochran, *Sampling Techniques*, 2nd edn. (New York, 1973). For other texts see S. R. Grossbart, 'Quantification and Social Science Methods for Historians: An Annotated Bibliography of Selected Books and Articles', *Historical Methods*, 25 (1992), 108–9.

[6] See D. A. Spaeth, 'Court Records and their Structures', in D. I. Greenstein (ed.), *Modelling Historical Data* (St Katharinen, 1991), 129–46.

[7] Jarausch and Hardy, *Quantitative Methods*, 68.

of political élites, for example, can only begin estimating the sampling universe by defining precisely what is meant by 'political élites'. Secondly, defining the sampling universe focuses an investigation on a particular set of records or source materials. The exercise is not always straightforward. With the Oxford data it was possible to estimate the total population of Oxford members, 1900–70, since basic information about every matriculant was readily to hand (e.g. name, year, and college at matriculation). In other cases, however, establishing the sampling universe may be more of an art than a science involving educated guesses, for example about the number and regional distribution of court proceedings in eighteenth-century England.

The statistician also refers to the 'sampling frame', or those cases in the sampling universe from which the sample is derived. In the Oxford study, the frame and the universe were identical; for every matriculant there was at least some information. In the study of eighteenth-century criminal justice, the universe and frame are different. The frame comprises only those court proceedings for which records exist. The universe, on the other hand, comprises all such proceedings whether records of them exist or not. Where the frame and the universe are different, it is important to know the relationship between them in order to assess the representativeness of any results obtained from the sample data. Pollsters' failure accurately to predict the 1932 US presidential election was partly due to the fact that the sampling frame drawn from city directories and car registration lists was at odds with the universe of potential voters in a way which biased the frame in favour of pro-Landon (Republican) voters. Clearly, where the sampling frame is contingent upon patchy evidence, as is the case with the eighteenth-century English court records, the relationship between the sampling frame and the sampling universe will be somewhat impressionistic.

## Sampling techniques

### 1. *Random Sampling*

Once the sampling frame is assembled, it is imperative to choose the technique which will select from it an unbiased sample or collection of cases. Random sampling is the most common technique. Here, each case in the frame has the exact same probability of being chosen for inclusion in the sample as any other. Random samples are taken by assigning a unique sequential number to every case in the sampling frame. When the sample size is known, the sample is populated with cases whose numbers are chosen at random. Take as an example, the study of early nineteenth-century transported British convicts that was referred to in Chapter 3.[8] A random sample of convicts could be produced by assigning a unique number to every one of the nearly 160,000 convicts, 1788–1853, whose biographical characteristics and offences are recorded in the *Convict Description* and *Colonial Offence Registers*. If a 1 per cent sample was deemed appropriate, then 1,600 numbers would be chosen at random from the range 1 to 160,000. The numbers could be selected from published tables of random numbers or with the aid of computer programs which produce random numbers to order (so-called random-number generators). One problem with random sampling is that it is not always practicable to administer. Imagine assigning a unique sequential number to the 160,000 convicts described in the colonial records just to select the 1 per cent random sample!

### 2. Systematic and cluster sampling

Systematic sampling can be more efficient than random sampling. Here, every *n*th case is taken from the sampling frame, where *n* is a value which when multiplied by the number of records in the sample produces the total number of cases in the sampling frame. Systematic sampling is most appropriate where information about cases is stored on discrete note cards, manuscript pages, or in individual folders or boxes.[9] Say, for example, that the historian interested in nineteenth-century poverty discovers an almshouse's admission records kept on large note cards arranged in file boxes by date of admission. A 3 per cent sample of these might be used to document the social composition of almshouse residents and

---

[8] See Ch. 3, pp. 74–80.

[9] The sampling technique adopted in Philip Taylor's study of the work-force at the electrical engineering firm of Mavor and Coulson is exemplary. The sampling frame consisted of the company's employee record cards kept for the period 1890–1931 in an alphabetically arranged card file. See P. Taylor, 'Management, Workforce and Community: Mavor and Coulson, 1896–1931' (Glasgow University M.Phil. thesis, 1990), Ch. 1.

the reasons for their admission. The sample could be compiled by taking every thirty-third note card. The problem here, is that any periodic variation would bias the sample. The sample would never pick up block admissions to the poor-house, for example, of families or of kin groups who applied and were admitted together.

Cluster sampling may in some cases make up for the shortcomings inherent in systematic sampling. Here, the researcher identifies whole areas or clusters within the data and takes the sample from them. Something approximating the same 3 per cent sample of poorhouse admissions could be compiled from records pertaining to those people who were admitted to the poorhouse on the first Saturday of every month in the period covered by the study. The problem here is that the chosen cluster or clusters may be unrepresentative. Saturday admissions might include more young, single, and intoxicated males than normal.

In some instances, it is appropriate to combine cluster and systematic or random sampling. A study based on city directories or other alphabetical lists of named individuals might take every *n*th person whose surname begins with the letter L or G. Letter-cluster sampling is especially useful where a project links nominal records found in two or more alphabetically arranged sources. It is only ever necessary to look through the Ls and the Gs in each source.[10] In some cases, however, letter-cluster sampling can prove disastrous. A demographic study of Liverpool which missed out people whose names begin with O and M would, for example, underrepresent the city's sizeable ethnic Irish and Scottish populations.

### 3. *Stratified sampling*

Finally stratified sampling may be necessary where small subgroups or strata exist within the sampling frame about which the researcher wants to know more and for which any of the other sampling techniques thus far described would produce too few

[10] S. Nenadic, 'The Structure, Values and Influence of the Scottish Urban Middle Class: Glasgow 1800–1870' (Glasgow University Ph.D. thesis, 1986), Appendix 6.2 and her 'Record Linkage and the Exploration of Nineteenth-Century Social Groups: A Methodological Perspective on the Glasgow Middle Class in 1861', *Urban History Yearbook* (Leicester, 1987), 32–43. Also see J. A. Phillips, 'Achieving a Critical Mass While Avoiding an Explosion: Letter Cluster Sampling and Nominal Record Linkage', *Journal of Interdisciplinary History*, 9 (1979), 493–508.

cases to sustain much in the way of analysis. This was the case
with the Oxford data. There, women contributed about 1,300 or
10 per cent to Oxford's total intake in the period 1900–13. Only
4.7 per cent of these women (61), that is 0.47 per cent of the
entire male and female intake, read science subjects. Random,
systematic, and cluster-sampling techniques designed to produce a
10 per cent sample of the entire intake would have added only
six women scientists to the sample for the period 1900–13. The
number is far too small to sustain much in the way of analysis.
Imagine a frequency distribution showing women scientists' final
examination results. The six cases would be spread over the four
examination classes. Imagine still further a joint-frequency distribution comparing women's educational backgrounds (in two categories, one each for maintained and independent schools), with
their examination results. Here the analysis would produce a
cross-tabulation with eight cells and the six cases distributed
amongst them.[11] The problem with both analyses is that as the
values observed in the cells of frequency and joint-frequency distributions decline, so does the probability that the result is meaningful or representative. The stratified sample overcomes this
problem by taking a larger proportion from smaller subgroups
than their contribution to the overall sampling frame would otherwise allow. In the Oxford study, all of the 61 women scientists
(100 per cent) were taken for the period 1900–13 compared to
10 per cent of all women arts undergraduates in the same period.
The method, however, complicates statistical analyses as the correct proportions have to be restored in the sample by weighting—
in this case, women arts students 1900–13, had to be weighted
by a factor of 10.[12]

### Sample size

Sample size is another issue which needs to be taken into account
and here, alas, there is no simple formula. There are two problems. First, ensuring that any one analysis involves enough observations to yield statistically meaningful results, and secondly that

---

[11] A similar analysis of Oxford men, 1900–39, is presented in Ch. 4, Figures
4.7 and 4.11.
[12] Each woman arts undergraduate counted as 10 in analyses while science
undergraduates counted as 1.

the results are representative of the whole population. The first of these problems can be addressed to some extent by considering early on how data will be analysed and the number of observations required to ensure confidence in any particular result. Where frequency and joint-frequency distributions are required, for example, the sample size should be determined to a certain extent by the number of cells in the envisaged cross-tabulations. Very generally speaking one wants to avoid frequency and joint-frequency distributions where 25 per cent or more of the observations are smaller than five. Clearly, considerations of this sort ramify for how data are categorized for analysis. A social mobility study involving 100 cases would be prudent to adopt an occupational classification scheme with five as opposed to sixty categories.

The second problem involving representativeness can be addressed in a rather more objective manner with statistical measures which show how results obtained from a sample vary from those expected from the whole population. It is on the basis of such measures that pollsters qualify their results by saying they are accurate to within plus or minus so many per cent. At the end of the day, however, sampling considerations will normally be determined by material constraints—a fact which is not easily disguised beneath technical jargon. According to Christian Johnson,

the overall selection of a sample design is governed by the comparative ratio of the variance characteristics of alternative designs to the cost of executing the sample design. In short, the goal is to obtain a probability sample with low variance for one's sampling dollar.[13]

### Sampling for textual analysis

Sampling is also important for textual analyses. How many and which eighteenth-century texts should be included in a study of an emerging American identity as apparent in anti-British broadsheets and published sermons from the period 1750–76? Which of Thomas Jefferson's works are sufficiently representative of his entire output to build up a stylistic profile and assess his influence

[13] R. C. Johnson, 'A Procedure for Sampling the Manuscript Census', *Journal of Interdisciplinary History*, 8 (1978), 515–30.

over later American political thinkers? In both cases it is necessary to define the sampling universe and the sampling frame. For
the Jefferson study, the sampling universe includes all texts,
extant or otherwise, written by Jefferson. The sampling frame
includes the subset of texts written by Jefferson from which the
sample will be drawn. It is also necessary to determine the sample
size. How many words written by Jefferson will be involved in the
study and from which texts will they be drawn? The sample size
may be determined in part with the aid of statistical measures
designed to estimate a sample's representativeness. But here as
elsewhere, sampling may be more of an art than a science. No
measure will determine beyond dispute that Cobbett's collected
works, for example, are representative of working-class political
sentiment in 1830s Britain. Nor will any measure determine
whether it is better to take 1,000 words from each of Jefferson's
known works or a small number of very lengthy works in their
entirety. Such questions can only be answered with reference to
the analytical aims of a project and the funding available to it.[14]

## SELECT THE RIGHT HARDWARE AND SOFTWARE

Computer hardware and software will be chosen only after the
source material and the sampling techniques are settled. In the
ideal world, the choices will be made freely. In fact they tend to
be constrained by what is available locally in the way of hardware and software, but also in the way of expertise and potential
support. Still, some guidance may be offered.

### Hardware

With hardware, the range of computers currently available on
the market is so great and functionality, power, and price so
much in flux as to mitigate against any but the most general discussion. It is worthwhile distinguishing two different computer
platforms: desktop computers (for example PCs or Macs) and computers to which desktops are linked via a network (so-called

---

[14] For information on sampling for textual analysis see A. J. Kenny, *The Computation of Style* (Oxford, 1982); C. Müller, *Initiation aux méthodes de la statistique* (Paris, 1979) and his *Principes et méthodes de statistique lexicale* (Paris, 1977).

'servers'). Servers are simply more powerful computers whose filestore, software, and processing power can be shared by several desktops simultaneously.[15] Obviously there is no clear distinction between desktops and servers. Well-funded organizations and individuals may purchase and use as stand-alone desktops computers which in other contexts act as servers for upwards of 100 or more users. Nor are these platforms mutually exclusive. When a desktop is linked to a more powerful server, it can be used as a stand-alone machine drawing exclusively on its filestore, processing power, and software, and/or as a terminal logged onto the server.

## 1. *Desktop computers*

In selecting the most appropriate platform, the researcher will normally want to weigh up the convenience of a desktop against the processing power and filestore available on a server. Affordable desktops are becoming sufficiently powerful to handle many if not most historical research projects. Moreover, as the dual trend of declining price and increasing power continues apace, more software has migrated to desktops and users have followed suit. Thus, database, statistical, and text retrieval software which was once only available on powerful servers is now readily available for the desktop.

A desktop computer's suitability to a project will depend almost entirely on three specifications including filestore, RAM, and processing capacity. Filestore—measured in terms of the space (in megabytes) available to store machine-readable information permanently—needs to accommodate a project's data and its software. RAM or 'random access memory' is also measured in megabytes and refers to the computer's electric memory into which software (and sometimes, data) is loaded when it is in use. The machine's RAM must be large enough to accommodate the project's software. Finally, processing power needs to be considered. This is measured in terms of the amount of information that can be processed by the computer in a given period of time. A desktop may have the filestore to accommodate relatively large data files and the RAM to accommodate sophisticated software packages but insufficient processing power to support extensive

---

[15] See Ch. 2, pp. 51–2.

text-searching or complex database commands. To determine whether a particular desktop will meet a project's requirements it is worth consulting a local expert taking care to outline the amount and kind of data involved and the kinds of computer processing—statistical, textual, database—that will be required.

Where desktop computers are used, the researcher will enjoy the privilege of free and easy computer access outside normal social hours; an advantage shared by laptop and portable computers as they catch up to desktops in their power, filestore, and speed. Problems with desktops occur when they have too little or too much computing power for the task to hand. Where desktops have too little power, the advantages of unrestricted access are outweighed by the necessity of having to wait several minutes and more to execute routine tasks. Where desktops are too powerful, their use can require a modicum of expertise or dependence on support staff, neither of which may be readily available.

*2. Shared servers*

Projects involving the management and manipulation of large quantities of data may require the filestore and processing power of a shared server. Similarly, projects where two or more researchers need simultaneous access to the same data will also want to consider servers. The server's disadvantage is that its use may incur a degree of dependence on shared facilities which constrains a project's conduct. For example, a project's choice of software might be constrained by what is available on a shared server irrespective of whether or not it is suited to the project's processing aims. Secondly, users compete for server resources—filestore, processing power, access to shared terminals—in a way which might inhibit a project's progress. Network traffic, like automobile traffic, tends to have peak periods. During these periods, communications and server responses can slow down considerably. Network failures are more unpredictable and more harmful to a project than network traffic because all server connections are terminated until the underlying faults are identified and corrected. Whatever platform is chosen, it is worth remembering that the decision is not irreversible. Normally it will be possible, in some cases even preferable, to move projects between computer platforms and/or to use several platforms. Projects which construct large-scale databases, for example, may enter data onto laptop computers which are taken from archive to archive, and later load these data into databases stored on desktops or shared servers.

## *Software*

Software decisions should be guided by a project's data management and analytical aims. At this level the decision is not between brand names but between different types of software or processing applications: spreadsheets, statistical packages, database management systems, free-text retrieval systems, text analysis software, word processors, line editors, and so on. The researcher interested in compiling concordances needs to know first that a spreadsheet is not the appropriate tool before shopping around for a particular product. At a secondary level, the selection of a particular brand name will be related at least in part to decisions about what computer to adopt. Where the project requires a statistical package and has opted to use a server, it will probably be constrained by the statistical software that is already available thereon. Thus a project might opt for the statistical package *SPSSx* over *SAS* simply because *SPSSx* is available on the shared server and *SAS* is not. Where a desktop is used the software choice will be constrained by what is available for that particular machine. For example, some software can only run on a Mac or on a PC. Another constraint is that a software package implemented on a desktop may not have the same range of functions available with the same package implemented on a more powerful computer. Thus, *SPSS-PC*, a statistical package available for PCs, has nowhere near the same range of data manipulation, graphical, and statistical facilities available with *SPSSx*, a version of the same software designed for more powerful computers.

Finally, it is prudent to choose software for which help is obtainable either from a local computing service or informally from colleagues with some experience. No manual or textbook will ever be as effective in helping a user come to terms with a particular product as personal tuition, live demonstrations, and an informal network of users through which useful tips, techniques, and shortcuts are disseminated. However the software and hardware selections are made, they should not be implemented without first conducting extensive pilot investigations designed to

test whether and how well different products meet a project's
requirements.[16]

## MODEL DATA

With the sources assembled and the hardware and software to
hand, it is necessary to give considerable thought to how the data
should be modelled, that is, how they should be structured and
represented in machine-readable form.[17] With databases and statistical packages modelling involves defining what tables are
required and their respective field structure. The correct model is
that which meets a project's data management and analytical
aims. For example, a project which requires retrieval and/or
analysis of geographical information by township as well as by
state and country will not enter the string 'Rochester, NY, USA'
into one field, but into three separate fields as follows:

| Town/city | State | Country |
| --- | --- | --- |
| Rochester | NY | USA |

...

With text retrieval and analysis, documents and elements need to
be identified and marked up, and here too, management and analytical aims must be determinate. Data also need to be modelled
with spreadsheets and word processors. Here the relative orienta-
tion of data displayed on the computer screen and/or on the
printed page is often of principal importance. On a spreadsheet of
municipal finance data, for example, the researcher might be
advised to emulate double-entry bookkeeping by separating
expenditures from receipts. In a word-processed article for a
learned journal, new paragraphs might begin with an extra blank
line and indented, and notes placed at the end of the document
rather than at the bottom of the page.

Data modelling will impinge greatly on a project's success. The

[16] See pp. 234–7.

[17] Data modelling is a recurring theme in this book. For more formal treatment
see Greenstein, *Modelling Historical Data*, and the general discussion in
T. Schijvenaars, 'Datamodelling of Sources in Dutch Historical Research Projects'
(Unpublished pamphlet, Department of Computer & Letteren, Faculty of Arts,
University of Utrecht, 1993), 3–21.

theme is a recurrent one, and preceding chapters have warned that mistakes made when modelling data may be expensive or even impossible to correct later on. Consequently, the researcher is advised to pilot or test a particular data model with a small amount of data. Enter ten or fifty records into a database or statistical package, a few short documents into a text analysis or text retrieval system, a sample portion of data into a spreadsheet. See if the data can be manipulated, analysed, graphed, and/or printed in the manner envisaged for the project irrespective of whether the results based on so few records are meaningful. If the model does not work with a fraction of the data, its failure will be spectacular when all the data are entered.

In reality, a project's analytical aims, its software, and its data modelling cannot be considered as independently as the preceding sections suggest—the three design stages are inextricably related. Ideally, the project's aims should determine its data model, and both its aims and data model should in turn direct software selection. A collective biography of French revolutionaries which models individual life histories as a sequence of one-to-many relationships connecting individuals to their educational experiences, jobs, familial relations, and the like, will require a multi-table database. Where scientific notation is required in printed documents, appropriate word processors or text formatters have to be chosen. Likewise, where text analysis or retrieval relies upon documents structured to comprise several layers of nested elements (e.g. the *Federalist Papers* structured as individual documents each with a text body comprising a preamble and a conclusion), software capable of recognizing hierarchical structures is required.

Unfortunately, one often finds that the best data model is rarely supported by the software product which offers the requisite analytical or processing facilities. There is no shortage of multi-table databases capable of managing the collective biography described above. Few furnish a datatype to handle dates from the French revolutionary calendar, however. Likewise, the text-formatting software which provides scientific notation may not support the nested footnotes which a formatted document requires. And the text-analysis package which comprehends a hierarchical model of the *Federalist Papers* may not offer the required analytical procedures. In all such cases, the user is advised to select the software which demands the least amount of compromise in how data are modelled and/or analysed. Still some compromise will probably be required in most projects. French revolutionary calendar dates may have to be translated into their Gregorian equivalents. Nested footnotes or scientific notation might have to be abandoned from a formatted document. And the *Federalist Papers* might have to be split up into three separate files—one each for the contributions of Madison, Hamilton, and Jay—in order to analyse the semantic content of the authors' respective preambles.

## ENTER DATA ACCURATELY

Data entry is treated at length here because of its critical importance to any project. It will absorb the lion's share of a project's costs wherever extant machine-readable data are unavailable for secondary analysis, or where such data can only contribute a fraction of those being collected and computerized. Planning ahead and planning carefully can yield significant economies. Moreover the reliability of a project's eventual results will be directly related to the accuracy with which data are transcribed from the printed or manuscript record to a machine-readable form. Data entry strategies will be contingent on the software and sources being used. None the less, they may be considered very generally under three heads: interactive data entry where data are entered directly into a software package; data exchange where data are exported from one software package into another; and scanning data with an optical character reader.

### Interactive data entry

Most software provides facilities for entering and editing data onto forms whose structure can be tailored to reflect the user's data model. With word processors the form looks like a printed page. Its dimensions (length, width, margins) and the format of the text entered onto it can all be determined. Spreadsheet forms look like matrices comprising cells organized into numbered rows and lettered columns. Cells can be chosen and used in any combination and the data entered into them can be formatted as appropriate. With databases and statistical packages, forms look like tables as

DATA ENTRY FORM FOR THE GORBALS DATABASE TABLE

| HNo | PNo | Surname | Forename | Address | Relation | Sex | Age | Occupation | TBirth | Rooms | HSize |
|-----|-----|---------|----------|---------|----------|-----|-----|------------|--------|-------|-------|
| 1 | 1 | Fletcher | John | 28 Norfolk St | Head | M | 28 | Ironworker | Ayr | 3 | 4 |
| 1 | 2 | Fletcher | Eliza | 28 Norfolk St | Wife | F | 28 | Seamstress | Edinburgh | 3 | 4 |
| 1 | 3 | Fletcher | John | 28 Norfolk St | Son | M | 8 | Scholar | Glasgow | 3 | 4 |
| 1 | 4 | Fletcher | James | 28 Norfolk St | Son | M | 6 | | | | |

| | | | | | | | |
|---|---|---|---|---|---|---|---|
| Save | | Insert | | Delete | | Blank | | Help | | Quit |

*Note*: The user has just entered three complete records into the Gorbals database table and is in the midst of entering a fourth. Selecting 'Save' from the menu line below saves the records and clears the form, preparing it to receive other records.

Fig. 6.1 Data entry using forms displaying data in a table

shown in Figure 6.1 or like a collection of the fields belonging to a single record as shown in Figure 6.2. Tabular forms allow several records to be entered or edited at once but may become awkward where the table is wider than the computer screen (normally 80 characters across). In such instances forms showing the fields of individual records may be more appropriate even as they only allow records to be added or edited one at a time. Because text retrieval and analysis packages normally have to accommodate elements with hundreds and even thousands of characters, only forms comprising the elements of a single document are available where interactive data entry is supported.

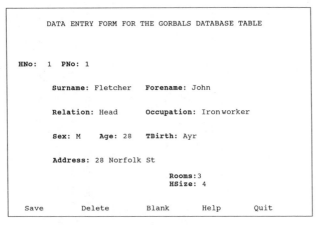

```
          DATA ENTRY FORM FOR THE GORBALS DATABASE TABLE


   HNo:   1   PNo: 1


        Surname: Fletcher    Forename: John


        Relation: Head       Occupation: Ironworker


        Sex: M     Age: 28   TBirth: Ayr


        Address: 28 Norfolk St

                             Rooms:3
                             HSize: 4

   Save        Delete      Blank      Help      Quit
```

*Note*: The user has just entered one record into the Gorbals database table. Selecting 'Save' from the menu line below saves the record and clears the form, preparing it to receive another record.

Fig. 6.2 Data entry using forms displaying data as single fields of information

Tabular forms and those showing the fields of individual records may be customized by determining the relative position of their fields, and by adding form titles (e.g. 'DATA ENTRY FORM FOR THE GORBALS DATABASE TABLE') and/or instructions (e.g. 'Paragraph breaks should be indented and preceded by a line break').[18] Data

---

[18] More dramatic visual effects also may be permitted, for example to highlight selected fields with reverse video, different colours, and blinking light.

validation may be available with which fields can be set up to accept only a specified range of values. It is especially useful where several people are involved in updating and amending data. The *Age* field in Figures 6.1 and 6.2, for example, might be set up to reject values outside the range 0 to 110, perhaps with a helpful message such as 'Ages must be between 0 and 110'.

More sophisticated database and text retrieval software provides so-called application-writing facilities with which forms can be linked together and a highly controlled environment created for anyone accessing a project's data. Such applications are useful in two ways. First, they help preserve data's integrity and accuracy. Secondly, with multi-table databases, applications permit the user to add, edit, and browse through data without knowing anything about how or why data are distributed across several tables. Though space does not permit a thorough review of applications programming, a general indication of what is possible can be provided with reference to the database about transported British convicts discussed in Chapter 3.

Figure 6.3 shows the five tables that make up the convicts database and how their records are related. Figures 6.4 to 6.6 show some of the forms or screens which confront a user browsing, entering, or editing data in the database. The first form that is encountered is shown in Figure 6.4. On it is entered the name and/or unique identifying tag of a convict in which the user is interested. The 'Go' command retrieves the rudimentary biographical information stored for that convict in the CONVICTS and OCCUPATIONS tables and displays it on the form shown in Figure 6.5. Once displayed, the biographical information can be edited or information about a new convict added to the system. Having finished with the biographical data, the user can move on to browse, edit, or add to the convict's criminal record by selecting 'More' and producing the form shown in Figure 6.6. There, data about the hearings in which a convict was involved including the offences tried and penalties imposed, are all displayed. The records can be edited and new ones added. The application protects the data's integrity (data validation is used on most fields) and provides easy access to biographical and criminal records stored in five different tables. At the same time it hides the fields whose values join related records stored in different tables (e.g in the *Pid* and *HNo* fields) or distinguish between those records in a table which

**CONVICTS**

| Pid | Surname | Forenames | Place | Age | Religion | Sex |
|---|---|---|---|---|---|---|
| D1256 | MacDonald | John | Born at sea | 37 | P | M |
| B349 | O'Brien | Ellen | Co Wicklow | 25 | RC | F |
| . . . | | | | | | |

**OCCUPATIONS**

| Pid | OccNo | Occupation | Employer | Place |
|---|---|---|---|---|
| D1256 | 1 | Stonemason | | |
| >>D1256 | 2 | Labourer | Mr Hudson | Anderston |
| B349 | 1 | Washerwoman | | |
| . . . | | | | |

**HEARINGS**

| Pid | HNo | Day | Month | Year | Place |
|---|---|---|---|---|---|
| D1256 | E08062104 | 8 | Jun | 1821 | Edinburgh |
| D1256 | V01012601 | 1 | Jan | 1826 | VDL |
| D1256 | V03012601 | 3 | Jan | 1826 | VDL |
| >>D1256 | V26022602 | 26 | Feb | 1826 | VDL |
| B349 | D18052203 | 18 | May | 1822 | Dublin |
| . . . | | | | | |

**PENALTIES**

| HNo | PNo | Penalty |
|---|---|---|
| E08062104 | 1 | 14 years' transportation |
| V01012601 | 1 | Admonished |
| V03012601 | 1 | 100 lashes |
| ->>V03012601 | 2 | Hard labour on the roads for 12 months |
| V26022602 | 1 | Solitary confinement for three days |
| D18052203 | 1 | 7 years' transportation |

**OFFENCES**

| HNo | ONo | Inf_Site | Infraction | Place |
|---|---|---|---|---|
| E08062104 | 1 | Near Edinburgh | Highway robbery | Edinburgh |
| V01012601 | 1 | Stonemason's yard | Refusing to work | VDL |
| V03012601 | 1 | Stonemason's yard | Striking overseer with hammer | VDL |
| ->>V26022602 | 1 | Notman's chain gang | Not emptying wheelbarrow | VDL |
| V26022602 | 2 | Notman's chain gang | Relieving himself vs orders | VDL |
| D18052203 | 1 | | Stealing trousers from line | Dublin |
| D18052203 | 2 | | On the town for three years | Dublin |

Note: The arrows show how records in the tables are joined by values stored in common fields.

Fig. 6.3 Five joined tables from the database of British convicts transported to the colonies in the nineteenth century

```
Use this form to enter the name and/or convict
identifying code (Pid) for the British convict in
whom you are interested, then select GO.


Pid:

Surname: MacDonald

Forenames: John


Go        Quit
```

*Note*: The user has entered the name 'John MacDonald' and is about to select 'Go' from the menu line (bottom) to see the biographical information about the John MacDonalds who are known to the database.

Fig. 6.4 First form of a data-entry application used with the convicts database

belong to the same object (e.g. offences which belong to the same hearing). These fields are entered and/or edited by the application as required but 'behind the scenes' and without the user's interference.

It is possible at this juncture to take up a question raised in Chapter 4 about when to use database as opposed to statistical software. As we have already seen, statistical packages are essential for projects requiring anything more advanced than the most basic aggregate measures and graphical displays. Database management systems simply do not have the full range of statistical and high-quality graphical routines. The question remains, however, when it is appropriate to use the statistical package for data entry, editing, and management as well as for data analysis. Although there is no fixed rule of thumb the following guide-lines may apply. Where data models involve several tables, it is often better to opt for the database management system over the statistical package at least for data entry and editing. Although statistical packages can retrieve and analyse related records stored in separate tables (as shown in Chapter 4), they do not provide the same level of sophistication in their data-entry facilities when compared with database management systems. Statistical packages are particularly weak in the kind of interactive multi-table data entry demonstrated in Figures 6.4 to 6.6. Indeed most statis-

```
Here is rudimentary biographical data for the convicts whose names
and/or Pid match those supplied on the previous form. Scroll through
selected convicts by choosing 'Next'. Change the information
pertaining to the convict shown on the form by editing the form and
selecting 'Update'. See more information about the convict shown on
the form by selecting 'More'. Add a new convict to the database by
clearing the form (select 'Blank'), entering the relevant information,
and selecting 'Create'.



CONVICTS' BIOGRAPHICAL DATA


Pid:  D1256

Surname: MacDonald   Forenames: John

    Age: 37  Sex: M

        Native Place: Born at sea   Religion: P


Occupations
┌─────────────────────────────────────┐
│ Labourer                            │
├─────────────────────────────────────┤
│ Stonemason                          │
├─────────────────────────────────────┤
│                                     │
├─────────────────────────────────────┤
│                                     │
└─────────────────────────────────────┘

More       Update       Blank       Create       Next       Quit
```

*Note*: The form displays biographical information stored in the CONVICTS and OCCUPATIONS tables for the convicts whose names and/or *Pid* match those supplied on the previous form (in this case 'John MacDonald'). The user can scroll through information pertaining to the selected convicts, see more information about the convict currently displayed on the form, edit the information pertaining to the convict shown on the form, or clear the form and add to the database information about a new convict.

Fig. 6.5 Second form of the data-entry application used with the convicts database

tical packages only allow data entry and editing with one table at a time. Where data have to be stored in several tables, data entry can become repetitive and prone to error.

Take the study of transported British convicts as an example. There, records in the OCCUPATIONS and HEARINGS tables are related to those in the CONVICTS table which share the same *Pid*, and records in the PENALTIES and OFFENCES tables are linked to those in HEARINGS

Here is a record of the selected convict's hearings showing
associated offences and penalties. Scroll through the hearings
in sequential (chronological order) by selecting 'Next'. If
necessary, edit information on the form and execute the changes
by selecting 'Update'. To add new hearing records, clear the form
(select 'Blank'), add the relevant information, and select 'Create'.

```
                    ┌────────────────────────────┐
                    │    John MacDonald          │
                    └────────────────────────────┘
```

Third hearing recorded in the Offence Register

**Hearing Information:**    **Day:** 03

                            **Month:** Jan

                            **Year:** 1826

                            **Place:** VDL

**Alleged Offences Tried:**

| Inf_Site | Infraction | Place |
|---|---|---|
| Stonemason's yard | Striking overseer with hammer | VDL |
| | | |
| | | |

**Penalties meted out (if any)**

| |
|---|
| 100 lashes |
| Hard labour on the roads for 12 months |
| |
| |

| Update | Create | Next | Blank | Quit |
|---|---|---|---|---|

*Note*: The user can scroll through the hearings sequentially, adding or editing information where necessary, selecting 'Quit' to return to the first form and get information on another convict or quit the application. Notice that the form is constructed to allow any one hearing to have several offences and/or penalties associated with it. Here, the user has scrolled through to the information pertaining to John MacDonald's third hearing.

Fig. 6.6 Third form of the data-entry application used with the convicts database, displaying information about the hearings where convicts were tried

which share the same *HNo*. If data had been entered into tables one at a time the *Pid* and *HNo* values belonging to joined records would have to be typed repeatedly. One typographical error could assign an occupational record to the wrong convict or a penalty record to no hearing in particular. In the multi-table data-entry application shown in Figures 6.4 to 6.6, on the other hand, the fields which link related records stored in separate tables or distinguish between records in the same table are entered automatically and accurately by the system. Statistical packages, then, are suitable for data entry as well as analysis where data fit easily and neatly into a small number of tables with tersely defined fields, and where a multi-table data structure is not required for bulk editing, data classification, or nominal record linkage as described in Chapter 3.

### Data exchange

Data exchange between software packages is of the utmost importance. It enables projects to migrate away from obsolete computers and outmoded software, to take advantage of different applications (for example by using a database to enter and manage data and a statistical package to analyse them), and to use data acquired from data and text archives. For whatever reasons data are exchanged, three conditions must be met if their transfer is to be successful. The data must be formatted and structured in a manner recognizable to both the source and the target software, and they must indicate their structure with symbols comprehensible to both packages.

Take file formats first. Most software packages save data in files which are not generally recognizable by other software packages. Thus in Chapter 5 we saw how files created in two different word processors were in the first instance mutually incomprehensible. The same may be said of spreadsheets, databases, statistical packages, and text retrieval and analysis packages, all of which store data using their own so-called internal file formats. This particular obstacle is easily overcome where target software recognizes the internal file format created by the source software. The exigencies of market competition if nothing else have forced software companies to make their products read and write data formats known to other like packages. Thus, a recent version of *Microsoft Word* reads internal format files created by competitor word processors (e.g. *Wordstar*, *WordPerfect*). It can also save its own files in formats immediately comprehensible to its competitors. Likewise, Microsoft's spreadsheet, *Excel*, can read and write the internal format files of its leading competitor *Lotus 1–2–3*. This kind of exchange facility is particularly well developed where software offers only very limited or primitive data entry and editing modules. The PC-based statistical package *SPSS-PC* is a good example. It does not enable interactive data entry but can read tabular data files prepared in leading spreadsheet and database products. Another means of exchanging data is by saving them in a standard format comprehensible to both target and source software. In most instances ASCII has been adopted as the *de facto* standard format. Here text analysis packages are a useful example. Many do not provide interactive data entry. Instead, they rely for data entry on reading ASCII files created in word processors or line editors.

Accurate and effective data exchange also requires that target software recognize how the data in the external file are structured. Spreadsheets need to be informed of data values' relative location so as to know in which cells to place them. A database or a statistical package needs to know where records and fields begin and end.[19] Likewise, text analysis and retrieval packages need to know where documents and their elements begin and end, and word processors where lines and paragraphs begin and end. Word processors also need to know about footnotes, page breaks, and a whole range of print-formatting conditions (e.g. where to begin and end italic or underlined characters). In some instances, it is simply impossible to explain data structures to target software in a manner which conforms to that software's view of what data are and how they can be modelled. Take the spreadsheet of municipal finance data shown in Figure 6.7.[20] Its structure cannot be explained in terms which are meaningful to databases and statistical packages, that is, as a table which in this case contains five records with three fields each. Should the data be imported into a database or statistical package they would be misinterpreted as shown in Figure 6.8. Similarly, no database or statistical package will comprehend and thus successfully import a word-processing file comprising the text of this chapter. The data model underlying this text is comprehensible to a word processor. It is incomprehensible to a database and a

---

[19] Where multi-table databases are involved it is also necessary to indicate which records belong to which tables.

[20] From *Annual Report of the Commissioners of the Sinking Fund for the year 1902* (Philadelphia, 1902), 588.

| | A | B | C |
|---|---|---|---|
| 1 | City loans at par | 6,645,300 | |
| 2 | 45,000 shares P&E railroad | 2,700,000 | |
| 3 | Total securities | | 9,345,300 |
| 4 | Cash balance | | 51,116 |
| 5 | Total cash and securities | | 9,396,416 |

Fig. 6.7 Sample spreadsheet of municipal finance data

| field 1 | field 2 | field 3 |
|---|---|---|
| City loans at par | 6645300 | 0 |
| 45,000 shares P&E railroad | 2700000 | 0 |
| Total securities | 0 | 9345300 |
| Cash balance | 0 | 51116 |
| Total cash and securities | 0 | 9396416 |

Fig. 6.8 The municipal finance data imported from a spreadsheet (Fig. 6.7) into a database table, where they are (wrongly) interpreted as comprising five rows with three fields each

statistical package, however, since both have a tabular view of the world.

This latter example is not meant to imply that data prepared in word processors and line editors cannot be imported into databases. On the contrary, word processors are frequently used for this purpose. To be successful, however, the word processor must create files in which records and fields are explicitly indicated to the intended database or statistical package. Thus records created in a word processor and saved as an ASCII file could be read into the Gorbals database table provided that in the ASCII file records were demarcated by line breaks and fields by delimiters or by their fixed length as shown in Figure 6.9. The command languages of most database and statistical software will be capable of specifying the structure of fixed-field or delimited ASCII files and thus reading records from those files. They will also permit data stored as database or statistical tables to be exported as fixed field or delimited ASCII files.

Finally, for data exchange to be successful, symbols which are used to indicate their structure must be comprehensible to both the source and target software. The data presented in the first example shown in Figure 6.9 are only comprehensible to a target

**Example 1. Records in a 'delimited' format:**

1@1@Fletcher@John@28 Norfolk St@Head@M@28@Ironworker@Ayr@3@4
1@2@Fletcher@Eliza@28 Norfolk St@Wife@F@28@Seamstress@Edinburgh@3@4
1@3@Fletcher@John@28 Norfolk St@Son@M@8@Scholar@Glasgow@3@4
. . .

**Example 2. Records in a 'fixed field' format:**

| 1 | 1 | Fletcher | John | 28 Norfolk St | Head | M | 28 | Ironworker | Ayr | 3 | 4 |
| 1 | 2 | Fletcher | Eliza | 28 Norfolk St | Wife | F | 28 | Seamstress | Edinburgh | 3 | 4 |
| 1 | 3 | Fletcher | John | 28 Norfolk St | Son | M | 8 | Scholar | Glasgow | 3 | 4 |

The same records when loaded into the Gorbals database table:

| HNo | PNo | Surname | Forename | Address | Relation | Sex | Age | Occupation | TBirth | Rooms | HSize |
|---|---|---|---|---|---|---|---|---|---|---|---|
| 1 | 1 | Fletcher | John | 28 Norfolk St | Head | M | 28 | Ironworker | Ayr | 3 | 4 |
| 1 | 2 | Fletcher | Eliza | 28 Norfolk St | Wife | F | 28 | Seamstress | Edinburgh | 3 | 4 |
| 1 | 3 | Fletcher | John | 28 Norfolk St | Son | M | 8 | Scholar | Glasgow | 3 | 4 |

*Note:* In the first example, line breaks and at-signs (@), respectively, indicate where records and fields begin and end. In the second, line breaks indicate where records begin and end; fields are demarcated by the number of character positions they take up on any line. The records as loaded into a database table are also shown. The same records when loaded into the Gorbals database table

Fig. 6.9 Two examples of records prepared in a word processor for entry into a database table

package which can comprehend line breaks and at-signs as record and field delimiters, respectively. Though an intuitively obvious condition, the use of standard symbols to indicate how data are structured is not yet an apparent trend within the industry. Tabular data are not so much a problem because their simple structure is easily described. Tables comprise only two features: fields and records. The data managed in text-processing packages are far more complex and as yet there is little agreement about the range of elements which should be demarcated (e.g. words, lines, paragraphs, preambles, footnotes) and how such elements should be demarcated (e.g. with descriptive tags enclosed in angle brackets as with SGML).[21] So long as different software packages prefer their own style of mark-up, the prospects for data exchange will remain limited. Fortunately, there seems to be a slow-moving tendency amongst software producers to prefer the descriptive mark-up language SGML for demarcating text elements. Agreement as to what elements to mark up is more of a problem, though here too there is evidence of some progress toward a standard, notably in the guide-lines prepared by the Text Encoding Initiative.[22]

In sum, then, data exchange enables a project to take advantage of more and better processing applications and to introduce efficiencies particularly where data entry is concerned. But there are constraints where packages comprehend data rather differently and/or use different mark-up to indicate their structure. Consequently, wherever data exchange is envisaged it must be tested, preferably before substantial time and money is invested in large-scale data entry.

### Data entry with optical character readers

Optical character readers (OCRs) scan printed information and turn it into machine-readable (normally ASCII) files.[23] Their speed

[21] See Ch. 5, pp. 68–73.

[22] C. M. Sperberg-McQueen and L. D. Burnard (eds.), *Guidelines for the Encoding and Interchange of Machine-Readable Texts*, edn. P2 (Oxford, 1993); for a report on the *Guidelines* and their usefulness in history see Greenstein, *Modelling Historical Data*.

[23] *Optical Character Recognition in the Historical Discipline: Proceedings of an International Workshop Organized by Netherlands Historical Data Archive, Nijmegen Institute for Cognition and Information* (St Katharinen, 1993); R. van Horik, 'Optical

and accuracy—ever improving but still contingent in large measure on the quality and clarity of the printed copy being scanned—promise to benefit projects which rely upon quantities of printed information. But OCRs only scan data; they do not indicate the data's structure. Consequently, scanned data need to be edited comprehensively before they can be imported into database or text retrieval software, for example. Comprehensive editing is desirable anyway as scanners' character recognition may not be 100 per cent accurate. Some editing can take place interactively with the OCR, which will throw lines of text up onto the computer screen as they are being scanned, giving the user a chance to correct or add to them wherever necessary. Files of scanned data can also be edited with word processors and line editors whose semi-intelligent editing procedures can be especially useful where the data's structure is simple and its demarcation requires only repetitive editing.[24]

In some circumstances computer programming also may be extremely useful. Computer programming is not an expertise which historians normally need to acquire and is therefore not discussed at length in this book. Since the late 1960s computer-literate historians have become increasingly reliant upon industry-standard as opposed to home-grown software, and the trend is likely to continue in this direction. Quite simply, commercial software is becoming more powerful and easier to use while similarly powered home-grown solutions require expertise and financial resources unavailable to most historians. None the less, simple programming can on occasion introduce huge efficiencies into a project. One further example from the study of Oxford members, 1900–70, demonstrates the point.[25]

Character Recognition and Historical Documents: Some Programs Reviewed', *History and Computing*, 4 (1992), 211–20; I. Lancashire (ed.), *The Humanities Computing Yearbook, 1989/90* (Oxford, 1991), 540–3; S. Hockey, 'OCR: The Kurzweil Data Entry Machine', *Literary and Linguistic Computing*, 1 (1986), 63–7. The technology is such that it already permits some manuscript texts to be scanned accurately.

[24] Semi-intelligent editing is demonstrated in Ch. 5, pp. 163–4 with the text of the *Federalist Papers*.

[25] Programming languages such as SNOBOL, SPITBOL, and ICON which specialize in character data are particularly useful since they are better suited to the manipulation of textual as opposed to strictly numeric data. See D. I. Greenstein, 'Programming in SPITBOL for Historians', *Humanistiske Data*, 2 (1987), 23–32; S. Hockey, *Snobol Programming for the Humanities* (Oxford, 1985); M. Olsen,

The Oxford study relied in the first instance on printed lists of twentieth-century matriculations and examination results. A list of examination results is shown in Figure 6.10. Though essential to the project, the information contained in such lists—some 263,000 records in all—would have been too time consuming and expensive to enter from the keyboard. OCR and some simple computer programming sped up the process immeasurably and decreased its overall cost. As lists were scanned, lines of text were thrown up onto the screen where they were edited. At this stage, extraneous information such as page headers and page numbers was deleted and symbols inserted to indicate the data's structure as shown in Figure 6.11. Thereafter, a computer program was written which could read the data, recognize their structure, and transform them so that information associated with each finalist (e.g. names and subject, year, and result of examination) was represented on a single line.[26] A partial result of the transformation is shown in Figure 6.12. Notice there that the information is given in the same order for every finalist. Notice, too, that the discrete pieces of information given for each finalist are separated from one another by at-signs (@). Presented in this fashion, the data are comprehensible to a database. In this instance, they were read into a database table shown in Figure 6.12, whence they were more comprehensively edited with the assistance of the multi-table database as described in Chapter 3.[27]

Obviously, not every project can benefit from optical scanning. Most manuscript sources are still unrecognizable to a scanner, so are some printed sources (especially those which are not in particularly good condition, and/or use eccentric or particularly small typefaces). Even where sources can be scanned, the machine-readable result may require so much editing as to make interactive data entry more cost effective. Here, as elsewhere, experimentation will help determine whether scanning is a feasible data-entry option for a given project.

'Beyond SNOBOL: The Icon Programming Language', *Computers and the Humanities*, 21 (1987).

[26] See Greenstein, 'Programming in SPITBOL for Historians'.

[27] Ch. 3, pp. 82–3.

*Over/* Fig. 6.10 Printed list of Oxford University finalists' examination results

*NOMINA CANDIDATORUM qui Termino Trinitatis,* A.D. 1912, *ab examinatoribus* IN SCIENTIIS MATHEMATICIS ET PHYSICIS *honore digni sunt habiti, in unaquaque classe secundum seriem literarum disposita.*

**CLASSIS I.**

Capon Robertus S. e Coll. D. Jo. Bapt.
Heywood Francus L. e Coll. Ball.

Mackie Joannes H. e Coll. Æn. Nas.
Pocock Robertus J. e Coll. Reg.

Pritchard Inkerman T. e Coll. Nov.

**CLASSIS II.**

Davis Georgius H. e Coll. Æn. Nas.
Elsdon Christophorus G. R. e Coll. Hertf.
Gimson Franklin C. e Coll. Ball.

Huson Arturus C. e Coll. Nov.
Martin Thomas H. e Coll. Æn. Nas.
Morgan Jacobus e Coll. Jesu.

Swinden Benjamin A. ex Æde Christi.
Verity Edgarus W. e Coll. Æn. Nas.
Wood Edgarus S. e Coll. Hertf.

**CLASSIS III.**

Border Georgius W. ex Æde Christi.
Dixon Lloyd e Coll. Ball.
Salmon Alanus H. M. e Coll. Vigorn.
Seed Cyrillus J. e Coll. D. Jo. Bapt.

Stephens Cyrillus R. e Coll. Jesu.
Vernon Henricus R. Schol. non Ascript.
Whitehead Percy e Coll. Hertf.

Wilson Aluredus K. e Coll. Reg.
Woodhead Alexander W. e Coll. Reg.
Woodhead Francus C. T. e Coll. Hertf.

**CLASSIS IV.**

E. B. ELLIOTT
E. H. HAYES } *Examinatores.*
H. T. GERRANS

*NOMINA CANDIDATORUM qui Termino Trinitatis,* A.D. 1912, *ab examinatoribus* IN SCIENTIA NATURALI *honore digni sunt habiti, in unaquaque classe secundum seriem literarum disposita.*

**CLASSIS I.**

Bourdillon Robertus B. e Coll. Ball. (Chem.)
Champion Harricus G. e Coll. Nov. (Chem.)
Chavasse Franciscus B. e Coll. Ball. (Physiol.)
East Arturus G. e Coll. D. Jo. Bapt. (Physiol.)
Ellwood Victor T. e Coll. Pemb. (Physiol.)
Gould Fridericus A. e Coll. Jesu (Phys.)

Grisman Joannes R. e Coll. Vigorn. (Phys.)
Kerry Arturus H. G. e Coll. D. Jo. Bapt. (Phys.)
Lambert Willelmus J. e Coll. Reg. (Chem.)
Medd Robertus T. e Coll. Æn. Nas. (Sci. Mach.)
Webb Fridericus J. e Coll. Æn. Nas. (Phys.)
Wood Cæcilius D. e Coll. Reg. (Physiol.)

**CLASSIS II.**

Apperly Francus L. e Coll. Linc. (Physiol.)
Aston Herbertus S. e Coll. Nov. (Chem.)
Ball Percy e Coll. Magd. (Chem.)
Baylis Harricus A. e Coll. Jesu (Zool.)
Britton Fridericus A. e Coll. Reg. (Phys.)
Brown Leonardus G. e Coll. Ball. (Physiol.)

Greenwood Mauricius e Coll. Trin. (Chem.)
Hartley Radulphus V. L. e Coll. D. Jo. Bapt. (Phys.)
Hodgkin Adrianus E. e Coll. Kebl. (Chem.)
Inman Robertus J. e Coll. Univ. (Physiol.)
Nelson Thomas S. e Coll. Univ. (Physiol.)
Otter Martinus J. B. e Coll. Pemb. (Bot.)

Carlton Carolus H. e Coll. D. Jo. Bapt. (Physiol.)
Carroll Edwardus W. e Coll. Hertf. (Bot.)
Collier Willelmus T. e Coll. Ball. (Physiol.)
Davies Lionellus M. e Coll. Linc. (Physiol.)
Davis Romney R. e Coll. D. Jo. Bapt. (Geol.)
Gardner Haroldus M. e Coll. Mert. (Bot.)
Gilbert Joannes G. e Coll. Linc. (Chem.)
Grant Arturus E. e Coll. Jesu (Phys.)

Parker Harding N. e Coll. Pemb. (Geol.)
Pratt Oliverus B. ex Æde Christi (Physiol.)
Shepherd Willelmus S. e Coll. Trin. (Geol.)
Sladden Cyrillus E. ex Æde Christi (Chem.)
Smith Leo e C.C.C. (Chem.)
Sprott Normanus A. ex Æde Christi (Physiol.)
Symonds Carolus P. e Coll. Nov. (Physiol.)
Whitelocke Hugo A. B. ex Æde Christi (Physiol.)

CLASSIS III.

Acland Lauchlan H. D. e Coll. Magd. (Chem.)
Aiengar Bangalore R. Schol. non Ascript. (Bot.)
Aldridge Montacutus Schol. non Ascript. (Chem.)
Baxter Robertus R. e Coll. D. Jo. Bapt. (Chem.)
Boldero Haroldus E. A. e Coll. Trin. (Physiol.)
Brooks Joannes B. ex Æde Christi (Bot.)
Broster Lennox R. e Coll. Trin. (Physiol.)
Constable Aluredus B. Schol. non Ascript. (Chem.)
Constable Mauricius G. e Coll. Mert. (Phys.)
Daly Josephus e Coll. D. Jo. Bapt. (Physiol.)
de Normanville Hugo ex Aul. Priv. Mag. Parker (Phys.)
Dixey Joannes C. e Coll. Æn. Nas. (Physiol.)
Dyott Kenelm M. Schol. non Ascript. (Physiol.)
Evans Horatius G. e Coll. Jesu (Chem.)

Gameson Lawrence e Coll. Reg. (Physiol.)
Gladstone Fridericus C. e Coll. Pemb. (Physiol.)
Haynes Joannes F. e Coll. Nov. (Physiol.)
Jones Odoenus P. e Coll. Jesu (Chem.)
Liddell Joannes A. e Coll. Ball. (Zool.)
Martin Philippus A. e Coll. Nov. (Physiol.)
Oddy Hubertus M. ex Æde Christi (Physiol.)
Pierce Haroldus W. e Coll. Linc. (Chem.)
Sells Clemens P. e Coll. Mert. (Physiol.)
Shardlow Joannes A. e Coll. Kebl. (Chem.)
Stark Robertus G. W. e Coll. D. Jo. Bapt. (Sci. Mach.)
Swinton Alanus E. e Coll. Nov. (Chem.)
Traill Antonius e Coll. Nov. (Physiol.)
Wiles Humphredus H. e Coll. Oriel. (Bot.)

CLASSIS IV.

Bassett-Smith Dudley W. e Coll. D. Jo. Bapt. (Chem.)
Blogg Willelmus G. V. e Coll. Kebl. (Physiol.)
Davies Willelmus A. Schol. non Ascript. (Chem.)
Labey Julius E. G. e Coll. Exon. (Phys.)
Lagden Ronaldus O. e Coll. Oriel. (Chem.)

Pidgeon Galfridus D. ex Æde Christi (Chem.)
Poole Joannes C. e Coll. Trin. (Bot.)
Tunbridge Willelmus S. e Coll. Linc. (Physiol.)
Wakeman Edwardus O. R. e Coll. D. Jo. Bapt. (Geol.)
Wigan Carolus R. e Coll. Univ. (Geol.)

| | |
|---|---|
| J. B. FARMER | C. G. DOUGLAS |
| R. E. BAYNES | C. F. JENKIN |
| F. D. CHATTAWAY | A. VAUGHAN |
| A. H. CHURCH | H. K. ANDERSON |
| E. S. GOODRICH | W. E. DALBY |
| J. S. E. TOWNSEND | J. JOLY |
| H. B. HARTLEY | C. H. LEES |
| G. W. SMITH | W. J. POPE |

Examinatores.

*Hunc ordinem ex Schedulis Examinatorum in singulis Scientiis Naturalibus accurate collectum esse testor*

R. E. BAYNES
Examinatorum præses.

$1912

@Maths

CLASSIS I.
Capon Robertus S. e Coll. D. Jo. Bapt.
Heywood Francus L. e Coll. Ball.

CLASSIS II.
Davis Georgius H. e Coll. AEn. Nas.
Elsdon Christophorus G.R. e Coll. Hertf.
Gimson Franklin C. e Coll. Ball
. . . names of other examinees in maths go here . . .

@Natural Science

CLASSIS I.
Bourdillon Robertus B. e Coll. Ball. (Chem.)
Champion Harricus G. e Coll. Nov. (Chem.)

. . . names of other examinees in natural science subjects go here . . .

*Note*: Columns of results were scanned separately. Examination lists were published with Latinized personal and college names. The Latin names were translated back into English, and college and subject names were standardized with bulk editing procedures similar to those described in Ch. 3.

Fig. 6.11 Scanned version of the printed list of Oxford finalists' examination results

## CONDUCT A PILOT PROJECT

Computer-aided work should never be launched before it has been thoroughly tested in a pilot project. This is nothing less than the whole project conducted from beginning to end with only a fraction of the total information ultimately envisaged. Thus, the pilot project for a computer-aided study of eighteenth-century English criminal justice will gather the full range of information desired for a small number of the court cases that the study hopes to examine. Once gathered, the data will be computerized, coded, and then analysed with the full battery of statistical, graphical, and tabular manipulations that are envisaged for the project in its entirety. A project which involves textual analysis will collect, computerize, and analyse a small portion of the texts that will be involved in the full-scale project. Even word processing demands piloting. The first time a journal article is prepared with a word processor, for example, it is worth experimenting with different page formats and footnote configurations before the entire text of the article is entered from the keyboard.

**(a) The scanned file after it was 'parsed' (processed) by a computer program**

c19121154@1912@Capon@Robertus@S@Jo. Bapt@Maths@I
c19121155@1912@Heywood@Francus@L@Ball@Maths@I
c19121156@1912@Davis@Georgius@H@Aen. Nas@Maths@II
c19121157@1912@Elsdon@Christophorus@G@Hertf@Maths@II
c19121358@1912@Gimson@Franklin@C@Ball@Maths@II
c19111359@1912@Bourdillon@Robertus@B@Ball@Chem@I
c19111360@1912@Champion@Harricus@G@Nov@Chem@I

. . . names of other examinees in natural science subjects go here. . . .

**(b) The parsed, scanned file after it was loaded into a database table**

| Exam_id | Year | Surname | Firstname | Secondname | College | Subject | Class |
|---|---|---|---|---|---|---|---|
| c19121154 | 1912 | Capon | Robertus | S | Jo. Bapt | Maths | I |
| c19121155 | 1912 | Heywood | Francus | L | Ball | Maths | I |
| c19121156 | 1912 | Davis | Georgius | H | AEn. Nas | Maths | II |
| c19121157 | 1912 | Elsdon | Christophorus | G | Hertf | Maths | II |
| c19121358 | 1912 | Gimson | Franklin | C | Ball | Maths | II |
| c19121359 | 1912 | Bourdillon | Robertus | B | Ball | Chem | I |
| c19121360 | 1912 | Champion | Harricus | G | Nov | Chem | I |

Fig. 6.12 Scanned examination results (Fig. 6.11) edited with a computer program in preparation for entry into a database table, and the same data shown imported into the EXAMS database table

In any case, the point of the pilot project is not to generate preliminary results or printed output; this will probably be meaningless anyway owing to the minuscule amount of data involved. Rather it is to design and test every aspect of the project which the researcher will ultimately be forced to consider. A pilot project will, by necessity, see the researcher through the selection of appropriate sources, sampling considerations, hardware and software choices, data modelling, data entry and exchange, and ultimately the production of results. It will enable the researcher to spot design flaws and to correct them at an early stage before they become costly or at worst irreparable.

At the same time, a pilot project will provide first-hand practical experience of the requisite procedural and analytical methods. In the pilot, the researcher will become familiar with the project's software and hardware without putting vast amounts of data at stake, and appropriate arrangements for saving and backing up data once entered can be devised.[28] Similarly, a pilot project will facilitate methodological experimentation. Where nominal record linkage is required, different methods may be tried; where data classification is required different schemes can be tested. Because computer-aided investigations involve procedures and analyses which have to be learned, their start-up costs are often high, forcing pilot studies to be dragged out over several weeks or even months. At the same time, researchers are prone to devote too little time to pilot investigation owing in part to the pressure to produce results with limited operating budgets. Much as this pressure can seem irresistible, it should not be allowed to cut into the time required to design and test a project's various methods and techniques. No saving made in this phase can possibly offset the cost incurred at a later stage where serious design flaws are discovered. The pilot study, then, is nothing less than the whole project in microcosm and its importance cannot be over emphasized. It is the only effective means of determining the overall feasibility of any project, and the tools and methods most appropriate for its conduct.

Pilot studies are important for another reason as well. For it is

---

[28] With the small handful of data involved in a pilot project, 'drop' or 'delete' commands can be used experimentally without disastrous consequences. The same would not be true if like commands were accidentally 'discovered' after several months of data entry had taken place.

here that the computer will prove its worth or not in the light of a given task. At this stage the naïve enthusiast recognizes the computer's inherent limitations while the naturally sceptical sees its strengths. And it is here as well that sceptics and enthusiasts alike will be forced to re-evaluate the myths and legends with which the book launched out in Chapter 1, and address the computer for what it is. That is, a tool, a rather powerful tool, which can in the 1990s be harnessed to the management and interpretation of historical data without threatening to distort them.

# Bibliography and Resource Guide

The bibliography and resource guide has four related aims. First, to point historians in the direction of more detailed help with respect to some of the specific technical and methodological problems they are likely to encounter (sections Iʌ and II). Secondly, to provide an index to available resources including electronic bulletin boards, on-line databases, and data and text archives (section III). Thirdly, to demonstrate the kinds of historical problems that historians have addressed with the aid of computers (sections Iʙ and IV). And finally, to provide ready access to the considerable debate that has been generated about the prospects and pitfalls of computer-aided and quantitative historical investigations (section IV).

Meeting these latter two aims in particular has entailed the inclusion of works which may at first glance seem somewhat out of date. Reports of very early forays into computer-aided content analysis or econometric research have nothing to offer the reader in search of the most up-to-date text-processing software or statistical measure. They will, however, give some indication of where computers have been integrated into historians' research agenda or illuminate some of the intellectual and conceptual problems which are involved whenever a computer-aided project is framed. There will of course be omissions and imbalances: non-English works are underrepresented; research into topics in modern history is overrepresented. None the less, it is hoped that there is something here for everyone which can help at least in a small way to ensure that time and effort are not wasted by the researcher solving anew problems which have been tackled successfully and written up elsewhere.

## I. TEXTBOOKS AND METHODOLOGICAL COMPILATIONS

### A. Computer textbooks

ANDREWS, D., and GREENHALGH, M., *Computing for Non-Scientific Applications* (Leicester, 1987).

BRENT, E. E. Jr., and ANDERSON, R. E., *Computer Applications in the Social Sciences* (Philadelphia, 1990).

MAWDSLEY, E., and MUNCK, T., *Computing for Historians: An Introductory Guide* (Manchester, 1993).

REIFF, J., *Structuring the Past: The Use of Computers in History* (Washington, DC, 1991).

SHORTER, E., *The Historian and the Computer: A Practical Guide* (Englewood Cliffs, NJ, 1971).

TANNENBAUM, R., *Computing in the Humanities and Social Sciences, i: The Fundamentals* (Rockville, Md., 1988).

WELFORD, R. (ed.), *Information Technology for Social Scientists* (Shipley, 1990).


B. *Methodological compilations (including compilations demonstrating results from computer-aided research)*

ALLEN, R. F., *Data Bases in the Humanities and Social Sciences* (Osprey, Fla., 1985).

AYDELOTTE, W. O., *Quantification in History* (Reading, Mass., 1971).

— *et al.* (eds.), *The Dimensions of Quantitative Research in History* (Princeton, NJ, 1972).

BEST, H., *et al.* (eds.), *Computers in the Humanities and the Social Sciences: Achievements of the 1980s: Prospects for the 1990s. Proceedings of the Cologne Computer Conference 1988 . . . September 1988* (Munich, 1991).

— and MANN, R. (eds.), *Quantitative Methoden in der Historisch-sozialwissenschaftlichen Forschung* (Stuttgart, 1977).

BOTZ, G., *et al.* (eds.), *'Qualität und Quantität': Zur Praxis der Methoden der Historischen Sozialwissenschaft* (Frankfurt, 1988).

BOWLES, E. A. (ed.), *Computers in Humanities Research* (Englewood Cliffs, NJ, 1967).

Centre National de la Recherche Scientifique, *L'Ordinateur et le métier d'historien. IVᵉ Congrès 'History and Computing': volume des actes* (Bordeaux, 1990).

CLUBB, J. M., and SCHEUCH, E. K. (eds.), *Historical Sociological Research: The Use of Historical Process Produced Data* (Stuttgart, 1980).

DENLEY, P. R., and HOPKIN, D. (eds.), *History and Computing* (Manchester, 1987).

— *et al.* (eds.), *History and Computing, II* (Manchester, 1989).

GENET, J.-P. (ed.), *Standardisation et échange des bases de données historiques* (Paris, 1988).

GRUNDLACH, R., and LUECKERATH, C. A., *Historische Wissenschaften und Elektronische Datenverarbeitung* (Frankfurt, 1976).

HOCKEY, S., *et al.* (eds.), *Research in Humanities Computing 1* (Oxford, 1991).

— *et al.* (eds.), *Research in Humanities Computing 2* (Oxford, forthcoming).

JARAUSCH, K. H. (ed.), *Quantifizierung in der Geschichtswissenschaft: Probleme und Möglichkeiten* (Düsseldorf, 1976).

Lorwin, V. R., and Price, J. M. (eds.), *The Dimensions of the Past: Materials, Problems, and Opportunities for Quantitative Work in History* (New Haven, Conn., 1972).

McCrank, L. J. (ed.), *Databases in the Humanities and Social Sciences* (Auburn, NY, 1987).

Mawdsley, E., *et al.* (eds.), *History and Computing III: Historians, Computers and Data. Applications in Research and Teaching* (Manchester, 1990).

Metz, R., *et al.* (eds.), *Historical Information Systems. Session B-12b. Proceedings, Tenth International Economic History Congress, Leuven, August 1990* (Leuven, 1990).

Miall, D. (ed.), *Humanities and the Computer: New Directions* (Oxford, 1990).

Rabb, T. K., and Rothberg, R. I., *The New Interdisciplinary History, the 1980s and Beyond: Studies in Interdisciplinary History* (Princeton, NJ, 1982).

Raben, J., and Marks, G., *Data Bases in the Humanities and Social Sciences* (Amsterdam, 1979).

Rahtz, S. (ed.), *Information Technology in the Humanities: Tools, Techniques and Applications* (Chichester, 1987).

Rowney, D. K., and Graham, J. Q. Jr. (eds.), *Quantitative History: Selected Readings in the Quantitative Analysis of Historical Data* (Homewood, Ill., 1969).

Smets, J. (ed.), *Histoire et informatique V$^e$ Congrès 'History and Computing': volume des actes* (Montpellier, 1992).

Thaller, M., and Müller, A. (eds.), *Computer in den Geisteswissenschaften: Konzepte und Berichte*, Studien zur Historischen Sozialwissenschaft 7 (Frankfurt, 1989).

Turk, C. (ed.), *Humanities Research Using Computers* (London, 1991).

Wrigley, E. A. (ed.), *Nineteenth Century Society: Essays in the Use of Quantitative Methods for the Study of Social Data* (Cambridge, 1972).

## II. METHODS AND APPLICATIONS

### A. Databases

Brent, E. E. Jr., 'Relational Data Base Structures and Concept Formation in the Social Sciences', *Computers and the Social Sciences*, 2 (1985), 29–50.

Burnard, L. D., 'The Principles of Database Design', in S. Rahtz (ed.), *Information Technology in the Humanities*, 54–68.

—— 'Relational Theory, SQL and Historical Practice', in P. R. Denley *et al.* (eds.), *History and Computing II*, 63–71.

DATE, C. J., *Database: A Primer*, 4th edn. (Reading, Mass., 1987).

— *A Guide to the SQL Standard*, 2nd edn. (Reading, Mass., 1988).

GREENSTEIN, D. I., 'Multi-Sourced and Integrated Databases for the Prosopographer', in E. Mawdsley *et al.* (eds.), *History and Computing III*, 60–6.

— 'A Source-Oriented Approach to History and Computing: The Relational Database', *Historical Social Research*, 14 (1989), 9–16.

HARTLAND, P., and HARVEY, C., 'Information Engineering and Historical Databases', in P. R. Denley *et al.* (eds.), *History and Computing II*, 44–62.

HARVEY, C., and PRESS, J., 'Relational Data Analysis: Value, Concepts and Methods', *History and Computing*, 4 (1992), 98–109.

OLDERVOLL, J. (ed.), *Eden or Babylon? On Future Software for Highly Structured Historical Sources* (St Katharinen, 1992).

PASLEAU, S., *Les Bases de données en sciences humaines* (Liège, 1988).

— *SQL langage et SGBD relationnels* (Paris, 1988).

— 'Historical Data Bases as a Field for Structured Query Language', *Historical Social Research*, 14 (1989), 23–9.

SPAETH, D. A., 'Computerizing the Godly: The Application of Small Databases to Anecdotal History', in E. Mawdsley *et al.* (eds.), *History and Computing III*, 156–62.

Thaller, M., *Einführung in die Datenverarbeitung für Historiker* (Cologne/Vienna, 1982).

— (ed.), *Datenbanken und Datenverwaltungssysteme als Werrkzeuge historischer Forschung*, Historisch-sozialwissenschaftliche Studien 20 (St Katherinen, 1986).

— 'The Historical Workstation Project', *Computing and the Humanities*, 25 (1991), 149–62.

— (ed.), *Kleio: A Database System* (St Katharinen, 1993).

## B. Measurement

### 1. *Inferential and descriptive statistics and sampling*

AGRESTI, A., and AGRESTI, B. F., *Statistical Methods for the Social Sciences* (San Francisco, 1979).

CLUBB, J. M., *et al.* (eds.), *The Process of Historical Inquiry: Everyday Lives of Working Americans* (New York, 1989).

DOLLAR, C. M., and JENSEN, R. J., *Historian's Guide to Statistics: Quantitative Analysis and Historical Research* (New York, 1971).

DRAKE, M., *The Quantitative Analysis of Historical Data* (Milton Keynes, 1974).

FLOUD, R., *An Introduction to Quantitative Methods for Historians* (Princeton, NJ, 1973).

# Bibliography and Resource Guide 243

HASKINS, L., and JEFFREY, K., *Understanding Quantitative History* (Cambridge, Mass., 1990).

HEFFER, J., ROBERT, J.-L., and SALY, P., *Outils statistiques pour les historiens* (Paris, 1981).

JARAUSCH, K. H., ARMINGER, G., and THALLER, M., *Quantitative Methoden in der Geschichtswissenschaft: Eine Einführung in die Forschung, Datenverarbeitung und Statistic* (Darmstadt, 1985).

— and HARDY, K. A., *Quantitative Methods for Historians: A Guide to Research, Data, and Statistics* (London, 1991).

LOETHER, H., and MCTAVISH, D. G., *Descriptive and Inferential Statistics: An Introduction*, 3rd rev. edn. (Boston, 1988).

OHLER, N., *Quantitative Methoden für Historiker* (Munich, 1980).

Sage University pamphlet series, *Quantitative Applications in the Social Sciences* (Beverly Hills, Calif., periodically).

WILLIAMS, F., *Reasoning with Statistics: How to Read Quantitative Research*, 3rd edn. (New York, 1986).

## 2. Statistics for lexical and linguistic (text) analysis

BERRY-ROGGHE, G. L. M., 'Computation of Collocations and their Relevance in Lexical Studies', in A. J. Aitken *et al.* (eds.), *The Computer and Literary Studies*.

BRUNET, E., 'What Do Statistics Tell Us?', in S. Hockey *et al.* (eds.), *Research in Humanities Computing 1* (Oxford, 1991), 70–92.

BUTLER, C., *Statistics in Linguistics* (New York, 1985).

HAYNES, J., *Introducing Stylistics* (London, 1989).

KENNY, A. J. P., *The Computation of Style: An Introduction to Statistics for Students of Literature and Humanities* (Oxford, 1982).

KRIPPENDORFF, K., *Content Analysis: An Introduction to its Methodology* (Beverly Hills, Calif., 1980).

MILIC, L., 'Progress in Stylistics: Theory, Statistics, Computers', *Computers and the Humanities*, 25 (1991), 393–400.

MÜLLER, C., *Principes et méthodes de statistique lexicale* (Paris, 1977).

— *Initiation aux méthodes de la statistique* (Paris, 1979).

OLSEN, M., and HARVEY, L.-G., 'Computers in Intellectual History: Lexical Statistics and the Analysis of Political Discourse', *Journal of Interdisciplinary History*, 18 (1988).

WEBER, R. P., *Basic Content Analysis* (Newbury Park, Calif., 1990).

## C. Text Processing

AITKEN, A. J., *et al.* (eds.), *The Computer and Literary Studies* (Edinburgh, 1972).

ASHFORD, J. H., and WILLETT, P., *Text Retrieval and Document Databases* (London, 1988).

BLAND, M., *et al.* (eds.), *Free Text Retrieval Systems: A Review and Evaluation* (London, 1989).

BURNARD, L. D., 'Tools and Techniques for Computer-Assisted Text Processing', in C. S. Butler (ed.), *Computers and Written Texts*, 1–28.

BURTON, D. M., 'Automated Concordances and Word-Indexes: The Process, the Programs, and the Products', *Computers and the Humanities*, 15 (1981), 139–54.

BUTLER, C. S. (ed.), *Computers in Linguistics* (Oxford, 1985).

— (ed.), *Computers and Written Texts* (Oxford, 1992).

CONRAD, P., and REINHARZ, S. (eds.), *Computers and Qualitative Data: A Special Issue of Qualitative Sociology*, 7 (1984).

CORNELIA, Z., WEBER, R. P., and NOBLER, P. P., *Computer-Aided Text Classification for the Social Sciences: The General Inquirer III* (Mannheim, 1989).

HUGHES, J. J., 'Text Retrieval Programs—A Brief Introduction', *Bits & Bytes Review* (July 1987), 1–16; (Aug. 1987), 1–19.

HOCKEY, S., *A Guide to Computer Applications in the Humanities* (London, 1980).

— *Snobol Programming for the Humanities* (Oxford, 1985).

HORIK, R. van, 'Optical Character Recognition and Historical Documents: Some Programs Reviewed', *History and Computing*, 4 (1992), 211–20.

JONES, A., and CHURCHHOUSE, R. F. (eds.), *The Computer in Literary and Linguistic Studies* (Cardiff, 1979).

OAKMAN, R. L., *Computer Methods for Literary Research* (Columbia, NY, 1980).

*Optical Character Recognition in the Historical Discipline: Proceedings of an International Workshop Organized by Netherlands Historical Data Archive, Nijmegen Institute for Cognition and Information* (St Katharinen, 1993).

RUDALL, B. H., and CORNS, T., *Computers and Literature: A Practical Guide* (Cambridge, Mass., 1987).

### D. Nominal record linkage

BASKERVILLE, S. W., HUDSON, P., and MORRIS, R. J. (eds.), *History and Computing Special Issue: Record Linkage*, 4 (1992).

BOUCHARD, G., 'The Processing of Ambiguous Links in Computerized Family Reconstitution', *Historical Methods*, 19 (1986), 9–19.

— 'Current Issues and New Prospects for Computerized Record Linkage in the Province of Québec', *Historical Methods*, 25 (1992), 67–74.

DE BROU, D., and OLSEN, M., 'The Guth Algorithm and the Nominal Record Linkage of Multi-Ethnic Populations', *Historical Methods*, 19 (1986), 20–4.

ITZCOVICH, O., 'Artigen: An Oracle Database for Mass Prosopography. Nominal Record Linkage and Kinship Network Reconstruction', in

Centre National de la Recherche Scientifique, *L'Ordinateur et le métier d'historien*, 155–62.

KATZ, M. B., and TILLER, J., 'Record Linkage for Everyman: A Semi-Automated Process', *Historical Methods*, 5 (1972), 144–50.

KITTS, A., *The Reconstitution of Viana Do Castel*, Research Studies in History and Computing 1 (Egham, 1990), 17–22.

NENADIC, S., 'Record Linkage and the Exploration of Nineteenth-Century Social Groups: A Methodological Perspective on the Glasgow Middle Class in 1861', *Urban History Yearbook* (1987), 32–43.

NYGAARD, L., 'Name Standardization in Record Linking: An Improved Algorithmic Strategy', *History and Computing*, 4 (1992), 63–74.

PERLMANN, J., 'Using Census Districts in Analysis, Record Linkage and Sampling', *Journal of Interdisciplinary History*, 10 (1979), 279–89.

PHILLIPS, J. A., 'Achieving a Critical Mass While Avoiding an Explosion: Letter Cluster Sampling and Nominal Record Linkage', *Journal of Interdisciplinary History*, 9 (1979), 493–508.

SCHOFIELD, R., 'Automatic Family Reconstitution: The Cambridge Experience', *Historical Methods*, 25 (1992), 75–9.

SKOLNICK, M., 'The Resolution of Ambiguities in Record Linkage', in E. A. Wrigley (ed.), *Identifying People in the Past*, ch. 5.

WINCHESTER, I., 'The Linkage of Historical Records by Man and Computer: Techniques and Problems', *Journal of Interdisciplinary History*, 1 (1970), 107–24.

— 'What Every Historian Needs to Know About Record Linkage in the Microcomputer Era', *Historical Methods*, 25 (1992), 149–65.

WRIGLEY, E. A., and SCHOFIELD, R. S., 'Nominal Record Linkage by Computer and the Logic of Family Reconstitution', in E. A. Wrigley (ed.), *Identifying People in the Past*, 64–101.

### E. Coding and encoding data

BLUMIN, S., 'The Classification of Occupations in Past Time: Problems of Fission and Fusion', in E. Mawdsley *et al.* (eds.), *History and Computing III*, 83–9.

BURNARD, L. D., 'What is SGML and How Does it Help?' in D. I. Greenstein (ed.), *Modelling Historical Data*, 65–80.

CLARK, M. A., 'Occupational Classification in the United States Census: 1870–1940', *Journal of Interdisciplinary History*, 9 (1978), 111–30.

GREENSTEIN, D. I. (ed.), *Modelling Historical Data: Towards a Standard for Encoding and Exchanging Machine-Readable Texts* (St Katharinen, 1991).

— 'Standard, Meta-Standard: A Framework for Coding Occupational Data', *Historical Social Research*, 16 (1991), 3–22.

— and BURNARD, L. D., 'Speaking with one Voice: Encoding Standards and the Prospects for an Integrated Approach to Computing in History', *Computers and the Humanities* (forthcoming).

HIGGS, E., 'Structuring the Past: The Occupational and Household Classification of Nineteenth-Century Census Data', in E. Mawdsley *et al.* (eds.), *History and Computing III*, 67–73.

KATZ, M. B., 'Occupational Classification in History', *Journal of Interdisciplinary History*, 3 (1972), 63–88.

MARKER, H. J., 'Encoding Standards for the "Generalist" and the "Specialist": Complex Compound Documents as a Test Case', in D. I. Greenstein (ed.), *Modelling Historical Data*, 147–62.

SCHÜRER, K., 'The Historical Researcher and Codes: Master and Slave or Slave and Master?', in E. Mawdsley *et al.* (eds.), *History and Computing III*, 74–82.

— and DIEDERIKS, H. (eds.), *The Use of Occupations in Historical Analysis* (St Katharinen, 1993).

SPERBERG-MCQUEEN, C. M., and BURNARD, L. D. (eds.), *Guidelines for the Encoding and Interchange of Machine-Readable Texts*, edn. P1 (Oxford, 1990).

— — (eds.), *Guidelines for the Encoding and Interchange of Machine-Readable Texts*, edn. P2 (Oxford, 1993).

THALLER, M., 'A Draft Proposal for the Coding of Machine Readable Sources', *Historical Social Research*, 40 (1986), 3–46.

— 'The Need for Standards: Data Modelling and Exchange', in D. I. Greenstein (ed.), *Modelling Historical Data*, 1–18.

TREIMAN, D. J., 'A Standard Occupational Prestige Scale for Use with Historical Data', *Journal of Interdisciplinary History*, 7 (1976), 283–304.

## III. RESOURCES

*A. Journals which regularly publish methodological and technical information*

*Canadian Humanities Computing*
*Computers and the Humanities*
*Computers and the Social Sciences*
*Computers in Genealogy*
*Computing and Medieval Data Processing*
*Genealogical Computing*
*Histoire et mésure*
*Historical Methods* (originally *History Methods Newsletter*)
*Historical Social Research* (originally *Quantum Information*)
*History and Computing* (originally *Computing and History Today*)

*Journal of Interdisciplinary History*
*Le Médiéviste et l'ordinateur*
*Medium Aevum Quotidianum Newsletter*
*Social Science History*
*Social Science Microcomputer Review*


## B. Data and text archives

CLUBB, J. M., 'Computer Technology and the Source Materials of Social History', *Social Science History* 10 (1986), 97–114.

GREENSTEIN, D. I., 'Historians as Producers or Consumers of Standard-Conformant, Full-Text Datasets? Some Sources of Modern History as a Test Case', in D. I. Greenstein (ed.), *Modelling Historical Data*, 179–94.

HAUSMANN, F., *et al.* (eds.), *Data Networks for the Historical Disciplines? Problems and Feasibilities in Standardization and Exchange of Machine Readable Data* (Graz, 1987).

ZWEIG, R. W., 'Virtual Records and Real History', *History and Computing*, 4 (1992), 174–82.

## 1. Data archives

*Danish Data Archives*, Munkebjergvaenget 48, DK-5230 Odense M, Denmark (Internet: DDA@VM.UNI-C.DK). Holds some 1,500 data sets mainly comprising survey data but also some significant historical compilations. Printed catalogue and newsletter are both available upon application.

*Danish Data Guide, 1986* (Odense, 1986).
*Danish Data Guide Update, 1988* (Odense, 1988).
*DDN-Nyt* (newsletter).


*Economic and Social Research Council Data Archive*, University of Essex, Wivenhoe Park, Colchester, Essex CO4 3SQ, UK (Internet: ARCHIVE@ESSEX.AC.UK). Holds nearly 3,500 data sets, many of them relating to the politics, economy, and society of twentieth-century Britain, but also a substantial and growing collection of historical data sets. Printed catalogue may be purchased from the archive. On-line catalogue available over JANET at UK.AC.SX.SOLB1 and over Internet at SOLB1.SX.AC.UK(username is biron, password is norib).

ANDERSON, S., 'The Future of the Present—The ESRC Data Archive as a Resource Centre of the Future', *History and Computing*, 4 (1992), 191–6.

ESRC Data Archive, *BIRON User Guide* (Essex, 1991).
— *Catalogue* (Colchester, periodically).
— *Data Catalogue and Index: Historical Data to 1939* (Colchester, 1991).

SCHÜRER, K., *et al.*, *A Guide to Historical Datafiles in Machine-Readable Form* (Cambridge, 1992).

*Inter-University Consortium for Political and Social Research (ICPSR)*, the University of Michigan, PO Box 1248, Ann Arbor, MI 48106, USA (Internet: ICPSR_NETMAIL@UM.CC.UMICH.EDU). Acts as a data archive for 350 member institutions. Holds and distributes 'machine-readable data on social phenomena occurring in over 130 countries'. Particularly strong on the USA, contemporary survey, and election and census data, but also has many historical data sets. Printed catalogue may be purchased from the archive. On-line catalogue accessible via Internet at ICPSR.ICPSR.UMICH.EDU.

Inter-University Consortium for Political and Social Research, *CDNet Search: Using SPIRES to Search the ICPSR Databases* (Ann Arbor, Mich., 1987).
— *Guide to Resources and Services, 1991–1992* (Ann Arbor, Mich., 1992).

*Netherlands Historical Data Archives*, Department of History, University of Leyden, PO Box 9515, 2300RA Leyden, The Netherlands (EARN: LETTPD@HLERUL2). The archive co-ordinates an international inventory of historical data sets.

*Norwegian Social Science Data Services*, Hans Holmboesgate 22, N-5007 Bergen, Norway (Internet: FNSBH@CC.UIB.NO). Holdings include the Norwegian Commune Database, 1769–1991, and biographical data on political élites, 1814–1990. Printed catalogue and newsletter both available upon application.

NSD, *Data Catalogue* (Bergen, 1991).
— *Annual Report.*
— *Brukermelding* (newsletter).

*Steinmetz Archive*, Herengracht 410–412, 1017 BX Amsterdam, the Netherlands (Internet: STEINM@SARA.NL). Over 2,100 data sets, most of them concerning contemporary social and behavioural phenomena. Printed catalogue and newsletters available on application.

Steinmetz Archive, *Catalogue and Guide* (Amsterdam, 1986).
— *Titels voor Sociaal-wetenschappelijk Onderzoek SWIDOC.*
— *Datanieuws: Bulletin van het Steinmetzarchief* (newsletter).

*Swedish Social Science Data Archive (SSD)*, Skanstorget 18, S-411 22 Goteborg, Sweden (Internet: SSD@RATATOSK.SSD.GU.SE). Holds mostly social-science survey data but contains historical statistics as well. Published catalogue and newsletter available upon application.

SSD, *Data Collections, 1990* (Gotenberg, 1990).
— *SSDkontakt* (newsletter).

*Zentralarchiv fur Empirische Sozialforschung (ZA)*, Universität Zu Köln, Bachemer Strasse 40, D-5000 Köln 41, Germany (EARN: MOCHMANN@DKOZA1). A data archive of over 1,700 machine-readable survey data sets relating to post-war Germany and to Germany in a comparative context. Published catalogue, updates, and newsletter available upon application.

ZA, *Umfragen aus der empirischen Sozialforschung, 1945–1982* (Cologne, 1986).
— *ZA-Information* (newsletter).
— *Zeitschrift für Soziologie* (journal).

2. *Text archives:*

*Center for Text and Technology*, Georgetown University, Reiss Science Building, Room 238, 37th and 0 Streets, NW, Washington DC 20057, USA (Internet: WILDER@GUVAX.GEORGETOWN.EDU). The Center is developing an on-line catalogue of text archives and projects that create and analyse electronic texts in the humanities. The catalogue is accessible via Internet on GUVAX3.GEORGETOWN.EDU, username is CPET, and no password is required.

The Center for Text and Technology of the Academic Computer Center, *The Georgetown University Catalogue of Projects in Electronic Text* (Washington, DC, 1991).

*Center for Electronic Text in the Humanities*, Alexander Library, Rutgers University, College Ave., New Brunswick, NJ 08903, USA (Internet: HOCKEY@ZODIAC.RUTGERS.EDU). The Center is part of an international network of text archives which aims to make machine-readable texts more generally accessible for teaching and research.

HOCKEY, S., 'Developing Access to Electronic Texts in the Humanities', in L. Saunders (ed.), *The Evolving Virtual Library: Visions and Case Studies* (forthcoming).

*Oxford Text Archive*, Oxford University Computing Service, 13 Banbury Road, Oxford OX2 6NN, UK (Internet: ARCHIVE@VAX.OXFORD.AC.UK). 'Offers scholars long term storage and maintenance of their electronic texts free of charge . . . [and] manages non-commercial distribution of electronic texts and information about them on behalf of its depositors.' Contains over a thousand titles including literary works in Greek, Latin, English, and other languages, linguistic corpora, and some standard reference works. Paper catalogue is available on application and in electronic form. Anonymous ftp at Internet site: BLACK.OX.AC.UK. Look in the directory OTA. For information on anonymous ftp see Ch. 2.

BURNARD, L. D., 'The Oxford Text Archive: Principles and Prospects', in J.-P. Genet (ed.), *Standardisation et échange*, 191–203.

*Project Gutenberg National Clearinghouse for Machine-Readable Texts* facilitates distribution of English-language machine-readable texts. Information may be obtained by mailing Michael Hart (Internet: HART@VMD.CSO.UIUC.EDU). The project operates several ftp installations and a discussion list. See Ch. 2.

## C. On-line databases

On-line database suppliers mentioned in this section include:

*BLAISE-LINE*. British Library, Bibliographic Services, 2 Sheraton St., London W1V 4BH, UK.

*BRS*. BRS Information Technologies, 8000 Westpark Drive, McLean, VA 22102, USA.

*DIALOG*. DIALOG Information Services, Inc., 3460 Hillview Ave., Palo Alto, CA 94304, USA.

*OCLC*. OCLC Online Computer Library Center, Inc., Frantz Rd., Dublin, OH 43017, USA.

*RLG/RLIN*. Research Libraries Group, Inc., 1200 Villa St. Mountain View, CA 94041–1100, USA.

*Wilson-Line*. H. W. Wilson Company, 950 University Ave., Bronx, NY 10452, USA.

*Academic Index* gives citations to articles and reviews in over 400 English-language, general interest, and scholarly periodicals mostly published since 1985; BRS and DIALOG.

*America History and Life* comprises references to publications on American and Canadian history and culture from nearly 2,000 journals; DIALOG.

*Arts & Humanities Search* consists of citations to articles and reviews from 1,300 arts and humanities journals, and citations to humanities articles from 5,000 social-science and scientific journals; BRS and DIALOG.

*Biography Master Index* comprises citations to biographical information in more than 700 English-language reference works and collective biographies corresponding to the printed Biography and Genealogy Master Index; DIALOG.

*BNBMARK* includes citations to books and journals published in Great Britain mostly after 1950 and corresponds to the printed British National Bibliography; BLAISE-LINE, OCLC, and RLG/RLIN. Also see S. Lehman and P. Renfro, 'Humanists at the Keyboard: The RLIN Database as a Scholarly Source in the Humanities and Social Sciences', *Computers and the Humanities*, 26 (1992), 181–94.

*British Library Catalogue: Humanities and Social Sciences* includes catalogue records for English and non-English materials acquired by the British Library's humanities and social science departments since 1976, and materials from the Oriental collections and from the India Office library; BLAISE-LINE.

*Current Contents Search: Arts and Humanities*, and *Current Contents Search: Social and Behavioural Sciences*, two different databases, include citations to articles in English and foreign-language periodicals in the arts and humanities, and in the social and behavioural sciences, respectively; BRS and DIALOG.

*Dissertation Abstracts On-line* comprises references to US doctoral dissertations since 1861 (including abstracts from June 1980). Selective US Masters theses and non-US doctoral dissertations are also included; BRS and DIALOG.

*Eighteenth-Century Short Title Catalogue* comprises bibliographic records of eighteenth-century publications printed in the British Empire and elsewhere; BLAISE-LINE.

*Historical Abstracts* has references from international publications on world history from 1450, excluding the USA and Canada (see *America History and Life*, above); DIALOG.

*OCLC On-line Union Catalogue* contains over 18 million cataloguing records for books, journals, manuscripts, sound recordings, and audiovisual materials located in more than 8,800 member libraries in the USA, Canada, and elsewhere; OCLC.

*RLIN Cataloguing Database*, partial list of holdings of participating libraries in the USA and Canada, and in the British Library; RLG/RLN.

*Social Science Index* includes citations to articles and reviews in 300 international English-language social science periodicals mostly from February 1983; Wilson Line.

*Social SciSearch* comprises references to the contents of over 1,500 English-language social-science articles from over 3,000 journals published since 1972; BRS and DIALOG.

### D. Electronic Bulletin Boards

Unless otherwise indicated, the addresses given below are known to BIT-NET. They may be accessible via other networks (e.g. Internet, EARN) perhaps with some alteration. To subscribe to a list send an electronic mail message to the so-called LISTSERV software which handles it. The message must include the name of the list to which you want to subscribe and your own name. To subscribe to HUMANIST, for example, I would send the message 'subscribe HUMANIST Daniel Greenstein' to the

BITNET accessible address, LISTSERV@BROWNVM. To cancel my subscription, I would send another message, 'unsubscribe HUMANIST Daniel Greenstein', to LISTSERV@BROWNVM. Please note that discussion lists do tend to come and go (either in and out of existence or from one computer installation to another). Moreover, electronic addresses sometimes change with network technology and protocols. Consequently, the addresses given below may require some modification before contact can be established.

| | |
|---|---|
| AFAM-L@UMCVMB | African-American Research |
| AFAS-L@KENTVM | African American studies and librarianship |
| AHC-L@DGOGWDG1 | The list of the mainly European Association for History and Computing |
| ALBION-L@UCSBVM | British and Irish history |
| AMLIT-L@MIZZOU1 | Very active list concentrating on American literature |
| AMERCATH@UKCC | History of American Catholicism |
| AMWEST-H@USCVM | Active list concentrating on the history of the American west |
| ANCIEN-L@ULKYVM | History of the ancient Mediterranean world |
| ANSAX-L@WVNVM | Very active list focusing on Anglo-Saxon scholarship |
| ANTHRO-L@UBVM | Anthropological research |
| ARCHIVES@INDYCMS | Active list for archives and archivists |
| ARCH-L@TAMVM1 | Archaeology list |
| ASEH-L@TTUVM1 | List of the American Society of Environmental Historians |
| BALZAC-L@CC.UMONTREAL.CA | French cultural studies. To contact send a message to: BALZAC-L-REQUEST@CC.UMONTREAL.CA |
| C18-L@PSUVM, | An active list focusing on eighteenth-century history and culture |
| CADUCEUS | List for historians of medicine. Send electronic mail via BITNET to IBOWMAN@UTMBEACH |
| CETH@PUCC | List of the Center for Electronic Texts. The Center promotes discussion relevant to the use of electronic texts in the humanities |
| CHINA@PUCC | Chinese studies |
| CLASSICS@UWAVM | Active list for classical Greek and Latin studies |

| | |
|---|---|
| DEUCHE-LISTE@CCU.UMANITOBA.CA | German literature and culture. To subscribe send message via Internet to: COLAPPE@CCU.UMANITOBA.CA |
| EARAM-L@KENTVM | List of the Society of Early Americanists |
| EMEDCH-L@USCVM | Early medieval China |
| EMHIST-L@USCVM | Early modern history |
| ERASMUS | Renaissance and reformation studies. To contact send a message via Internet to: BOWEN@VM.EPAS.UTORONTO.CA |
| ESPORA-L@UKANVM | Spanish and Portuguese studies |
| FOLKLORE@TAMVM1 | Folklore |
| FRANCEHS@UWAVM | French history |
| GRMNHIST@USCVM | German history. To subscribe send the message 'sub grmnhist <your name>' via EARN to LISTSERV@DGOGWDG1 |
| HABSBURG@PURCCVM | Austrian history since 1500 |
| H-CIVWAR@UICVM | US Civil War |
| H-DIPL@UICVM | Diplomatic history, foreign affairs, international relations |
| H-ETHNIC@UICVM | American ethnic and immigration history |
| H-IDEAS@UICVM | Intellectual history |
| HISLAW-L@ULKYVM | History of law |
| HISTEC-L@UKANVM | History of evangelical Christianity |
| HISTOWNR@UBVM | List for editors of history lists |
| HISTORY@PSUVM | General history discussion list |
| HISTORY@FINHUTC | A general history discussion list located in Finland; EARN |
| H-LATAM@UICVM | Latin American history |
| H-LAW@UICVM | Legal and constitutional history |
| HOLOCAUS@UICVM | Holocaust studies, anti-Semitism, and related themes |
| HN-ASK-L@UKANVM | Information on history lists and communications |
| HOPOS-L@UKCC | History of Science |
| HPSST-L@QUCDN | History and philosophy of science |
| H-RURAL@UICVM | Rural and agricultural history |
| H-SOUTH@UICVM | History of the US south |
| HTECH-L@SIVM | Active list focusing on the history of technology |
| HUMANIST@BROWNVM | Active list focusing on all aspects of humanities computing |
| H-URBAN@UICVM | Active and lively urban history list |
| H-WOMEN@UICVM | Women's history |

| IBYCUS-L@USCVM | Ancient Greek |
| IEAHC-NET@UICVM | American colonial history, sponsored by the Institute of Early American and Cultural Studies at Williamsburg |
| IOUDAIOS@YORKVM1 | Judaism in the first century |
| ISLAM-L@ULKYVM | History of Islam |
| L-CHA@UQAM | List of the Canadian Historical Association on Computing |
| MEDFEM-L@INDYCMS | List for feminist medieval historians |
| MEDIEV-L@UKANVM | Medieval history |
| MEDTEXTL@UIUCVMD | Lists for scholars interested in medieval texts, philology, and codicology |
| MILHST-L@UKANVM | Active, semi-popular list focusing on military history |
| POLI-SCI@RUTVM1 | Political science digest |
| PSRT-L@MIZZOU1 | For book reviews in political science and in constitutional law |
| RENAIS-L@ULKYVM | Renaissance studies |
| ROOTS-L@NDSUVM1 | Very active list for genealogists |
| RUSHIST@DOSUNI1 | Russian history list |
| SEASIA-L@MSU | South-east Asian studies |
| SEDIT-L@UMDD | For editors of scholarly editions |
| SHARP-L@IUBVM | History of authorship and reading |
| SHOTHC-L@SIVM | History of computing |
| SOCHIST@USCVM | Social history |
| SOVHIST@DOSUNI1 | Soviet history |
| VICTORIA@IUBVM | Victorian studies |
| VWAR-L@UBVM | Very active list focusing on the history and popular culture of the Vietnam War |
| WMST-L@UMDD | Women's studies list |
| WORLD-L@UBVM | Very active and non-Eurocentric world history list. |
| WWII-L@UBVM | Second World War studies |

### *E. Software reviews and bibliographies*

DEEGAN, M., and LEE, S. (eds.), *CTI Centre for Textual Studies Resources Guide* (Oxford, 1991).

FITCH, N. E., 'Statistical and Mathematical Methods for Historians: An Annotated Bibliography of Selected Books and Articles', *Historical Methods*, 13 (1980), 222–31.

GROSSBART, S. R., 'Quantification and Social Science Methods for Historians: An Annotated Bibliography of Selected Books and Articles', *Historical Methods*, 25 (1992), 100–20.

*History and Computing* (software review section).
*History Micro Review* (hardware and software reviews).
LANCASHIRE, I. (ed.), *The Humanities Computing Yearbook 1989/90: A Comprehensive Guide to Software and other Resources* (Oxford, 1991).
MATSUBA, S. N., 'Computer Application in the Humanities: A Reading List', *Canadian Humanities Computing*, 4 (1990), 1–8.
MIDDLETON, R., and WARDLEY, P., 'Annual Review of Information Technology Developments for Economic and Social Historians', *Economic History Review* (1990– ).
SPAETH, D. A., *A Guide to Software for Historians* (Glasgow, 1991).

## IV. HISTORIOGRAPHY

### A. Quantitative and computer-aided history: for and against

AYDELOTTE, W. O., 'Quantification in History', *American Historical Review*, 71 (1966), 803–25.
BARZUN, J., 'History: The Muse and Her Doctors', *American Historical Review*, 77 (1972), 36–64.
— *Clio and the Doctors* (Chicago, 1974).
BEACH, W. W., 'A Second Look: "The Agenda for Social Science History"', *Social Science History*, 4 (1980), 357–64.
BENSON, L., 'Quantification, Scientific History, and Scholarly Innovation', *AHA Newsletter* (June 1966).
BERINGER, R. E., *Historical Analysis: Contemporary Approaches to Clio's Craft* (Malabar, Fla., 1986).
BOGUE, A. G., 'Great Expectations and Secular Depreciation: The First 10 Years of the Social Science History Association', *Social Science History*, 11 (1987).
BRIDENBAUGH, C., 'The Great Mutation', *American Historical Review*, 68 (1963).
BULLOUGH, V. L., 'The Computer and the Historian: Some Tentative Beginnings', *Computers and the Humanities*, 1 (1966), 61–4.
CLUBB, J. M., 'The New History as Applied Social Science: A Review Essay', *Computers and the Humanities*, 9 (1975), 247–51.
— 'The "New" Quantitative History: Social Science or Old Wine in New Bottles?', in J. M. Clubb and E. K. Scheuch (eds.), *Historical Sociological Research*, 19–24.
— and ALLEN, H., 'Computers and Historical Studies', *Journal of American History*, 54 (1967), 599–607.
— and BOGUE, A. G., 'History, Quantification, and the Social Sciences', *American Behavioural Science*, 21 (1977), 167–86.

256 *Bibliography and Resource Guide*

Cobb, R., 'Historians in White Coats', *Times Literary Supplement* (3 Dec. 1971).

Dollar, C. M., 'Innovation in Historical Research: A Computer Approach', *Computers and the Humanities*, 3 (1968), 139–51.

Douglas, L. H., 'Computers and Historians: The Results of Two National Surveys', *History Micro Review*, 2 (1986), 16–18.

Erikson, C., 'Quantitative History', *American Historical Review*, 80 (1975), 351–65.

Finley, M. I., 'Progress in Historiography', *Daedalus*, 106 (1977), 125–42.

Fitch, N., 'Statistical Fantasies and Historical Facts: History in Crisis and its Methodological Implications', *Historical Methods*, 17 (1984), 239–54.

Floud, R., 'Quantitative History and People's History: Two Methods in Conflict?', *Social Science History*, 8 (1984), 151–68.

Fogel, R. W., 'The Limits of Quantitative History', *American Historical Review*, 80 (1975), 329–50.

— '"Scientific History" and Traditional History', in L. J. Cohen (ed.), *Logic, Methodology, and Philosophy of Science VI: Proceedings of the Sixth International Congress of Logic, Methodology, and Philosophy of Science, Hannover, 1979* (Amsterdam, 1982), 15–61.

— and Elton, G. R., *Which Road to the Past? Two Views of History* (New Haven, Conn., 1983).

Furet, F., 'Quantitative History', *Daedalus*, 100 (1972), 151–67.

Greenstein, D. I., 'A Matter of Method', *History and Computing*, 2 (1990), 210–15.

Handlin, O., 'The Capacity of Quantitative History', *Perspectives in American History*, 9 (1975), 7–26.

Herlihy, D., 'Computation in History: Styles and Methods'. *Computers and the Humanities*, 11 (1978), 8–18.

Himmelfarb, G., *The New History and the Old* (Cambridge, Mass., 1987).

Jaritz, G., 'Medieval Image Databases: Aspects of Cooperation and Exchange', *Literary and Linguistic Computing*, 6 (1991), 15–19.

Jensen, R., 'The Microcomputer Revolution for Historians', *Journal of Interdisciplinary History*, 14 (1983), 91–111.

Johnson, E. A., 'Reflections on an Old "New History": Quantitative Social Science History in the Post Modern Middle Age', *Central European History*, 22 (1989), 408–26.

Kedourie, E., 'New Histories for Old', *Times Literary Supplement* (7 Mar. 1975), 238.

Kocka, J., 'Theory and Quantification in History', *Social Science History*, 8 (1984), 167–78.

Kousser, J. M., 'The Agenda for Social Science History', *Social Science History*, 1 (1977), 383–91.

— 'Quantitative Social Science History' in M. Kammen (ed.), *The Past Before Us: Contemporary Historical Writing in the United States* (Ithaca, NY, 1980), 433–56.

— 'History QUASSHed: Quantitative Social Science History in Perspective', *American Behavioral Scientist*, 23 (1982), 885–904.

— 'The Revivalism of Narrative: A Response to Recent Criticisms of Quantitative History', *Social Science History*, 8 (1984), 133–49.

— 'The State of Social Science History in the Late 1980s', *Historical Methods*, 22 (1989), 13–20.

LAMPARD, E. E., 'Two Cheers for Quantitative History: An Agnostic Forward', in L. F. Schnore (ed.), *The New Urban History* (Princeton, NJ, 1975).

McCLOSKEY, D., 'Ancients and Moderns', *Social Science History*, 14 (1990), 289–303.

MILIC, L. T., 'The Next Step', *Computers and the Humanities*, 1 (1966), 3–6.

MONKKONEN, E. H., 'The Challenge of Quantitative History', *Historical Methods*, 17 (1984), 86–94.

RABB, T. K., 'The Development of Quantification in Historical Research', *Journal of Interdisciplinary History*, 13 (1983), 591–601.

RABEN, J., 'Humanities Computing 20 Years Later', *Computers and the Humanities*, 25 (1991), 341–50.

SCHLESINGER, A. Jr., 'The Humanist Looks at Empirical Social Research', *American Sociological Review*, 27 (1962).

SILBEY, J., 'Clio and the Computers: Moving into Phase II, 1970–2', *Computers and the Humanities*, 7 (1972), 67–79.

SPRAGUE, D. N., 'A Quantitative Assessment of the Quantitative Revolution', *Journal of Canadian History*, 13 (1978), 177–92.

STONE, L. (ed.), *The Past and the Present* (Boston, 1981).

SWIERENGA, R. P., 'Clio and Computers: A Survey of Computerized Research in History', *Computers and the Humanities*, 5 (1970), 1–21.

THALLER, M., 'Methods and Techniques of Historical Computation', in P. R. Denley and D. Hopkin (eds.), *History and Computing*, 147–55.

— 'The Need for a Theory of Historical Computing', in P. R. Denley *et al.* (eds.), *History and Computing II*, 2–11.

TILLY, C., 'Computers in Historical Analysis', *Computers and the Humanities*, 7 (1973), 323–35.

ZEMSKY, R., 'Numbers and History: The Dilemma of Measurement', *Computers and the Humanities*, 4 (1969–70), 31–40.

### B. Economic history

ANDREANO, R. (ed.), *The New Economic History: Recent Papers in Methodology* (New York, 1970).

COCHRAN, T. C., 'Economic History, Old and New', *American Historical Review*, 74 (1968-9), 1561-72.

CRAFTS, N. F. R., *et al*. (eds.), *Quantitative Economic History* (New York, 1991).

DAVIS, L. E., 'And It Will Never Be Literature: The New Economic History: A Critique', *Explorations in Entrepreneurial History*, 6 (1968), 75-92.

— and ENGERMAN, S. L., 'The State of the Science (or is it Art or, perhaps Witchcraft?)', *History Methods Newsletter*, 20 (1987).

— HUGHES, J. R. T., and REITER, S., 'Aspects of Quantitative Research in Economic History', *Journal of Economic History*, 20 (1960), 539-47.

DELBECKE, J., and VAN DER WEER, H., 'Quantitative Research in Economic History in Europe After 1945', in R. Freindling and P. K. O'Brien (eds.), *Productivity in the Economies of Europe* (Stuttgart, 1983), 11-29.

ENGERMAN, S. L., *et al*. (eds.), *The Reinterpretation of American Economic History* (New York, 1971).

FLOUD, R. (ed.), *Essays in Quantitative Economic History* (Oxford, 1974).

FOGEL, R. W., 'A Provisional View of the New Economic History', *American Economic Review*, 54 (1964), 77-89.

— 'History and Retrospective Econometrics', *History and Theory*, 3 (1970), 245-64.

— 'The New Economic History: Its Findings and Methods', in D. K. Rowney and J. Q. Graham, Jr. (eds.), *Quantitative History*, 320-35.

HIDY, R. W., 'The Road We Are Traveling', *Journal of Economic History*, 32 (1972), 3-14.

LANDES, D. S., 'On Avoiding Babel', *Journal of Economic History*, 38 (1978).

MCCLELLAND, P. D., *Causal Explanation and Model Building in History, Economics and the New Econometric History* (Ithaca, NY, 1975).

MCCLOSKEY, D. M., 'The Achievements of the Cliometric School', *Journal of Economic History*, 38 (1978).

MURPHEY, G. G. S., 'The "New" History', *Explorations in Entrepreneurial History*, 2nd Series, 2 (1965), 132-46.

NORTH, D. C., 'Quantitative Research in American Economic History', *American Economic Review*, 53 (1963), 128-30.

— 'The State of Economic History', *American Economic Review*, 55 (1965), 86-91.

PARKER, W. N., 'From Old to New to Old in Economic History', *Journal of Economic History*, 31 (1971).

REDLICH, F., '"New" and Traditional Approaches to Economic History and their Interdependence', *Journal of Economic History*, 25 (1965), 480-95.

SUPPLE, B., 'Economic History in the 1980s: Old Problems and New Directions', *Journal of Interdisciplinary History*, 12 (1981), 199-205.

TEMIN, P. (ed.), *The New Economic History* (Harmondsworth, 1973).

— 'Economic History in the 1980s: The Future of the New Economic History', *Journal of Interdisciplinary History*, 12 (1981), 179–97.

## C. Political history

Bogue, A. G., 'The "New" Political History', *Journal of Contemporary History*, 3 (1968), 5–22.

— (ed.), *Emerging Models in Social and Political History* (Beverly Hills, Calif., 1973).

— *Clio and the Bitch Goddess: Quantification in American Political History* (Berkeley, Calif., 1983).

— 'The Quest for Numeracy: Data and Methods in American Political History', *Journal of Interdisciplinary History*, 21 (1990), 89–116.

— 'United States: The "New" Political History', in D. K. Rowney and J. Q. Graham, Jr. (eds.), *Quantitative History*, 109–26.

Bourke, P. F., and DeBats, D. A., 'Individuals and Aggregates: A Note on Historical Data and Assumptions', *Social Science History*, 4 (1980), 229–50.

Kousser, J. M., 'The New Political History: A Methodological Critique', *Reviews in American History* (4 Mar. 1976), 1–14.

— and Lichtman, A. J., '"New Political History": Some Statistical Questions Answered', *Social Science History*, 7 (1983), 321–44.

McCormick, R. L., 'Ethno-Cultural Interpretations of Nineteenth-Century American Voting Behaviour', *Political Science Quarterly*, 89 (1974), 351–77.

McCormick, R. P., 'New Perspectives on Jacksonian Politics', *American Historical Review*, 65 (1960).

O'Gorman, F., 'Electoral Behaviour in England, 1700–1872', P. R. Denley *et al.* (eds.), *History and Computing II*, 220–38.

Shade, W. G., '"New Political History": Some Statistical Questions Raised', *Social Science History*, 5 (1981), 171–96.

Silbey, J. H., 'Delegates from the People? American Congressional and Legislative Behavior', *Journal of Interdisciplinary History*, 13 (1983), 603–27.

Speck, W. A., and Gray, W. A., 'The Computer Analysis of Poll Books: An Initial Report', *Bulletin of the Institute of Historical Research*, 48 (1975), 105–12.

Vandermeer, P., 'The New Political History: Progress and Prospects', *Computers and the Humanities*, 11 (1978), 265–78.

## D. Medieval history

Bullough, V. L., *et al.*, 'Computers and the Medievalist: A Report', *Speculum* (1974).

BULST, N., 'Prosopography and the Computers: Problems and Possibilities', in P. R. Denley *et al.* (eds.), *History and Computing, II*, 12–18.

FOSSIER, L. (ed.), *Le Traitement automatique des documents diplomatiques du Haut-Moyen-Âge* (Nancy, 1973).

— 'L'Informatique documentaire: nouvelles perspectives', in *Mémoires de la Société pour l'Histoire du Droit et des Institutions des Anciens Pays Bourguignons, Comtois et Romands: études d'histoire du droit médiéval en souvenir de Josette Metman* (Dijon, 1988), 145–53.

— *et al.* (eds.), *Informatique et histoire médiévale* (Rome, 1977).

GENET, J.-P., and BULST, N. (eds.), *Medieval Lives and the Historian: Studies in Medieval Prosopography. Proceedings of the First International Interdisciplinary Conference on Medieval Prosopography* (Kalamazoo, 1986).

GILMOUR-BRYSON, A., *Medieval Studies and the Computer* (Oxford, 1978).

— (ed.), *Medieval Studies and the Computer: Computing and the Humanities Special Issue*, 12 (1978).

— 'Computers and Medieval Historical Texts: An Overview', in P. R. Denley and D. Hopkin (eds.), *History and Computing*, 3–9.

— *Computer Applications to Medieval Studies* (Kalamazoo, 1984).

HERLIHY, D., 'Computer-Assisted Analysis of Statistical Documents of Medieval Society', in J. M. Powell (ed.), *Medieval Studies: An Introduction* (Syracuse, 1976), 185–212.

— 'Quantification and the Middle Ages', in V. R. Lorwin and J. M. Price (eds.), *The Dimensions of the Past*, 13–52.

MILLET, H., 'La Rencontre prosopographie et informatique', *Histoire moderne et contemporaine informatique*, 5 (1984), 111–14.

— *Informatique et prosopographie* (Paris, 1985).

PARISSE, M., 'A propos du traitement automatique des chartes: chronologies du vocabulaire et repérage des actes suspects', *La Lexicologie du Latin médiéval et ses rapports avec les recherches actuelles sur la civilisation du Moyen Âge* (Paris, 1981), 241–9.

REUTER, T., 'Computer-Assisted Editions of Medieval Historical Texts', in P. R. Denley and D. Hopkin (eds.), *History and Computing*, 251–5.

SCHWOB, A., *et al.* (eds.), *Historische Edition und Computer: Möglichkeiten und Probleme interdisziplinärer Textverarbeitung und Textbearbeitung* (Graz, 1989).

THALLER, M., 'The Daily Life in the Middle Ages: Editions of Sources and Data Processing', *Medium Aevum Quotidianum Newsletter*, 10 (1987), 6–28.

— (ed.), *Database Oriented Source Editions: Papers from Two Sessions at the 23rd International Congress on Medieval Studies, Kalamazoo, Michigan, 5–8 May, 1988* (Göttingen and Kalamazoo, 1988).

— (ed.), *Images and Manuscripts in Historical Computing* (St Katharinen, 1992).

WERNER, K. F. (ed.), *Medieval History and Computers: l'histoire médiévale et les ordinateurs, rapports d'une table ronde internationale, Paris, 1978* (Munich, 1981).

### E. National histories

BEST, H., 'Technique or Method? Quantitative Historical Social Research in Germany', *Computers and the Humanities*, 25 (1991), 163–72.

BOGUE, A. G., 'Quantification in the 1980s: Numerical and Formal Analysis in US History', *Journal of Interdisciplinary History*, 12 (1981).

BOONSTRA, O., and GALES, B., 'Quantitative Social Historical Research in the Netherlands: Past, Present and Future', *Historical Social Research*, 9 (1984).

BORDELAIS, P., 'French Quantitative History: Problems and Promises', *Social Science History*, 8 (1984), 179–92.

GENET, J.-P., 'L'Historien et l'ordinateur', *Historiens et Géographes*, 270 (1978), 125–42.

HARRIS, J., 'Computer Analysis in German History', *Computers and the Humanities*, 13 (1979), 37–39.

HERLIHY, D., 'Quantification in the 1980s: Numerical and Formal Analysis in European History', *Journal of Interdisciplinary History*, 12 (1981), 115–35.

IGGERS, G. G., *New Directions in European Historiography* (London, 1985).

IMHOF, A. E., 'The Computer in Social History: Historical Demography in Germany', *Computers and the Humanities*, 12 (1978), 227–36.

JARAUSCH, K. H., 'The International Dimension of Quantitative History: Some Introductory Reflections', *Social Science History*, 8 (1984), 123–32.

— 'International Styles of Quantitative History', *Historical Methods*, 18 (1985), 13–19.

JENSEN, R., 'Quantitative American Studies: State of the Art', *American Quarterly*, 16 (1971), 225–40.

JOHNSON, E. A., 'Counting "How it Really Was": Quantitative History in West Germany', *History Methods Newsletter*, 21 (1988).

KRAUSE, J. (ed.), *Computers and the Humanities in Germany. Computing and the Humanities Special Double Issue*, 25 (1991).

LINZ, J. L., 'Five Centuries of Spanish History: Quantification and Comparison', in V. R. Lorwin and J. M. Price (eds.), *The Dimensions of the Past*, 177–262.

PEREZ-BRIGNOLI, H., and RUIZ, E. A., 'History and Quantification in Latin America: An Assessment of Theories and Methods', *Social Science History*, 8 (1984), 201–15.

ROTHSTEIN, M., *et al.*, 'Quantification and American History: An Assessment', in H. J. Bass (ed.), *The State of American History* (Chicago, 1970), 298–329.

ROWNEY, D. K. (ed.), *Soviet Quantitative History* (Berkeley, Calif., 1983).

SHEEHAN, J. J., 'Quantification in the Study of Modern German Social and Political History', in V. R. Lorwin and J. M. Price (eds.), *The Dimensions of the Past*, 301–32.

SPINOSA, G. (ed.), *Humanities Computing in Italy. Computing and the Humanities Special Double Issue*, 24 (1990).

SWIERENGA, R. P. (ed.), *Quantification in American History* (New York, 1970).

— 'Computers and American History: The Impact of the New Generations', *Journal of American History*, 60 (1974), 1045–70.

TILLY, C., 'Quantification in History as Seen From France', in V. R. Lorwin and J. M. Price (eds.), *The Dimensions of the Past*, 93–126.

VAN DER VOORT, R. C. W., 'The Growth of Historical Information Systems in Historical Sciences', in R. Metz *et al.* (eds.), *Historical Information Systems*, 3–9.

### F. Other historical subject areas

CONZEN, K. N., 'Quantification and the New Urban History', *Journal of Interdisciplinary History*, 13 (1983), 653–77.

EVERSLEY, D., and WRIGLEY, E. A. (eds.), *An Introduction to English Historical Demography from the Sixteenth Century to the Nineteenth Century* (London, 1966).

HAWGOOD, D., *Computers for Family History: An Introduction* (London, 1989).

SCHNORE, L. F. (ed.), *The New Urban History: Quantitative Explorations by American Historians* (Princeton, NJ, 1975).

SCHÜRER, K., 'Historical Demography, Social Structure and the Computer', in P. R. Denley and D. Hopkin (eds.), *History and Computing*, 33–45.

— 'Theory and Methodology: An Example from Historical Demography', in P. R. Denley *et al.* (eds.), *History and Computing II*, 130–42.

STEARNS, P., 'Towards a Wider Vision: Trends in Social History', in M. Kammen (ed.), *The Past Before Us*, 205–30.

STONE, L., 'Family History in the 1980s: Past Achievements and Future Trends', *Journal of Interdisciplinary History*, 12 (1981), 51–87.

SWIERENGA, R. P., 'Computers and Comparative History', *Journal of Interdisciplinary History*, 5 (1971), 267–86.

TILLY, L., and COHEN, M., 'Does the Family Have a History? A Review of Theory and Practice in Family History', *Social Science History*, 6 (1982), 131–80.

VINOVSKIS, M. A., 'Quantification and the Analysis of American Antebellum Education', *Journal of Interdisciplinary History*, 13 (1983), 761–87.

WRIGLEY, E. A. (ed.), *Identifying People in the Past* (London, 1973).
— 'Population History in the 1980s: The Prospect for Population History', *Journal of Interdisciplinary History*, 12 (1981), 207–26.

# Index

266                           *Index*

data entry (*cont.*):
  into spreadsheets 137–9, 216
  into statistical software 145–6,
    222–5
  into text editors 163
  into word processors 216
  with an optical character reader 29,
    229–34
data modelling 214–16
  for bibliographic databases 40–2
  for databases (general) 62–3, 66–8,
    106–7, 175–7, 226–7
  for databases (multi-table) 74–80
  for full-text retrieval software
    168–72, 178–81, 196, 226
  for research-note databases 44
  for spreadsheets 147, 155, 157,
    214, 226–7
  for statistical software 144, 147,
    155, 157, 226
  for word processors 214, 216
data types:
  in databases 66–8, 107
  in full-text retrieval software
    177–8
  in spreadsheets 136
  in statistical software 145–6
desktop computer 43, 47, 48–51, 52,
    211–12
DIALOG, *see* on-line database
discussion list 52, 55
disk management 33, 48–51
diskette 51
  *see also* disk management

EARN, *see* network
ECCE 162–3
  *see also* text editor
econometrics 17–18
Economic History Association 21
electronic mail 53–4
*Excel* 225
  *see also* spreadsheet

file server 52, 212–13
file storage 29, 211
  *see also* disk management
file transfer protocol 58–60
floppy disk, *see* diskette
frequency distribution 116–17
  prepared with statistical software
    152–3
  represented graphically 118–19

full-text retrieval software:
  data exchange with: a text editor
    163–4, 226; a word processor 226
  description of 177–8
  data model for 168–72, 178–81,
    196, 226
  limitations 183
  use: as bibliographic database
    182–3; data classification with
    196–7; data entry in 163–4, 178,
    218, 219, 227, 229; retrievals
    with 179–83
ftp, *see* file transfer protocol

graphs:
  preparation of 39–40; with
    spreadsheets 140; with statistical
    software 153–5
  types of: bar chart 37, 38, 118;
    histogram 120–1; line graph 37,
    119, 123, 125; pie chart 37, 38,
    418; scattergram 128–30; stacked
    bar chart 123–5; uses 36–7

hardware:
  selection of 210–13
  *see also* desktop; file server; file
    storage; laptop; magnetic tape

ICPSR (previously ICPR), *see* Inter-
  University Consortium for Political
  and Social Research
Internet, *see* network
Inter-University Consortium for
  Political and Social Research 21
interval scale variable, *see* variables

JANET, *see* network
joint-frequency distribution, *see* cross
  tabulation

KWIC, *see* concordance
KWOC, *see* concordance

LAN, *see* network
laptop 212
linguistic content analysis, *see* content
  analysis
*Lotus 1–2–3* 226
  *see also* spreadsheet

Mac, *see* desktop computer
magnetic tape 51
  *see also* disk management